THE
Explosive Child

THE
Explosive Child

A New Approach
for Understanding and Parenting
Easily Frustrated,
Chronically Inflexible Children

Second Edition

Ross W. Greene, Ph.D.

Quill
An Imprint of HarperCollins*Publishers*

In memory of Irving A. Greene

HarperCollins books may be purchased for educational, business, or sales promotional use. For information please write: Special Markets Department, HarperCollins Publishers Inc., 10 East 53rd Street, New York, NY 10022.

First Quill edition published 2001.

Designed by Elina D. Nudelman

Library of Congress Cataloging-in-Publication Data is available.

ISBN 0-06-093102-7

01 02 03 04 05 ❖/RRD 10 9 8 7 6 5 4 3 2 1

Anyone can become angry, that is easy . . .
but to be angry with the right person, to the right degree,
at the right time, for the right purpose, and in the right
way . . . this is not easy.

—*Aristotle*

Man masters nature not by force but by understanding.
—*Jacob Brownowski*

Contents

Acknowledgments

This book is about helping inflexible, easily frustrated, explosive children and their parents think and interact more adaptively. My own thinking has been influenced by two of the world's pre-eminent clinician/researchers in child psychopathology, Drs. Thomas Ollendick and Joseph Biederman. It has been my incredible good fortune to work with these two distinguished scholars. Tom, my mentor while I was in graduate school at Virginia Tech, taught me how to think critically; Joe, my colleague at Massachusetts General Hospital, has furthered the process. Although both would appreciate the need to subject much of what is written in this book to rigorous scientific evaluation (a process that is currently underway), I suspect they would be reassured by the belief that children and their families might be helped by its contents.

Though I have benefited from my interactions with many mental health and education professionals over the years, two psychologists who supervised me during my training years were particularly influential: Drs. George Clum at Virginia Tech and Mary Ann McCabe at Children's National Medical Center in Washington, DC. I've also found much wisdom in the writing of several authors, including Ruth Charney (author of *Teaching Children to Care: Management in the*

Responsive Classroom); Dr. Stanley Turecki (author of *The Difficult Child*); Dr. Thomas Gordon (author of *P.E.T.: Parent Effectiveness Training*); and Dr. Myrna Shure (author of *Raising a Thinking Child*). And I probably wouldn't have gone into psychology in the first place if I hadn't stumbled across the path of Dr. Elizabeth Altmaier when I was an undergraduate at the University of Florida.

Love helps, too, and I get lots from my wife Melissa, daughter Talia, son Jacob, mother, brother, aunt, and grandmothers. I also got lots from those whose deaths preceded the publication of this book: my father (to whom this book is dedicated), grandfathers, and, of course, Nene and Lucy B. Greene.

My agent, Wendy Lipkind, believed in this book the minute she saw the first draft. So did Joelle Delbourgo at Harper-Collins. Their collective vision for this book was critical to its development and success. The patience and superb editing skills of Tim Duggan and energy and enthusiasm of Betsy Areddy, both at HarperCollins, have been indispensable as well.

Needless to say, those who were most central to the evolution of many of the ideas in this book, and to whom I owe the greatest debt of gratitude, were the many parents who entrusted me with the care of their children and families.

While there are many inflexible-explosive girls, for ease of exposition most of this book is written in the masculine gender. The names and identifying information of all the children in this book are completely fictitious. Most of the names are, in fact, those of friends, nonspecific cartoon characters and rock musicians, and my wife's ex-boyfriends. Any resemblance to actual children of the same names is, as the saying goes, purely coincidental.

Preface

Welcome to the second edition of *The Explosive Child*. I have been enormously gratified by the response to the first edition of this book and, while the message remains very much the same, I have made a variety of changes and additions to the text for the purpose of helping the concepts and strategies come through even more clearly.

As the title suggests, this book is about explosive, inflexible, easily frustrated children. These children often exhibit severe behaviors—intense temper outbursts, noncompliance, volatility, mood instability, and verbal and physical aggression—that have the potential to make life extraordinarily challenging and frustrating for themselves, their parents, siblings, teachers, and others who interact with them. Though they have been described in many ways—difficult, strong-willed, manipulative, attention-seeking, contrary, intransigent—and may carry any or many of various psychiatric diagnoses, such as oppositional-defiant disorder (ODD), attention-deficit/hyperactivity disorder (ADHD), intermittent explosive disorder, Tourette's disorder, depression, bipolar disorder, nonverbal learning disability, Asperger's disorder, and obsessive-compulsive disorder (OCD), I believe their behavior is still poorly understood and therefore difficult to change.

For a long time the prevailing view of such behavior has been that it is attention-seeking, coercive, and the byproduct of inept parenting practices. But research of the past two decades suggests to me that inflexible and explosive behavior is a lot more complex than previously thought, and may emanate from a variety of different factors. Thus, there is no "one size fits all" approach to helping these children.

In writing and revising *The Explosive Child*, my intent has been to provide a more up-to-date conceptualization of such behavior, and to describe a new, practical, comprehensive approach aimed at decreasing adversarial interactions between explosive children and the adults who strive to ensure their well-being at home and school; reducing family hostility; and improving these children's capacities for flexibility, frustration tolerance, communication, problem solving, conflict resolution, and self-regulation. My goals are to help you appreciate the manner by which your explanations for and interpretations of a child's inflexible and explosive behavior can influence how you respond to it; to help you understand the factors that may lead to inflexible and explosive behavior in children; and to highlight the importance of finding the right treatment to fit the needs of individual children and families. Most of all, my goal is to help you break down the barriers imposed by a child's inflexibility and explosiveness and begin interacting in ways that feel better to you both.

This approach has evolved over the twenty or so years that have elapsed since I worked with my first explosive child. I don't think the kids have changed all that much since then, but my approach to helping them and their parents and teachers looks a lot different. And I think it works a lot better.

As always, the only prerequisite is an open mind.

Ross W. Greene, Ph.D.
Boston, Massachusetts

THE
Explosive Child

The Waffle Episode

Jennifer, age eleven, wakes up, makes her bed, looks around her room to make sure everything is in its place, and heads into the kitchen to make herself breakfast. She peers into the freezer, removes the container of frozen waffles, and counts six waffles. Thinking to herself, "I'll have three waffles this morning and three tomorrow morning," Jennifer toasts her three waffles and sits down to eat.

Moments later, her mother and five-year-old brother, Adam, enter the kitchen, and the mother asks Adam what he'd like to eat for breakfast. Adam responds, "Waffles," and the mother reaches into the freezer for the waffles. Jennifer, who has been listening intently, explodes.

"He can't have the frozen waffles!" Jennifer screams, her face suddenly reddening.

"Why not?" asks the mother, her voice and pulse rising, at a loss for an explanation of Jennifer's behavior.

"I was going to have those waffles tomorrow morning!" Jennifer screams, jumping out of her chair.

"I'm not telling your brother he can't have waffles!" the mother yells back.

"He can't have them!" screams Jennifer, now face-to-face with her mother.

The mother, wary of the physical and verbal aggression of which her daughter is capable during these moments, desperately asks Adam if there's something else he would consider eating.

"I want waffles," whimpers Adam, cowering behind his mother.

Jennifer, her frustration and agitation at a peak, pushes her mother out of the way, seizes the container of frozen waffles, then slams the freezer door shut, pushes over a kitchen chair, grabs her plate of toasted waffles, and stalks to her room. Her brother and mother begin to cry.

Jennifer's family members have endured literally thousands of such episodes. In many instances, the episodes are more prolonged and intense, and involve more physical or verbal aggression than the one described above (when Jennifer was eight, she kicked out the front windshield of the family car). Mental health professionals have told Jennifer's parents she has something called oppositional-defiant disorder. For the parents, however, a simple label doesn't begin to explain the upheaval, turmoil, and trauma that Jennifer's outbursts cause. Her siblings and mother are scared of her. Her extreme volatility and inflexibility require constant vigilance and enormous energy from her mother and father, thereby lessening the attention the parents wish they could devote to Jennifer's brother and sister. Her parents frequently argue over the best way to handle her behavior, but agree about the severe strains Jennifer places on their marriage. Although she is above average in intelligence, Jennifer has no close friends; children who initially befriend her eventually find her rigid personality difficult to tolerate.

Over the years, Jennifer's parents have sought help from countless mental health professionals, most of whom advised them to set firmer limits and be more consistent in managing Jennifer's behavior, and instructed them on how to implement formal behavior management strategies. When such strategies failed to work, Jennifer was medicated with innumerable combinations of drugs, without dramatic effect. After eight years of medicine, advice, sticker charts, time-outs, and reward programs, Jennifer has changed little since her parents first noticed there was something "different" about her when she was a toddler.

"Most people can't imagine how humiliating it is to be scared of your own daughter," Jennifer's mother once said. "People who don't have a child like Jennifer don't have a *clue* about what it's like to live like this. Believe me, this is not what I envisioned when I dreamed of having children. This is a nightmare."

"You can't imagine the embarrassment of having Jennifer 'lose it' around people who don't know her," her mother continued. "I feel like telling them, 'I have two kids at home who don't act like this—I really *am* a good parent!'"

"I know people are thinking, 'What wimpy parents she must have ... what that kid really needs is a good thrashing.' Believe me, we've tried everything with her. But nobody's been able to tell us how to help her ... no one's really been able to tell us what's the *matter* with her!"

"I hate what I've become. I used to think of myself as a

kind, patient, sympathetic person. But Jennifer has caused me to act in ways I never thought I was capable of. I'm emotionally spent. I can't keep living like this."

"I know a lot of other parents who have pretty difficult children . . . you know, kids who are hyperactive or having trouble paying attention. I would give my *left arm* for a kid who was just hyperactive or having trouble paying attention! Jennifer is in a completely different league! It makes me feel very alone."

The truth is, Jennifer's mother is not alone; there are a lot of Jennifers out there. Their parents quickly discover that strategies that are usually effective for shaping the behavior of other children—such as explaining, reasoning, reassuring, nurturing, redirecting, ignoring, rewarding, and punishing—don't have the same success with their Jennifers. Even formal behavior management programs—sticker charts, contingent rewarding and punishing, and time-outs—and commonly prescribed medications have not led to satisfactory improvement. If you started reading this book because you have a Jennifer of your own, you're probably familiar with how frustrated, confused, angry, bitter, guilty, overwhelmed, worn out, and hopeless Jennifer's parents feel.

Besides oppositional-defiant disorder, children like Jennifer may be diagnosed with any of a variety of psychiatric disorders and learning inefficiencies, including attention-deficit/hyperactivity disorder (ADHD), mood disorders (bipolar disorder and depression), Tourette's disorder, anxiety disorders (including obsessive-compulsive disorder), language-processing impairments, sensory integration dysfunction, nonverbal learning disability, reactive attachment disorder, and Asperger's disorder. Such children may also be described as having difficult temperaments. Whatever the label, children like Jennifer are distinguished by a few characteristics—namely, striking inflexibility and low frustration tolerance—that make life significantly more difficult and challenging for them and for the people who interact with them.

These children have enormous difficulty thinking clearly in the midst of frustration and often respond to even simple changes and requests with extreme inflexibility and often verbal or physical aggression. For reasons that will become clear, I've come to refer to such children as "inflexible-explosive"—not because I'm interested in inventing yet another syndrome (there are plenty already)—but because I think it's more accurate and descriptive and therefore gives us a better idea about what they need help with.

How are inflexible-explosive children different from other kids? Let's take a look at how different children may respond to a fairly common family scenario. Imagine that Child 1—Hubert—is watching television and his mother asks him to set the table for dinner. Hubert has a pretty easy time shifting from his agenda—watching television—to his mother's agenda—setting the table for dinner. Thus, in response to, "Hubert, I'd like you to turn off the television and come set the table for dinner," he would likely reply, "OK, mom, I'm coming" and would set the table shortly thereafter.

Child 2—Jermaine—is somewhat tougher. He has a harder time shifting from his agenda to his mother's agenda but is able to manage his frustration and shift gears (often with a threat hanging over his head). Thus, in response to, "Jermaine, I'd like you to turn off the television and come set the table for dinner," Jermaine might initially shout, "*No way*, I don't want to right now!" or complain, "You *always* ask me to do things right when I'm in the middle of something I like!" However, with some extra help (Mother: "Jermaine, if you don't turn off the television and come set the dinner table right now, you're going to have to take a time-out"), these "somewhat tougher" children do shift gears.

And then there is Jennifer, Child 3, the inflexible-explosive child, for whom shifting gears—from her agenda to her mother's agenda—often induces an unimaginable, intense, debilitating level of frustration. In response to, "Jennifer, I'd like you to turn off the television and come set the table for dinner," these children get stuck and often simply explode, at which point all bets are off on what they may say or do.

> *Whatever the label, children like Jennifer are distinguished by a few characteristics—namely, striking inflexibility and low frustration tolerance—that make life significantly more difficult and challenging for them and for the people who interact with them.*

Inflexible-explosive children come in all shapes and sizes. Some blow up literally dozens of times every day; others only a few times a week. Many "lose it" only at home, others only at school, some both at home and school. Some scream when they become frustrated but do not swear or become physically or verbally aggressive. One such child, Richard, a spunky, charismatic fourteen year old who was diagnosed with ADHD, began to cry in our first session when I asked if he thought it might be a good idea for us to help him start managing his frustration so he could begin getting along better with his family members. Others scream and swear but do not lash out physically (including Jack, an engaging, smart, moody ten year old, diagnosed with ADHD and Tourette's disorder, who had a very reliable pattern of becoming inflexible and irrational over the most trivial matters and whose inflexibility and irrationality tended to elicit similar behaviors from his parents). Still others combine the whole package, such as Marvin, a bright, active, impulsive, edgy, easily agitated eight year old with Tourette's disorder, depression, and ADHD, who reacted to unexpected changes with unimaginable screaming, swearing, and physical violence (on one occasion, Marvin's father innocently turned off an unnecessary light in the room in which Marvin was playing a video game, prompting a massive one-hour blowup).

What should become quite clear as you read this book is that these children have wonderful qualities and tremendous potential. In most ways, their general cognitive skills have developed at a normal pace. Yet their inflexibility and low tolerance for frustration often obscure their more positive traits and cause them and those around them enormous pain. I can think of no other group of children who are so misunderstood. Their parents are typically caring, well-intentioned people who often feel guilty that they are no longer able to feel great love for their children.

"You know," Jennifer's mother would say, "each time I start to get my hopes up . . . each time I have a pleasant interaction with Jennifer . . . I let myself become a little optimistic and start to like her again . . . and then it all comes crashing down with her next explosion. I'm ashamed to say it, but a lot of the time I really don't like her and I definitely don't like what she's doing to our family. We are in a perpetual state of crisis."

Clearly, there's something different about the Jennifers of the world. This is a critical, often painful, realization for parents to come to. But there is hope, as long as their parents, teachers, relatives, and therapists are able to come to grips with a second realization: Inflexible-explosive children often require different disciplinary practices than do other children. Unfortunately, there is no bible on how to deal with these children, particularly if medication and standard behavior management strategies fail to resolve their difficulties. Thus, the parents, teachers, relatives, and therapists of such children often aren't sure what to do or where to turn.

What I've found is that dealing more effectively with inflexible and explosive behavior requires, first and foremost, a new *understanding* of what these children are about. Once people have a better sense about why these children behave as they do, strategies for helping things improve become clearer. In some instances, achieving a more accurate understanding of a child's difficulties can, by itself, lead to improvements in adult-child interactions, even before formal strategies are tried. The first chapters of this book are devoted to helping you think about why these children adapt so poorly to changes and requests, are so easily frustrated, and explode so quickly and so often. Along the way, you'll read about why popular strategies for dealing with difficult children may be less effective than expected. In later chapters, you'll read about alternative strategies that have been helpful to many of the children, families, and teachers with whom I've worked over the years.

If you are the parent of an inflexible-explosive child, this book may restore some sanity and optimism to your family and help you feel that you can actually handle your child's difficulties confidently and competently. If you are a relative, friend, teacher, or therapist, this book should, at the least, help you understand. There is no panacea. But there is hope.

2

Terrible Beyond Two

One of the most amazing and gratifying things about being a parent is watching your child develop new skills and master increasingly complex tasks with each passing year. Crawling progresses to walking and then advances to running; babbling slowly develops into full-blown talking; smiling progresses to more sophisticated forms of socialization; learning the letters of the alphabet leads to reading whole words and then sentences, paragraphs, and books.

It is also amazing how unevenly different children's skills develop. Some children learn to read more readily than they learn to do multiplication. Some children turn out to be excellent athletes, while others may be less athletically skilled. When children's skills in a particular area lag well behind their expected development, we often give them special help. This special help may be informal, such as Steve's baseball coach suggesting extra batting practice, or formal, such as Ken's school giving him remedial assistance with reading. In some cases, skills may lag because of a child's lack of exposure to the appropriate material (for example, maybe Steve was never actually taught how to hit a baseball). More commonly, children have difficulty learning a particular skill even though they have the desire to master the skill and have been provided with the instruction typically needed to master it. It's not that they don't *want* to learn; it is simply that they are not learning as readily as expected. Sometimes, with intensive instruction, extra effort, and a lot of support and encouragement, children can improve their skills in areas in which they are having difficulty. And sometimes children's skills improve to some extent but never reach the desired level of mastery. In other words, some children—no matter how hard they and their parents, teachers and coaches try—are just not "built" to be great athletes, readers, or spellers.

Flexibility and *frustration tolerance* are also skills we expect to develop in children as they grow past the toddler years. Many children go through a phase called the Terrible Twos, in which they are increasingly inflexible and easily frustrated. During this phase, there is often a marked increase in the frequency and intensity of a child's tantrums; indeed, at this stage of development, tantrums are a common, if not particularly pleasant, way for children to say things like, "I'm hungry," "I'm tired," "I'm confused," "I don't know how to handle this problem," or "I'm not happy with what's going on at the moment." To the tremendous relief of parents, this phase is usually relatively short-lived.

Why do most children eventually progress beyond the Terrible Twos? They do so because they gradually develop the ability to express their needs and desires more effectively, tolerate frustration and delay gratification more readily, "shift gears" more efficiently when events vary from the original plan, resolve problems by thinking through possible solutions, and move beyond "black-and-white" thinking by demonstrating the ability to appreciate the "gray" in many situations. In most cases, children need some initial guidance from adults to recognize the necessity of these skills ("George, don't *hit* Carolyn! Use your *words*!" "Fred, if you won't let Cindy take a turn at the Nintendo, then I'm going to turn the whole thing off and neither of you will get to play." "Tom, I don't think Mary is enjoying watching you play with the Legos. Why don't you ask her if there's something she'd like to build.")

Mastery of these hurdles is crucial to a child's overall development because interacting adaptively with the world requires the continuous ability to solve problems, work out disagreements, and control the emotions one experiences when frustrated. Indeed, it's difficult to imagine many situations in a child's day that don't require flexibility, adaptability, and frustration tolerance. When two children disagree about which game to play, we hope both children possess compromising and problem-solving skills that will help them resolve the dispute in an agreeable, mutually satisfactory manner. When bad weather forces parents to cancel their child's much-anticipated trip to the amusement park, we hope the child has the ability to express his disappointment appropriately, shift gears, and delay the trip and settle on an alternative plan. When a child is engrossed in a video game and it's time to set the table for dinner, we hope the child is able to interrupt his game, manage his natural feelings of frustration, and think clearly enough to recognize that he can return to the game later. And when a child decides she'll have three frozen waffles for breakfast today and three tomorrow and her younger brother decides he wants three frozen waffles today, too, we hope the child can move beyond black-and-white thinking ("I am *definitely* going to have those three waffles for breakfast tomorrow so there's no way my brother can have them") and recognize the gray in the situation ("I guess I don't have to eat those *exact* waffles . . . I can ask my mom to buy more . . . anyway, I might not even feel like eating waffles tomorrow").

Just as some children lag in acquiring reading skills and other children do not develop great athletic skills, still others—the children this book is about—do not progress to the degree we would have hoped in terms of flexibility and frustration tolerance. Thus, a major premise of this book is that these children do not *choose* to be explosive and noncompliant—any more than a child would choose to have a reading disability—but are delayed in the process of developing the skills that are critical to being flexible and tolerating frustration (or have significant difficulty applying these skills when they most need to). A second important premise of this book is that the inflexibility and explosiveness of these children have a lot to do with how they're "built" (and, of course, with how you respond to how they're built—we'll get to that later).

When people say a child is "built" to be one way or another, they are often referring to the workings of the child's brain. Our understanding of these "workings" is still fairly elementary, though we live in an age in which science is quickly unraveling the chemical and physiological bases for human behavior. As we learn more, many popular explanations for behavior become obsolete. Old explanations for disorders, such as schizophrenia and depression, have fallen by the wayside as convincing evidence has emerged that in many cases there is a neurobiochemical predisposition to these disorders that is often genetically transmitted.

Nevertheless, the human brain is a remarkably complex entity, so it's hard to get a precise handle on things, especially in children, whose brains aren't fully developed. Science has not advanced to the degree that we can speak with perfect accuracy about the specific neurobiochemical brain mechanisms underlying many childhood psychiatric disorders. Still, there's some fairly compelling evidence to suggest that, for example, irregularities in the prefrontal and frontal regions of the brain and other brain structures connected to these regions may contribute to impairments in "executive" thinking skills often seen in children with ADHD. As you'll read, these skills—including mental flexibility, the ability to shift from one mind-set to another, problem solving, planning, organizing one's thoughts, and controlling one's impulses—are critical to one's capacity for flexibility and frustration tolerance. Other brain irregularities involving the neurotransmitter serotonin have been implicated in depression, aggression, and obsessive-compulsive disorder, all of which can be associated with inflexibility and explosiveness. Still other irregularities—largely in the right hemisphere of the brain—are thought to underlie impaired "nonverbal skills," which may contribute to a pattern of poor problem-solving skills; difficulty understanding cause-and-effect relationships; trouble adapting to unfamiliar,

A major premise of this book is that these children do not choose to be explosive and noncompliant—any more than a child would choose to have a reading disability—but are delayed in the process of developing the skills that are critical to being flexible and tolerating frustration (or have significant difficulty applying these skills when they most need to).

unexpected, or complex situations; and poor social perception and social judgment. As you'd imagine, impaired nonverbal skills can contribute to inflexible-explosive behavior as well. Finally, irregularities in certain regions of the left hemisphere of the brain may affect language functioning. Children with impaired language-processing skills often have difficulty sorting through and expressing their thoughts so as to solve problems and handle frustration adaptively.

One of the nice things about uncovering these physiologic connections—imprecise as some still are—is that they help move us away from the standard, knee-jerk explanations for why some children keep doing things we wish they wouldn't; for instance, "He's doing it for attention" or "He could do better if he really wanted to." It's becoming less common these days to hear someone suggest, for example, that a child with ADHD is "intentionally" being hyperactive, impulsive, and inattentive or that the vocal tics of a child with Tourette's disorder are "for attention." Of course, we are left to ponder why such knee-jerk explanations are still commonly invoked to explain the inflexibility and explosiveness that often accompanies these otherwise "unintentional" disorders.

The main point is this: There's a big difference between viewing inflexible-explosive behaviors as the result of a brain-based failure to progress developmentally and viewing them as planned, intentional, and purposeful. That's because your interpretation of a child's inflexible-explosive behaviors will be closely linked to how you try to change these behaviors. In other words, *your interpretation will guide your intervention*.

If you interpret a child's behavior as planned, intentional, and purposeful, then labels such as "stubborn," "manipulative," "coercive," "bratty," "attention-seeking," "controlling," "resistant," and "defiant" will sound perfectly reasonable to you, and popular strategies aimed at motivating compliant behavior and "teaching the child who's boss" will make perfect sense. If this has been your interpretation of your child's explosive behavior, you're not alone. You're also not alone if this interpretation hasn't led you to a productive outcome. Throughout this book, I encourage you to put this explanation on the shelf and give some consideration to an alternative explanation: that your child's explosive behavior is unplanned and unintentional and reflects a developmental delay in the skills of flexibility and frustration tolerance. From this perspective, putting a lot of energy into motivating your child and teaching him who's boss may actually be counterproductive. Indeed, these goals can actually fuel an adversarial pattern that may make progress much more difficult to achieve.

Is this alternative, contemporary view more accurate in many instances? If so, is there a better way of describing these children? And are there alternative strategies that may better match the needs of inflexible-explosive children and their families?

Yes, yes, and yes.

To begin with, here's the diagnostic criteria for oppositional-defiant disorder, which, as you read in Chapter 1, is the standard diagnosis for children whose temper outbursts, excessive arguing, and defiance persist well beyond the Terrible Twos:

Partial Diagnostic Criteria
for Oppositional-Defiant Disorder*

A pattern of negativistic, hostile, and defiant behavior lasting at least six months, during which four (or more) of the following are present:

- often loses temper
- often argues with adults

- often actively defies or refuses to comply with adults' requests or rules
- often deliberately annoys other people
- often blames others for his or her mistakes or misbehavior
- is often touchy or easily annoyed by others
- is often angry or resentful
- is often spiteful and vindictive

*Reprinted with permission from the *Diagnostic and Statistical Manual of Mental Disorders, Fourth Edition. Copyright 1994 American Psychiatric Association.

I'm not invested in these criteria because I don't think they do justice to the actual processes of inflexible-explosive behavior. These criteria also imply that oppositional behavior is deliberate, and I don't think this is true in many instances. If my first goal is to help you come to a more accurate understanding of your child's behavior, I'd better give you a more accurate way of describing it. The characteristics discussed next may be helpful:

Common Characteristics of Inflexible-Explosive Children

1. The child has difficulty managing and controlling the emotions associated with frustration and has difficulty "thinking through" ways of resolving frustrating situations in a rational, mutually satisfactory manner. Thus, frustration (caused by disagreements, changes in plan, demands for "shifting gears") often leads to a state of cognitive debilitation in which the child has difficulty remembering how to stay calm and problem-solve, has

difficulty recalling the consequences of previous inflexible-explosive episodes, may not be responsive to reasoned attempts to restore coherence, and may deteriorate even further in response to limit-setting and punishment.

2. An extremely low frustration threshold. The child becomes frustrated far more easily and by far more seemingly trivial events than other children of his or her age. Therefore, the child experiences the world as one filled with insurmountable frustration and has little faith in his ability to handle such frustration.

3. An extremely low tolerance for frustration. The child is not only more easily frustrated, but also experiences the emotions associated with frustration more intensely and tolerates them far less adaptively than do other children of the same age. In response to frustration, the child becomes extremely agitated, disorganized, and verbally or physically aggressive.

4. Remarkably limited capacity for flexibility and adaptability; the child often seems unable to shift gears in response to commands or a change in plans.

5. The tendency to think in a concrete, rigid, black-and-white manner. The child does not recognize the gray in many situations ("Mrs. Robinson is *always* mean! I *hate* her!" rather than "Mrs. Robinson is usually nice, but she was in a really bad mood today"); may apply oversimplified, rigid, inflexible rules to complex situations; and may impulsively revert to such rules even when they are obviously inappropriate ("We *always* go out for

recess at 10:30. I don't *care* if there's an assembly today, *I'm* going out for recess!").

6. The persistence of inflexibility and poor response to frustration despite a high level of intrinsic or extrinsic motivation. The child continues to exhibit frequent, intense, and lengthy melt-downs even in the face of salient, potent consequences.

7. Explosive episodes may have an out-of-the-blue quality. The child may seem to be in a good mood, then fall apart unexpect-edly in the face of frustrating circumstances, no matter how trivial.

8. The child may have one or several issues about which he or she is especially inflexible—for example, the way clothing looks or feels, the way food tastes or smells, the order or manner in which things must be done.

9. The child's inflexibility and difficulty responding to frustration in an adaptive manner may be fueled by behaviors—moodi-ness/irritability, hyperactivity/impulsivity, anxiety, obsessive-ness, social impairment—commonly associated with other disorders.

10. While other children are apt to become more irritable when tired or hungry, inflexible-explosive children may completely fall apart under such conditions.

What I hope these unofficial characteristics will help you begin to do is understand and describe your child's explo-sions and inflexibility differently. It's hard to imagine how a child could be actively "yanking your chain" or know "just the right buttons to push" when he's not thinking rationally in the midst of frustration. It's harder still to imagine why a child would intentionally behave in a way that makes other people respond in a manner that makes him miserable. I also don't think these kids are especially angry, though I do think they're extremely frustrated. When the term angry applies to them, it's often because they're angry at being misunderstood. They typically don't understand their own behavior, but they're quite certain no one else does either.

In their own incredible frustration and confusion over the constant inflexibility and explosiveness being exhibited by their child, parents frequently demand that the child provide a logical explanation for his actions. The dialogue often goes something like this:

Parent: "We've talked about this a million times . . . WHY DON'T YOU DO WHAT YOU'RE TOLD? WHAT ARE YOU SO ANGRY ABOUT?"

Inflexible-Explosive child: "I don't know."

The child's maddening response usually has the effect of further heightening his parents' frustration. It's worth noting, of course, that the child is probably telling the truth.

In a perfect world, the child would respond with something like, "See, Mom and Dad, I have this little problem. You guys—and lots of other people—are constantly asking me to shift from Agenda A to Agenda B, and I'm not very good at it. In fact, when you ask me to make these shifts, I start to get frustrated. And when I start getting frustrated, I have trouble thinking clearly and then I get even more frustrated. Then you guys get mad. Then I start doing things I wish I didn't do and saying things I wish I didn't say. Then you guys get even madder and punish me, and it gets really messy. After the dust settles—you know, when I start thinking clearly again—I end up being really sorry for the things I did and said. I know this isn't fun for you, but rest assured, I'm not having any fun either."

It's hard to imagine how a child could be actively "yanking your chain" or know "just the right buttons to push" when he's not thinking rationally in the midst of frustration. It's harder still to imagine why a child would intentionally behave in a way that makes other people respond in a manner that makes him miserable.

Alas, we live in an imperfect world. Inflexible-explosive children are rarely able to describe their difficulties with this kind of clarity. Nonetheless, this ideal response provides a good opportunity to take a closer look at where I'm heading in this book, for it describes the downward spiral that often typifies inflexible-explosive episodes. Indeed, the child's response suggests that there is a distinct progression to many such episodes. Here's what I mean:

When you ask me to make these shifts, I start to get frustrated . . . and when I start getting frustrated, I have trouble thinking clearly, and then I get even more frustrated.

In the early phase of an inflexible-explosive episode, the child is presented with an environmental demand to shift gears and experiences the natural frustration associated with doing so. But because of his deficits in the domains of flexibility and frustration tolerance, he has trouble tolerating the frustration and responding adaptively to the demand. It is in this early phase that he exhibits the early warning signs that he's stuck. The trouble is, he's likely to tell you he's stuck in a way that is offensive. I've come to refer to this early phase of an inflexible-explosive episode as *vapor lock* (a metaphor originated by Dr. Steve Durant, a colleague of mine at Mass General).

Let's elaborate on the theme of vapor lock for a moment by thinking of your child's brain as working in the same way as a car's engine. Vapor lock in engines is caused by excessive heat. The excessive heat causes a bubble in the gas line that prevents gas from flowing to the engine and causes the engine to stall. No matter how many times the driver pumps the gas pedal or turns the ignition, the car won't start again until the engine cools down. In a similar manner, frustration often causes a breakdown in an inflexible-explosive child's capacity to think clearly, causing him to become more overwhelmed and less rational. No matter how many times adults pump the gas pedal—scream, berate, reason, insist, reward, punish, or whatever—the child probably won't start thinking clearly again until someone helps him cool down.

A child I worked with had his own term for this phenomenon: *brain lock*. He explained that he locked on to an idea and then had tremendous difficulty unlocking, regardless of how reasonable or rational the attempts of others to unlock him. A few other children have referred to this early phase as "short-circuiting" to describe the difficulty they have at unjamming their brain circuits in order to think clearly and rationally. One computer-savvy child told me he wished his brain had a Pentium processor so he could think faster and more efficiently when he became frustrated. Regardless of the term you use, the important point is that during vapor lock, a child may still be capable of rational thought; therefore, it may still be possible to prevent a full-blown catastrophe.

. . . then you guys get mad . . .

Now we've moved to the second phase of an inflexible-explosive episode: the *crossroads* phase. This is the parents' chance to respond to their child's frustration in a manner that facilitates either (1) communication, collaborative problem solving, and resolution or (2) further deterioration. As you've probably found, getting mad has probably been moving your child closer to "2" than to "1" because getting mad probably doesn't reduce your child's frustration or help him think more clearly. Luckily, there's a whole universe of things you can do during this phase besides getting mad. As you shall see.

Then I start doing things I wish I didn't do and saying things I wish I didn't say . . . then you guys get even madder and punish me, and it gets really messy.

A deteriorating inflexible-explosive child is neither a pretty sight nor a pleasant experience. If the child deteriorates past the point of rescue, he'll become completely overwhelmed by frustration and lose his capacity for coherent, rational thought. At that point, the final phase of the episode has been reached: *meltdown*. Others have referred to this phenomenon as "disintegrative rage"; Dr. Daniel Goleman, author of *Emotional Intelligence*, referred to it as a "neural hijacking." It is during meltdowns that inflexible-explosive children are likely to lapse into their most destructive, abusive behavior. I use the term *mental debris* to describe the horrible words that may come out of a child's mouth during these incoherent moments.

Obviously, *meltdown* is not an original term; go to any playground frequented by two year olds and you'll hear their parents describing, often with good humor, their children's latest "meltdown of the week." The meltdowns of inflexible-explosive children often look very much the same as those of two year olds. But the parents of inflexible-explosive children do not describe meltdowns with good humor. They've been enduring them for a long time, and the meltdowns have become much more frequent, intense, and uncontrollable.

The trouble is, little or no learning occurs for a child while he is in the midst of a meltdown (as far as I can tell, very few people are receptive to learning when they are in an incoherent state). In fact, attempts to continue teaching the child how to behave while he is in the midst of a meltdown—even trying to talk reasonably—have an excellent chance of increasing his frustration and making it that much more difficult for him to regain coherence. Punishing a child during a meltdown has the potential to fuel his frustration even further and, as you may have found, may not decrease the odds of a meltdown the next time he's frustrated.

> After the dust settles—you know, when I start thinking clearly again—I end up being really sorry for the things I did and said.

This statement speaks to the fact that once coherence has been restored, these children often express deep remorse for what they've said or done, although many have difficulty recalling events that occurred during the meltdown or what they were so upset about in the first place.

OK, now we've given you a jump-start on a new way of interpreting and describing your child's behavior and an appreciation for the general sequence of events. But this sequence can be useful in another way: it can help you think about *when* you should be intervening, and, once that's been established, *how* you should do it. You'll get more details on the when and how as you continue reading. Briefly, though, what I've found is that many parents of inflexible-explosive children put most of their energy into intervening during and after the meltdown phase. I call this reactive intervention, or intervening on the back end, and, in the case of inflexible-explosive children, I have little faith that intervening at these moments will be productive. The emphasis in this book is on helping you respond to your child *before* he's at his worst—in other words, proactively, on the front end. Thus, an important focus of this book is to help you learn how to anticipate and recognize situations that routinely lead to vapor lock—so you can respond before vapor lock sets in—and to help you become more aware of the things you can do during the vapor lock and crossroads phases to prevent meltdowns.

*

You've just been given a lot of new ideas to digest. Perhaps the following summary of this chapter will be helpful:

· Flexibility and frustration tolerance are critical developmental skills that some children fail to develop as they move beyond the Terrible Twos. Inadequate development of these skills can contribute to a variety of behaviors—sudden outbursts, prolonged tantrums, and physical and verbal aggression, often in response to even the most benign of circumstances—that frequently have a traumatic, adverse impact on these children's interactions and relationships with parents, teachers, siblings, and peers.

- How you interpret your child's inflexible-explosive behavior and the language you use to describe it will directly influence the strategies you use to help your child change this behavior.

- Putting your old interpretation on the shelf will also mean putting your old parenting practices on the shelf. In other words, helping your child be more flexible usually means you will have to be more flexible first. This isn't as unfair or unreasonable a statement as it may sound, for you've already experienced the futility of responding inflexibly to a child who is, by nature, inflexible.

- One of the most important things you can do to help your child explode less often is to approach his difficulties proactively (before the fact) rather than reactively (after the fact)—as you shall see.

3

Pathways to Inflexibility-Explosiveness

The last chapter provided a brief discussion of various factors that may compromise your child's capacity to handle the emotions associated with frustration in an adaptive manner, think through problems, and deal effectively with curves in the road. Let's take a closer look at some of the specific pathways that may set the stage for a chronic pattern of vapor lock and meltdowns, including difficult temperament, ADHD, social skills deficits, language-processing impairments, mood and anxiety disorders, nonverbal learning disability, and sensory integration dysfunction.

Difficult Temperament

Dr. Stanley Turecki has written an excellent book on children with difficult temperaments entitled *The Difficult Child*. He defines temperament as *the natural, inborn style of behavior of each individual* and adds that this style of behavior is *innate and . . . not produced by the environment*. On the basis of the work of Drs. Alexander Thomas, Herbert Birch, Stella Chess, and others, Turecki delineated nine characteristics of temperamentally difficult children: high activity level, distractibility, high intensity, withdrawal from or poor reaction to new or unfamiliar things, poor adaptability (reacting badly to changes in routine), negative persistence (strong willed, whiny, rigid), low sensory threshold (for example, clothes that don't "feel" right), and negative mood (cranky, irritable).

Does this sound like your child? Here's something you probably already know: These temperamental features are often evident, in one form or another, at infancy (although I've come across a fair number of children who were described as relatively "easy" infants but became much more difficult somewhere between one and four years old). Temperamentally difficult infants may react poorly to changes in routine; are restless and squirmy; protest when first introduced to new foods, places, or people; can be fussy or colicky; are poorly regulated with regard to feeding and sleeping; over-react to noises, lights, and discomfort (hunger, cold, a wet diaper, etc.), and may not settle down easily even after their needs have been met. But I've yet to hear a temperamentally difficult infant described as "manipulative," "coercive," "bratty," or "controlling." Rather, it is generally assumed that temperamentally difficult infants are simply built that way. I can't explain why the explanations become a lot less compassionate as such children get older. I often tell parents that their inflexible-explosive child is simply a slightly older version of the temperamentally difficult infant or toddler they were blessed with a few years back.

How are difficult temperament and inflexibility-explosiveness connected? Here's the basic recipe: Mix high intensity with a poor reaction to new or unfamiliar things, add poor adaptability and negative persistence, stir in low sensory threshold and negative mood. Season with hyperactivity (optional). Heat (briefly). You've just cooked up an inflexible-explosive child. Inflexibility-explosiveness may best be viewed as the most toxic manifestation of a difficult temperament.

In keeping with the credo that very few things in psychology are always true, not all inflexible-explosive children have or had difficult temperaments. Nonetheless, you'll see a lot of overlap between the characteristics of temperamentally difficult children and the behaviors, described next, that define many of the diagnostic labels that end up on their insurance forms.

ADHD and Executive Function Deficits

A lot of temperamentally difficult children and many of the inflexible-explosive children I work with are diagnosed with ADHD at some point along the way. ADHD is the diagnostic label used to describe children who exhibit developmentally extreme levels of inattention or hyperactivity-impulsivity, or both. ADHD has received more research attention than any other childhood psychiatric disorder. But some of the most exciting research on ADHD has occurred over the past fifteen years. This research has shown that children with ADHD often have deficits in a crucial set of thinking skills commonly referred to as "executive functions." There's no universal agreement on the specific skills that comprise executive functions, nor a complete consensus on the regions of the brain that govern these skills (although much research has zeroed in on the frontal, prefrontal, and frontally interconnected subcortical regions of the brain fueled by the neurotransmitter dopamine). Nonetheless, executive functions can help us understand not only the behaviors that are included in the diagnosis of ADHD—such as difficulty sustaining attention and effort, lack of attention to details, seeming not to listen, difficulty following through on tasks or instructions, disorganization, distractibility, motoric restlessness, talking excessively, difficulty awaiting one's turn, interrupting or intruding on others—but also the poor tolerance for frustration, inflexibility, temper outbursts, and unstable mood commonly seen in inflexible-explosive children.

Specifically, executive functions include cognitive skills such as *shifting cognitive set* (the ability to shift efficiently from one mind-set to another), *organization and planning* (organizing a coherent plan of action to deal with a problem or frustration), *working memory* (performing multiple thinking tasks simultaneously), and *separation of affect* (the ability to separate your emotional response to a problem from the thinking you need to perform to solve the problem). What I like about these terms is that they help us understand what's going on (or, perhaps more accurately, what's *not* going on) inside the heads of many inflexible-explosive children. Let's take a closer look at each.

Moving from one environment (such as recess) to a completely different environment (such as a reading class) requires a shift from one mind-set ("In recess it's OK to run around and make noise and socialize") to another ("In reading, we sit at our desks and read quietly and independently"). If a child has difficulty shifting cognitive set, there's a good chance he'll still be thinking and acting like he's in recess long after reading class has started. This circumstance helps explain why children with ADHD have such trouble making transitions from the rules and expectations of one activity to the rules and expectations of another.

But inefficient shifting of cognitive set may also explain why a child may become so frustrated when, for example, his parents ask him to stop watching television and come in for dinner. If a child is an inefficient "shifter" and if other factors—like the parents insisting that he comply with their requests or shift gears quickly—compound the child's mounting frustration or compromise his capacity for clear thought, even seemingly simple requests may set the stage for serious explosions. Such children are not intentionally trying to be noncompliant; rather, they have trouble flexibly and efficiently shifting from one mind-set to another.

Parent: "My child does just fine unless something doesn't go his way."

Me: "Precisely."

Parent: "Doesn't that mean he just wants his way?"

Me: "We all just want our way. Your child lacks some of the skills he needs to handle the fact that things aren't going to go the way he had envisioned."

How do we know a child is having difficulty shifting cognitive set? He tells us! That's the good part. The unfortunate part is that he may not articulate this difficulty in an appropriate way. Let's listen in:

Parent: Please turn off the TV and come in for dinner.

Casey [early vapor lock]: No! My show's not over yet!

Parent [crossroads]: Turn off the TV and come in for dinner now!

Casey [advanced vapor lock]: I can't come in!

Parent: What do you mean, you "can't come in"? Dinner's getting cold . . . get in here!

Casey: Shut up! I'm not listening!

As this dialogue suggests, if you respond to a child who's having difficulty shifting cognitive set as if he were being intentionally noncompliant, you probably won't help him shift gears any faster.

"I may want to sit. Just give me a chance to process this."

Organization and impulse control are also critical to the process of thinking through one's options for dealing with problems or frustrations. Children with ADHD are notorious for being disorganized and impulsive. This explains why many of them have so much trouble bringing the appropriate homework materials home from school, completing homework, and getting ready for school in the morning (tasks that involve a high level of organization and planning of multiple sequenced smaller tasks), and why children with ADHD so often call out answers in class, have difficulty awaiting their turns, and interrupt and intrude on others.

However, disorganization and poor impulse control may also explain the difficulty many children with ADHD have in responding effectively to life's daily barrage of problems and frustrations. Such children are often taken by surprise at problems because they're not good at anticipating them in advance, even when certain problems seem to occur over and over. Furthermore, to deal effectively with frustration one must organize a coherent plan of action—in other words, think clearly. Now, most of us don't do our clearest thinking when we're frustrated. Indeed, it's when we're frustrated that we're most likely to lash out, swear, and behave unreasonably. If you're disorganized and impulsive to begin with, you're entering each frustrating situation with a limited capacity to think clearly and organize a coherent plan of action, and—like the rest of us—the frustration is likely to make things that much worse.

I've seen a few interesting patterns in the disorganized, impulsive children with whom I've worked. The first I call "impulsive negativity." This refers to the tendency for the child to instantaneously say "no!" every time someone asks him to do something. An eight-year-old boy with ADHD and Asperger's disorder used to exhibit this pattern in my office almost weekly. He knew that I was going to spend the first ten minutes of each session talking with his mother while he played in my waiting room. He also knew that after ten minutes I'd invite him to come into my office to play a game. He liked being in my office more than he liked playing in my waiting room, so he was motivated to come in. But, with amazing dependability, every time I would open my door and say, "OK, Tom, it's your turn, come on in," he'd respond, "No!" After about 30 seconds, without another word being uttered, he'd come into my office. His initial "No!" was simply his way of letting me know he needed a little extra time to organize a coherent response.

The second pattern I've seen in such children is what might be called "repertoire shrinkage." Few problems are simple enough to have straightforward solutions; rather, most problems we face are complex and have similarly complex solutions. In other words, most problems aren't successfully resolved with one quick thought. But if you respond to problems impulsively rather than reflecting on your full range of response options, you tend to respond in a very rigid, circumscribed manner. This may explain why some children continue to swear or hit or throw things in the midst of frustration, even though (in calmer moments) they can think of much more adaptive ways to respond.

An executive skill that operates in tandem with organization and planning is working memory. Working memory refers to a person's capacity to "multi-task." For example, you're multi-tasking when you're driving a car because you're watching the road in front of you, attending to whether you're exceeding the speed limit, conscious of what the cars around you are doing, listening to the radio, and thinking about the activities you have planned after work. Difficulties with working memory can make it appear as if a person has a "one-track mind." Borrowing from computer lingo, such a person might run into trouble if a task required them to open and work with more than one "file" at a time. I once asked Jack, a fourteen-year-old boy with ADHD, why he was calling out so often in class, and he unknowingly responded in a manner that told me he had difficulty with working memory: "If I have to wait until I'm called on, I'll forget what I wanted to say . . . and if I try to remember what I want to say, I won't be able to follow the discussion that's going on, so when I'm finally called on, my answer seems off-base."

How might impaired working memory compromise a child's capacity for flexibility and frustration tolerance? Well, returning to computer lingo, when you're faced with a problem or frustration, there are at least three "files" you need to open in your brain. The first is the "problem definition" file, which helps you identify what problem it is that you're actually trying to solve. (Can you imagine trying to solve a problem without first opening this file?) The second file to open is the "hindsight" file, which helps you access information about how you've handled similar problems in the past ("How have I successfully handled this problem before?" "What previous actions have I taken in response to this problem that have *not* been as successful?"). But you must keep the problem definition file open while you're simultaneously accessing the hindsight file, or you'll lose track of what problem it was that you were trying to access previous information about! The third file to open—while keeping the first two open at the same time—is the "forethought" file. This file permits you to project each possible solution to the problem into the future so as to select the best option ("Under the present circumstances, which of the possible solutions to this problem will work out the best?"). Naturally, accessing the forethought file wouldn't be particularly helpful if you weren't able to keep the problem definition and hindsight files open simultaneously.

If you can't keep all three files open while you're trying to think through potential solutions, the "thinking-through" process is likely to stall, and you're likely to respond in the same way many people do when, in the midst of frustration, their brains fail them: by crying or exploding. Children with poor working memory are not intentionally trying to be non-compliant; rather, they have trouble efficiently and flexibly sorting through different solutions to frustrating problems. A typical scenario may sound something like this:

Parent: I'm running a little behind today. Finish your breakfast, put your dishes in the sink, and get ready for school.

Child [early vapor lock]: But I'm not through eating yet.

Parent [crossroads]: Why don't you grab an apple or something. Come on, hurry! I have to drop some things at the post office on the way there.

Child [advanced vapor lock]: I can't do that!

Parent: You can't do what? Why do you always do this when I'm in a hurry? Just this once, could you please do what I say without arguing?

Child: I don't know what to do!

Parent: I just told you what to do! Don't push me today!

Child: [meltdown]

As this dialogue suggests, if you respond to a child who's having difficulty with working memory as if he were being intentionally noncompliant, you probably won't help him problem-solve any better.

Thinking clearly is a lot easier if a child has the capacity to separate or detach himself from the emotions caused by frustration, an executive skill sometimes referred to as "separation of affect." This skill permits people to put their emotions on the shelf so as to think through solutions to problems more objectively, rationally, and logically. Children whose skills in this domain are lacking or inefficient tend to respond to frustrating situations with less thought and more emotion. They may actually feel themselves "heating up" but often aren't able to stem the emotional tide until later, when the emotions have subsided and rational thought has kicked back in. They may even have the knowledge to deal successfully with problems (under calmer circumstances, they can actually demonstrate such knowledge), but at the moment they're frustated, their powerful emotions prevent them from using the information. Such children are not intentionally trying to be noncompliant; rather, they become overwhelmed with the emotions associated with frustration. You know what this is like:

Parent: It's time to stop playing Nintendo and get ready for bed.

Child, responding with more emotion than thought: Damn it! I'm right in the middle of an important game!

Parent: You're always right in the middle of an important game. Get to bed! Now!

Child: Damn! You made me mess up my game!

*Parent: I messed up your game? Get your butt in gear
before I mess up something else!*

Child: [meltdown]

As this dialogue suggests, if you respond to a child who's
having difficulty separating affect as if he were intentionally
being noncompliant, you probably won't help him manage his
emotions and start thinking rationally. Quite the opposite, in
fact. I often tell inflexible-explosive children and their parents
and teachers that treatment consists of two simple goals: Goal
number two: *think clearly in the midst of frustration*. Goal
number one: *stay calm enough to achieve goal number two*.

Executive function deficits can also explain why children
with ADHD may demonstrate so little insight about themselves and equally minimal awareness of the impact of their
behavior on other people. Indeed, children with executive
function deficits often come off as demanding, self-centered,
and lacking in empathy and social tact. Self-awareness and
empathy require a fairly continuous process of reflecting on
and rethinking of past experience and perspective taking, and
this process may be short-circuited by deficits in executive
skills. As you'll read in later chapters, helping inflexible-
explosive children achieve a basic level of insight into their difficulties can help them respond to frustration more adaptively.
Of course, helping *you* achieve greater insight about these difficulties is our goal right now.

Social Skills Deficits

I can think of few human activities that require more flexibility, complex thinking, and rapid processing than social interactions. Thus, it should come as no surprise that children whose thinking is rigid and inefficient find their social interactions to be frustrating, and this frustration may fuel many of their explosions. In collaboration with several of his colleagues, Dr. Ken Dodge, a researcher at Duke University, has delineated a set of specific thinking skills—known as "social information processing skills"—that are thought to be involved in even the most trivial of social interactions. A brief review of these thinking skills will help you understand just how labor-intensive social interactions can be, especially for children who aren't good at them.

Let's say a boy is standing in a hallway at school and a peer comes up and, with a big smile on his face, whacks the boy hard on the back and says, "Hi!" The boy who was whacked on the back now has a split-second to attend to and try to pick up on the important qualities of the social cues of this situation ("Who just whacked me on the back? Aside from the person's smile, is there anything about his posture or facial expression or this context that tells me whether this was a friendly or unfriendly smile and whack?"). At the same time he must connect those cues with his previous experiences ("When have other people, and this person in particular, whacked me on the back and smiled at me before?") so as to interpret the cue ("Was this an overexuberant greeting or an aggressive act? How do I feel about it?"). Then he has to think about what he wants to have happen next ("That was a mean thing to do . . . I'd like to avoid getting into a fight with this person" or "That was a nice greeting . . . I'd like to play a game with him").

Then, on the basis of his interpretation of the cue and the outcome he desires, the boy must begin to think about how to respond, either by remembering his experiences in similar situations or by thinking of new responses. Then, he must evaluate the different possible responses, consider the likely outcomes of each ("If I smile back, he'll probably ask me to play a game with him"), choose a response, enact it, monitor the course of events throughout, and adjust the response accordingly.

Sounds like a lot of thinking for one event, yes? The key point is that this process is nonstop and requires a lot of efficiency. It's barely noticeable to people who do it without even thinking about it, but it's very frustrating when it doesn't happen automatically. As children get older, social interactions become increasingly complex and require even greater efficiency of thought.

Many inflexible-explosive children are quite unskilled at recognizing the impact of their behavior on others; may apply the same rigid, rote interpretation (for example, "He doesn't like me" or "That's not fair") to diverse, complex social situations; and may have a limited repertoire of responses and end up applying the identical response (hitting, screaming, crying, exploding) to a wide range of social situations. If a child isn't "built" to reflect on the accuracy of his interpretations, the effectiveness of a given response, or the manner in which his behavior affects others—a circumstance Daniel Goleman has referred to as "emotional illiteracy"—he is likely to find social interactions extremely frustrating. This can, at the least, contribute to the child's general level of frustration; at worst, it may lead to a chronic pattern of explosions. There are two books by Drs. Stephen Nowicki and Marshall Duke—*Helping the Child Who Doesn't Fit In* and *Teaching Your Child the*

Language of Social Success—that describe these and other social difficulties, and how to help, more fully.

Sometimes a child's social functioning is so severely impaired that the diagnosis of pervasive developmental disorder (PDD) may be considered. PDD is the category under which disorders such as autism and Asperger's disorder are subsumed. These disorders are characterized both by marked delays in social interaction and communication skills and greatly restricted or repetitive interests, activities, and behaviors. Depending on the specific form of PDD, these features may occur with or without impaired functioning in other cognitive domains. As you might imagine, the constellation of difficulties typifying PDD can also severely compromise a child's ability to deal adaptively with frustration.

Language Processing

It may have occurred to you as you read the foregoing that a lot of the thinking and communicating we do involves language. Many prominent theorists—with well-known names such as Vygotsky, Piaget, and Luria—have underscored the importance of language skills in setting the stage for many forms of thinking, including reflecting, self-regulating, goal setting, problem solving, and managing emotions. Thus, as you may imagine, children who are less efficient at understanding language, categorizing and storing current and previous experiences (in language), thinking things through (in language), or expressing themselves (via language) are at risk for being less effective at dealing adaptively with frustration.

Let's take these basic language skills one at a time. Children who have difficulty understanding the complex array of verbal events going on around them often become confused and frustrated by these events. In other words, understanding language is often the first necessary step in responding to people around you and the world in general. It's hard to formulate an adaptive response to a given situation when you don't fully comprehend things in the first place.

Some children understand language just fine but have trouble categorizing and labeling their emotions. This is another skill needed for responding to the world in an adaptive manner. If a child isn't skilled at categorizing or labeling previous experiences, he may not know how he's feeling at any given moment and may therefore have difficulty remembering how he previously responded when he felt the same way. Can you imagine *feeling* all the sensations associated with frustration—hot-faced, agitated, tense, explosive, and so on—without being able to label and categorize what you're feeling? You'd probably become even more frustrated, and your ultimate response would likely be quite counterproductive. I've worked with many children who lacked even a rudimentary vocabulary for describing their emotions. Helen, age seven—about whom you'll read more in Chapter 4—was one such child:

Me: Helen, what types of things make you happy?

Helen [long pause]: I don't know.

Me: Well, then, what types of things make you sad?

Helen: [shrug]

Me: Before you came in today, your mom told me about how she got mad at you for leaving your clothes on the *floor in your room. How did her being mad at you make you feel?*

Helen: I don't know.

Me: Hmm. From what I hear, you became very upset and ran out of the house when she got mad at you. You don't know what you were feeling?

Helen [long pause]: Upset?

Me: When you say you were upset, what do you mean?

Helen: I don't know.

Because children like Helen have a limited repertoire of "feeling" words, they may use other words in the midst of frustration instead, such as "I hate you," "Shut up," "Leave me alone," or worse. In Chapter 9, I'll talk about things that can be done to expand the "feeling" vocabularies of such children.

Some children do just fine at understanding language and labeling their feelings but have trouble figuring out, or coming up with the words to tell you, what's the matter. This may also need to be trained. Others can figure out and tell you what's the matter but have trouble thinking things through to arrive at an adaptive response. These children may be very good at telling you, "I'm very *mad* right now," but may become confused and frustrated when they try to think about what to do next. All that some of them can "think" of (if you want to call it thinking) to do next when they're frustrated is to hit someone, break something, or call someone a name. What they probably need most from adults is some help in expanding their "what to do next when you're mad" repertoire.

Of course, life isn't always so simple as "I'm mad" anyway. If a child says, "I'm mad," the world—his parents, teachers, siblings, peers, soccer coaches—is bound to respond in some way. Then the child has some more thinking, feeling, and expressing to do. The trouble is, "I'm mad" is about all some children can muster in the "expressing your feelings" department. So if the world asks for clarification or a more sophisticated articulation of "I'm mad" or demands additional thinking through, these children may become confused, disorganized, overwhelmed, and—you guessed it—*explosively* frustrated.

Me: George, I understand you got pretty frustrated at soccer the other day.

George: Yep.

Me: What happened?

George: The coach took me out of the game, and I didn't want to come out.

Me: I understand you told him you were very mad.

George: Yep.

Me: I think it's probably good that you told him. What did you do next?

George: He wouldn't put me back in, so I kicked him.

Me: You kicked the coach?

George: Yep.

Me: What happened next?

George: He kicked me off the team.

Me: I'm sorry to hear that.

George: I didn't even kick him that hard.

Me: I guess it wasn't important how hard you kicked him. I'm just wondering if you can think of something else you could have done when you were mad besides kick the coach.

George: Like what?

Me: I don't know; I wasn't there. Can you think of any times you've been mad and did something that made things turn out better than getting kicked off the soccer team?

George: Nope.

Me, to parents: Thinking back, has George ever responded to frustration in an adaptive way?

Father: Now that you mention it, no.

Mother: But it was never this bad.

Me: How do you mean?

Mother: When he was smaller, he didn't swear at us like he does now.

Me: What did he do instead?

Mother: Well, instead of screaming things like "Screw you!" he'd scream things like "I hate you!" or "I want to kill you!"

Me: But, when he's been frustrated, he's never said things like, "I don't know what to do," "That's bothering me," or "I need help"?

Father: Absolutely not.

Mother: No way. So is there any hope?

Me: Sure there's hope. Just don't expect him to learn a vocabulary he's never had overnight.

Mood

After a long day at work, I'm often hungry, tired, emotionally spent, and irritable. Any problems or frustrations—even those that require minimal thought—seem like major obstacles. My sense is that most of us have our irritable, agitated, tired moods; if we're lucky, these moods are relatively short-lived, and people around us know what to do to help restore our "normal selves." But there are some people—including children—who are *constantly* in an irritable, agitated, cranky, fatigued state of mind. This chronic mood state can severely compromise a person's capacity to be flexible and deal adaptively with frustration, and children who are so afflicted may react to even minor problems and frustrations as if they were major obstacles.

Are these children depressed? Some mental health professionals reserve the term *depression* for children who are routinely blue, morose, sad, and hopeless, which actually seems *not* to be the case for many of the irritable inflexible-explosive children I know. Some inflexible-explosive children who exhibit the constellation of extreme irritability, agitation, and mood instability are instead diagnosed as having bipolar disorder or manic-depression. This is still a controversial diagnosis in children; it has been suggested that what some researchers and clinicians call bipolar disorder is similar to what others call "difficult temperament" and still others have called "really bad ADHD" or "ADHD plus depression." Regardless of the label one chooses, in my experience—and the research of my colleagues at Mass General confirms this impression—children who meet criteria for bipolar disorder exhibit more severe behavior, are more impaired psychosocially, and have poorer long-term outcomes than do those with ADHD alone.

When children don't seem to meet the official criteria for either depression or bipolar disorder but still exhibit some unmistakable components of one or the other, my tendency is to suggest that there is a clear "mood component" contributing to their difficulties. What's crystal clear is that the inflexibility-explosiveness of these children is being fueled by a chronic state of irritability, agitation, volatility, and mood instability that makes it hard for them to respond to life's routine frustrations in an adaptive, rational manner.

Mother: Mickey, why so grumpy? It's a beautiful day outside. Why are you indoors?

Mickey [slumped in a chair, agitated]: It's windy.

Mother: It's windy?

Mickey [more agitated]: I said it's windy. I hate wind.

Mother: Mickey, you could be out playing basketball, swimming . . . you're this upset over a little wind?

Mickey [very agitated]: It's too windy, dammit! Leave me alone!

Anxiety

I used to be flight-anxious. That's right, scared of flying. I'm still not the world's greatest flyer, but I'm nowhere near as bad as I used to be. No, I wasn't intentionally being anxious (sweaty palms, racing heart, catastrophic thoughts) so flight attendants would pay attention to me. I was truly unnerved to find myself five miles above the earth going 500 miles per hour in an aluminum contraption filled with gasoline, with my life in the hands of people (the pilots and air traffic controllers) I'd never met. To control this anxiety, I engaged in a few important rituals to ensure the safe progress of my flight: I had to sit in a window seat so I could scan the skies for oncoming aircraft, and had to review the emergency instruction card before the plane took off. I knew these rituals worked because all the flights I'd been on had delivered me safely to my destination.

Did these rituals cause me to behave oddly at times? You

bet. On one flight, the plane was cruising along at 33,000 feet or so and I was, as usual, vigilantly scanning the horizon for threatening aircraft. Then the unthinkable happened: I spotted an aircraft far off in the horizon ascending in the direction of my airplane. By my expert calculation, we had about five minutes before the paths of the two planes crossed and my life would come to an abrupt, fiery end. So I did what any very anxious, increasingly irrational, human being would do: I rang for the flight attendant. There was no time to spare. "Do you see that airplane down there?" I sputtered, pointing toward the speck miles off in the distance. She peered out the window. "Do you think the captain knows it's there?" I demanded. The flight attendant tried to hide her amusement and said, "I'll be sure to let him know." I was greatly relieved, albeit certain that my heroism was not fully appreciated by either the flight attendant or the passengers seated near me (who were now scanning the aircraft for empty seats to move to). The plane landed safely, of course, and as I was leaving the airplane at the end of the flight, the flight attendant and pilot were waiting at the door and smiled as I approached. The flight attendant tugged on the pilot's sleeve and introduced me: "Captain, this is the gentleman who was helping you fly the plane."

The point is that severe anxiety has the potential to make rational, coherent thought much more difficult. And as fate would have it, it's when we're severely anxious about something that clear thinking is most crucial. This combination of anxiety and irrationality causes some children (the lucky ones) to cry. But a substantial number of them (the unlucky ones) explode. We adults tend to take things far less personally and respond far more empathically to children who cry when they're frustrated instead of explode, even though the two behaviors often flow from the same source. Also, I've become convinced that some of the obsessive-compulsive children I've seen began ritualizing because, in the absence of rational thought, the rituals were the only things they could come up with to reduce their anxiety, albeit only temporarily.

I'm proud to note that I no longer feel compelled to sit next to the window or review the emergency manual and have survived flights on which I did neither. How did I get over my flight anxiety? Experience. And by thinking (clearly). An Air Florida pilot got the process going. As I was boarding this Air Florida flight, the captain was greeting passengers at the door of the aircraft. I seized the opportunity. "You're going to fly the plane safely aren't you?" I sputtered. The pilot's response was more helpful than he knew: "What, you think *I* want to die, buddy?"

That the pilot wasn't particularly interested in dying was an important revelation, and it got me thinking. About the thousands of planes in the air across the world at any given time and the slim odds of something disastrous happening to the plane that I was on. About the millions of flights that arrive at their destinations uneventfully each year. About the hundreds of flights I have been on that arrived safely. About the thousands of flights my brother and brother-in-law have flown without incident. About how calm the flight attendants look. About how many of my fellow passengers are fast asleep. Even when there's turbulence. Quite unintentionally, that Air Florida pilot gave me a "cognitive anchor"—a way of thinking, or mental roadmap—that was helpful to me during moments when I was inclined to become highly irrational. Instead of staring out the window thinking, "What if the wing falls off?" I could instead think a less anxiety-provoking thought such as, "The pilot doesn't want to die" or, "The likelihood of something catastrophic happening to my aircraft is really quite slim." As you'll see, one of the most valuable things we can do for an inflexible-explosive child is to provide him with cognitive roadmaps that help him stay rational at moments when he's likely to become explosive.

My flight anxiousness never caused me to become explosive. But some children do explode when they get anxious. They stop thinking clearly, become overwhelmed with anxiety, and veer off right into an explosion.

Nonverbal Learning Disability

Although any learning disability has the potential to make life a lot more frustrating for a child, one learning disability may actually set the stage for inflexible-explosive behavior. Nonverbal learning disability has drawn increased attention from researchers, and refers to a syndrome in which children have poorer nonverbal than verbal skills (often seen in the form of poorer Performance versus Verbal scale scores on the Wechsler Intelligence Scale for Children); poor mathematical skills; difficulty comprehending reading material despite good skills at reading single words; poor nonverbal memory and visual perception; significant difficulty on tasks or in situations requiring problem-solving, flexibility, and adaptability (especially in response to abstract or unfamiliar stimuli); and difficulties in social perception, social judgment, and social interaction skills. Some children do not manifest the full syndrome but still exhibit several of these difficulties.

Children with this syndrome tend to be strong at learning rote material and often approach the world in a rigid, concrete, black-and-white, literal manner. Unfortunately, the world—and social interactions in particular—require a lot more problem solving, flexibility, and adaptability than rote memorization and concrete thinking. You see, while some situations require minimal flexibility and problem-solving skills ("Johnny, sharpen your pencil and sit back down at your desk"), others require a higher level of these skills ("Johnny, I want you, Francis, Lisa, and Bob to work together and come up with a presentation on the early explorers of Florida"). The former situation usually requires only a rote response, which is easier for a concrete thinker. But concrete, rigid thinking can cause such children to respond to the latter situation in a maladaptive manner ("I can't do this! They're not doing the presentation the right way!"), demonstrating an incapacity to deal adaptively with circumstances that involve greater complexity and require greater cognitive flexibility. Such children have great difficulty moving beyond their original configuration of how a problem should be resolved. Unpredictable situations often cause these children to fall apart completely.

Thus, children with nonverbal difficulties may experience enormous frustration as they struggle to apply concrete rules to a world where few such rules apply:

Child [in a car]: Dad, this isn't the way we usually go home. (early vapor lock)

Father [driving]: I thought we'd go a different way this time, just for a change of pace.

Child [advanced vapor lock]: But this isn't the right way!

Father: I know this isn't the way we usually go, but it may even be faster.

Child [crossroads]: We can't go this way! It's not the same! I don't know this way!

Father: Look, it's not that big a deal to go a different way every once in awhile.

Child: [meltdown]

Sensory Integration Dysfunction

One final area worthy of mention as a potential pathway to inflexibility-explosiveness is sensory integration dysfunction. In addition to helping us humans sort through our thoughts, the central nervous system is also important for helping us screen, sort through, and respond to—in other words, integrate—the barrage of sensory information from the external environment. As children mature, their capacity to sort through incoming sensations and ability to direct their own motor movements develop rapidly. These skills do not develop as readily in some children, however. Occupational and physical therapists—the professionals who generally assess and diagnose sensory integration disorders—typically focus on the different ways in which a child may be having difficulty integrating various sensory systems, such as touch, movement and coordination, body position and awareness, sight, and sound. Children who are underreactive to various sensations may fluctuate between under- and overresponsiveness, whereas children who are overly sensitive to these sensations may avoid certain clothes and textures, overreact to loud noises, and react poorly to seemingly routine movements.

Sensory integration difficulties may have adverse effects on motor planning (such as using scissors, getting on a bicycle, and manipulating eating utensils), academic skills (like handwriting), and self-care skills (including tying shoes and buttoning and zipping clothes), and such children may have strong sensitivities to clothing (such as being sensitive to collars hitting the neck, sleeves hitting wrists, and seams and tags in clothing) and food (for example, temperature, texture, and certain smells or flavors). Although the overlap between sensory integration dysfunction and executive functions is not well-studied, a variety of behaviors typically associated with deficits in executive functions—disorganization, distractibility, poor planning skills, failing to anticipate the results of one's actions, difficulty adjusting to new situations or following directions, frustration, and aggression—have also been attributed to sensory integration dysfunction. Regardless of the label one applies, many of the inflexible-explosive children with whom I've worked have sensory integration problems, and these difficulties caused them significant frustration and clearly compromised their ability to be flexible and to tolerate frustration. A book called *The Out of Sync Child* by Carol Stock Kranowitz describes sensory integration dysfunction in greater detail, along with how children so diagnosed can be helped.

Other Factors Contributing to Cumulative Frustration

We all have a "frustratometer"—that unofficial meter inside our heads that gauges our present and cumulative levels of frustration. Although the pathways described above can best be conceptualized as contributing to a "limited-capacity frustratometer," other issues may be important because they add to a child's cumulative level of frustration.

In other words, while a difficult temperament, irritable or unstable mood, anxiety, and deficits in executive functions, social skills, language processing, nonverbal skills, and sensory integration can make it difficult for a child to be flexible and to tolerate frustration, a variety of other problems may make things even worse by pushing a child that much closer to the edge.

Learning disabilities—in reading, math, writing skills, for example—can add substantially to a child's cumulative level of frustration. A child who has a lot of vocal tics may be frustrated and embarrassed by them and may expend a substantial amount of energy trying to inhibit them. An inflexible-explosive child of divorced parents may have difficulty adapting to the disparate demands imposed by different home environments. One wonderful boy with whom I was working was very short; although he did a good job of dealing with the teasing and his own self-doubts most of the time, his short stature continually contributed to his cumulative level of frustration. Difficult interactions with a teacher, parent, stepparent, or coach can add to a child's frustration; so can difficult interactions with peers or siblings, or poor athletic skills. Although many of these frustrations might be considered normal for most children, a limited-capacity frustratometer can make them feel like an insurmountable burden.

It should be clear that multiple factors may compromise a child's capacity for flexibility and frustration tolerance.

> *It should be clear that multiple factors may compromise a child's capacity for flexibility and frustration tolerance. Perhaps the most important thing the pathways described in this chapter can help us understand is that flexibility and frustration tolerance are not skills that come naturally to all children.*

Perhaps the most important thing the pathways described in this chapter can help us understand is that flexibility and frustration tolerance are not skills that come naturally to all children.

We tend to think that all children are created equal in these capacities, and this tendency causes many adults to believe that inflexible-explosive children must not want to be compliant and handle frustration in an adaptable way. As you now know, in many cases, this simply isn't true.

I should emphasize that there's a big difference between interpreting the pathways described in this chapter as "excuses" rather than as "explanations." When the pathways are invoked as *excuses*, the door slams shut on the process of thinking about how to help a child. Conversely, when the pathways are used as *explanations* for a child's behavior, the door to helping swings wide open, for our explanations should provide us with an improved understanding of the child's needs and a clearer sense of how we can be helpful. It is almost impossible to be helpful without a comprehensive, in-depth understanding of a child's difficulties.

Not all children with difficult temperaments; mood and anxiety disorders; nonverbal learning disabilities; or deficits in executive functions, social information processing, language processing, or sensory-integration ultimately become inflexible-explosive. Perhaps it is the *severity* of a child's difficulties that leads to inflexibility-explosiveness in some instances and the *combination* of difficulties that leads to it in other instances. And, in many cases, perhaps it is the manner in which the world responds to a child's inflexibility-explosiveness that makes all the difference. This response, as you may suspect, is what the rest of the book is about.

4

Inflexible-Explosive Faces

As you'd imagine—given the multiple pathways you just read about—inflexibility and low frustration tolerance can look different in different children. Some children have such incredibly short fuses that in many instances the slightest frustration spins them into immediate vapor lock. Others have longer fuses but still aren't adept at thinking things through; their descent into a meltdown may be more prolonged but just as nasty once they get there. Some kids are pretty good at letting you know when their circuits have started jamming ("I can't talk about that right now!"); others let you know in less desirable ways ("Shut up!" "Screw you!" "I hate you!" or "Leave me alone!"). Some children don't warn of an impending meltdown with words but rather with a sudden onset of irritability, whining, or fatigue; others don't give much warning at all. Many are able to hold it together at school but then melt down almost instantaneously when they get home; some melt down both at home and school. Some children throw things or hit during meltdowns, others scream and swear, and still others cry; I've known others who curled up into a ball on the floor.

So that the characteristics you've read about start to come to life, it's useful for you to have a good idea of how inflexibility-explosiveness appeared in some of the children with whom

I've worked. My bet is that you'll see similarities between the children described in this chapter and the inflexible-explosive child you're trying to parent or teach. These children and their families are revisited in one way or another throughout the book.

Casey

Casey was a six-year-old boy who lived with his parents and younger sister. In our first session, his parents reported that, at home, Casey was hyperactive; had difficulty falling asleep at night; was unable to play by himself (but had equal difficulty engaging in cooperative play); had a lot of difficulty with transitions (getting him to come indoors after playing outside was often a major ordeal); was restricted and rigid in the clothes he was willing to wear and the food he was willing to eat (he often complained that certain fabrics were annoying to him and that many common foods "smelled funny"); became anxious when presented with new tasks or situations; was frequently in an irritable, agitated mood; and melted down many times each day. Most of these characteristics had been present since Casey was a toddler.

His parents noted that Casey seemed to be quite bright, in that he had excellent memory for factual information, but thought that his fine and gross motor skills were somewhat delayed compared to other boys his age. Casey had never undergone a complete psychoeducational evaluation, but was evaluated by an occupational therapist when he was three years old. The therapist thought that Casey had difficulties with sensory integration and began working with him in occupational therapy at that time. His parents had previously consulted a psychologist, who helped them establish a reward and punishment program. The parents vigilantly implemented the program but found that Casey's hyperactivity and irritability were more potent than his clear desire to obtain rewards and avoid punishments. Indeed, the program actually seemed to frustrate him further, but the psychologist encouraged the parents to stick with it, certain that Casey's behavior would improve. It didn't, so the parents discontinued the program after about three months.

The parents had read a lot about ADHD and thought that this diagnosis fit Casey, but that many of his characteristics fell outside the realm of this disorder. They thought the term *control freak* fit their son better than any traditional diagnosis. They often tried to talk to Casey about his behavior, but even when he was in a good mood, his capacity for thinking about his own behavior seemed limited; after a few seconds, he would yell, "I can't talk about this right now!" and run out of the room.

"We can live with a lot of Casey's behaviors," said his mother. "But his explosions . . . and the way they disrupt our entire family . . . and our concern about what's going to happen to him if we don't help him . . . really worry us."

Casey had difficulties at school, too. His first-grade teacher reported that Casey would occasionally hit or yell at other children during less structured play or academic activities, particularly when he did not get his way. Like the parents, Casey's teacher was impressed by his factual knowledge but concerned by his poor problem-solving skills. When lessons called for recall of rote information, Casey was the star of the class. When lessons required the application of this information to more abstract, complex, real-life situations, his responses were disorganized and off the mark.

When he was frustrated by a particular classroom situation or task he would yell, "I can't do this!" and would become quite agitated or start crying; sometimes he would run out of the classroom. On several occasions, he ran out of the school, which caused great concern for his safety. Sometimes he regained his composure quickly; other times it took twenty to thirty minutes for him to calm down. Afterwards, Casey was either remorseful ("I'm sorry I ran out of the classroom . . . I know I shouldn't do that") or had difficulty remembering the episode altogether. The teacher reported that she could often tell from the moment Casey walked through the door in the morning that he was going to have a tough day. But she also observed that Casey was capable of falling apart even when his day seemed to be going smoothly. The teacher was becoming increasingly concerned about Casey's relationships with other children; Casey seemed to lack an appreciation for the impact of his actions on others and seemed unable to use the feedback he received from others to adjust his behavior.

In my first session with Casey, he was very hyperactive and seemed unwilling or unable to talk about the important issues that he might need help with. He bounced from one toy to another in my office. When his parents were brought into the session, he settled down just long enough to hear that the reason he was in my office was that he sometimes became upset when things didn't go exactly the way he thought they would. He agreed that this was sometimes a problem. When the parents tried to get Casey to talk about this issue, he buried his face in his mother's shoulder; when the parents persisted, he warned, "I can't talk about this right now!" When they persisted further, he became red-faced and agitated and ran out of the office.

"Was that pretty typical?" I asked the parents.

"No, at home he'd have become a lot more frustrated," replied his mother. "He doesn't usually hit us—although he has hit kids at school—but he falls apart completely . . . turns red, screams or cries, yells 'I hate you!'"

"You know, in some ways his running out of the room is adaptive," I commented.

"How's that?" asked the father, a little surprised.

"Well, based on what you've told me, it seems pretty clear that he has a lot of trouble thinking and talking about his own behavior and tolerating the frustration he feels when we ask him to do one of those things," I said. "While we wish he would 'use his words' to discuss things with us, his running out of the room probably keeps him from doing other things—swearing, throwing things, becoming physically threatening—that would be a lot worse."

Was Casey inflexible-explosive? It seemed so to me. Using the unofficial criteria presented in Chapter 2, he seemed to fit the bill on many counts. He clearly had a limited capacity for flexibility and adaptability and had difficulty thinking rationally in the midst of severe frustration; had an extremely low frustration threshold and very low frustration tolerance; remained inflexible and easily frustrated even when faced with salient, meaningful consequences; fell apart over seemingly benign events; and had several issues about which he was especially inflexible. There appeared to be a combination of possible pathways to inflexibility-explosiveness that required further evaluation, including ADHD, mood and anxiety issues, sensory integration dysfunction, nonverbal learning disability, and other learning problems. Thus, my short-term goal was to achieve greater clarity on these potential pathways by having Casey comprehensively assessed.

My general long-term goals were (1) to provide his parents and teachers with a framework for creating environments at school and home that would set the stage for improved flexibility and frustration tolerance; (2) to help Casey feel comfortable enough, focus long enough, and stay calm enough to articulate his frustration so he could begin talking things through and be more open to adult assistance when he became frustrated; (3) to determine, over the longer term, whether Casey could begin to deal with frustration more independently; and (4) to explore whether medications for reducing hyperactivity and impulsivity and reducing irritability should be considered at some point. These goals and strategies for achieving them are described in greater detail in later chapters.

Let's turn to another child and see what her inflexibility-explosiveness looked like.

Helen

I first met with Helen and her mother and father when she was seven years old. Helen was described as a charming, sensitive, creative, energetic, sociable girl. Her parents also described her as intense, easily angered, argumentative, resistant, and downright nasty when frustrated. They had observed that Helen seemed to have a lot of trouble making the transition from one activity to another and tended to fall apart when things didn't go exactly as she had anticipated. They reported that weekends were especially difficult; although Helen didn't love going to school, unstructured weekend time seemed to make her very irritable and difficult to please. A child psychiatrist had given Helen a tentative diagnosis of ADHD, but had conceded that ADHD didn't seem to encompass the full range of behaviors Helen was exhibiting. Her second-grade teacher reported that Helen had a tendency to grumble when new lessons were introduced. Her piano teacher observed that Helen tended to become easily frustrated and often balked at trying new pieces of music. Psychoeducational testing by school personnel indicated that while Helen was of above-average intelligence, her expressive language skills were delayed.

In one of my early meetings with Helen's parents, they recounted one of her meltdowns during the previous week. "On Tuesday, Helen told me she'd like to have chili for dinner the next night," recounted her father. "So, on Wednesday afternoon, I left work a little early and made her the chili she had asked for. When she got home from swimming late Wednesday afternoon, she seemed a little tired; when I announced to her that I had made her the chili she wanted, she grumbled, 'I want macaroni and cheese.' This took me a little bit by surprise, since I know she really loves chili. It was also a little irritating, since I had put time into doing something nice for her. So I told her she would have to eat the chili. But she seemed unable to get macaroni and cheese out of her head, and I continued to insist that she eat the chili for dinner. The more I insisted, the more she fell apart. Eventually, she lost it completely. She was screaming and crying, but I was determined that she would eat the chili I had made her."

"What did you do then?" I asked.

"We confined her to her bedroom and told her she had to stay there until she was ready to eat the chili," said Helen's mother. "For the next hour she screamed and cried in her room; at one point, she was banging on her mirror and broke it. Can you imagine? All this over chili! I went up to her room a few times to see if I could calm her down, but it was impossible. Helen was totally irrational—the amazing thing is that, at one point, she couldn't even remember what she was upset about."

I then asked the parents a question you'll see lots more of in later chapters. "How important was it to you that she eat the chili instead of the macaroni and cheese?"

"I couldn't have cared less," the father quickly responded, knowing where I was heading. "In retrospect, I honestly didn't care which of the two she ate." The mother confirmed this point of view.

Then came another question you're going to see a lot more of: "Do you think that your enduring this meltdown—having Helen go nuts in her room for an hour, breaking her mirror, and ruining your evening—made it any less likely that she'll melt down the next time she's frustrated over something similarly unimportant?"

"No," was the instantaneous, unanimous response.

"What was Helen like when the episode was all over?" I asked.

"Very remorseful and very loving," the mother responded. "It's hard to know whether to reciprocate her being loving or to hold a grudge for a while to cement the point that we don't like that kind of behavior."

"Well," I replied, "if you don't think that inducing and enduring meltdowns is going to help her deal better with frustration the next time, then it follows that holding a grudge probably isn't going to help either."

"Yes, but how will she learn that that kind of behavior is unacceptable?" asked the mother.

"There are a lot of things that might help, though I'm not yet sure which ones," I replied. "But from what I've heard, the fact that you disapprove of that kind of behavior is pretty well cemented in her mind already . . . so I doubt that we'll be needing more cement. She also seems genuinely motivated to please you both . . . and seems as unhappy about her meltdowns as you are . . . so I'm not sure she needs additional motivation. What we have to figure out is why, under certain circumstances, a kid who knows you disapprove of her temper outbursts and is eager to please you continues to have temper outbursts that displease you."

Later that session, Helen and I played Connect Four, a game she already knew how to play. I noticed that even after several games, Helen seemed to have a lot of trouble deciding on a strategy. Each time it was her turn, she begged me to tell her what to do for her next move. Sometimes she refused to make a move without being guided on strategy. Game after game, it seemed that although Helen plainly *understood* the rules of Connect Four, she was unable to organize and plan a coherent strategy and didn't seem able to think about potential moves for more than a moment before begging for guidance.

At the end of this session, I described to the parents my early impression of their daughter's difficulties. "Based on what you've told me and what I've observed myself, Helen seems to have a lot of trouble thinking clearly when a situation is new, unfamiliar, or uncertain or requires extensive thinking and planning. When we play Connect Four, she seems practically paralyzed unless I give her some sort of help. Have you ever noticed that she becomes very disorganized and frustrated when she's uncertain about something?"

"Absolutely," the mother replied. "When we're helping her

with her homework, she needs a lot of organizing and reassurance for her to stick with tasks she's uncertain about. If we don't help her, she starts falling apart."

"From the stories you've told me, it sounds like the same thing happens when she's uncertain in other situations," I commented. "She seems to be lacking a framework for thinking about things when she's uncertain. She's also easily overwhelmed by frustration, and once she's overwhelmed, it's practically impossible for her to think rationally until she calms down again.

"Let's start talking about what we can do to help her," I continued. "Her language-processing issues and ADHD seem to be the primary factors fueling her difficulties, although there may be a mood component as well. Let's talk about the language piece first. A lot of the thinking people do in their heads relies heavily on language skills. In other words, most of our thoughts are words and feelings and categories and actions that involve language. From what I've heard and seen, Helen doesn't seem to have the words to let us know what's the matter or the problem-solving skills to figure out what to do, and this is even more true when she's frustrated. Her ADHD adds disorganization and an impulsive response style to the mix. I think the testing her school did is probably fine for now, although at some point we may want to evaluate other aspects of her cognitive functioning more fully, just to make sure nothing's been overlooked.

"I think it's important for us to understand that a lot of the things Helen says or does when she's frustrated are clear evidence that she's having trouble thinking rationally and to recognize that you can play an important role in keeping her from becoming quickly overwhelmed when she's uncertain or frustrated. To assist her in this way, we'll need to work toward helping Helen come to view you both as people who can help her to think things through—rather than seeing you as adversaries—when she's starting to become upset. In other words, when she's in what I call the 'red haze of frustration,' it will be easier to restore her to rationality if she sees you as potential helpers, not as enemies. We also need to see if we can give her some sort of framework for thinking things through when she's uncertain and disorganized. If we can help her take some baby steps in this direction and then slowly add some new skills, over time I'm optimistic she'll be able to start thinking through frustrating situations on her own, rather than needing you both to do the thinking for her."

Anthony

Anthony was an eight-year-old second grader when I first met him and his parents. I remember that at that time, his father described Anthony as "a piece of work." Anthony was a socially engaging child who had average verbal skills and well below average nonverbal skills. He was functioning below grade level in practically all academic skill areas. He also had sensory integration and language-processing difficulties, had extremely poor organizational skills, and was excessively distractible. Though he was a very concrete child (he was much more comfortable when things were predictable), Anthony had a lot of trouble remembering things he'd learned. But perhaps the most striking thing about Anthony was his high level of anxiety, especially when things were unpredictable. Anthony worried about just about anything and everything. And there was one thing he was especially worried about.

"He's worried about the weather," said his mother in our first meeting. "If he hears it's going to snow, his day is ruined. Same thing with rain. It would be funny if it didn't happen so often and if he didn't become as upset as he does."

"Why's he so worried about the weather?" I asked.

"If it snows, he's afraid the snow will accumulate on the power lines and we'll lose power," the mother replied.

"Do you guys have a generator?" I asked.

"Of course," the mother said. "But he's afraid the generator will run out of gas."

"I'm sure you have extra gas for the generator," I said.

"Lots," Anthony's father replied. "But he's afraid we'll run out and won't be able to get more because gas stations can't pump gas without power."

"Well, he certainly has all his power-outage disasters covered," I said. "What's his deal with rain?"

"Lightning knocks out power," the mother replied. "Generator runs out of gas. Gas station can't pump more gas. Same deal. I've practically become a Weather Channel addict because I'm worried about him having a bad day! They do their five-day forecast and I'm on the edge of my seat!"

"Am I safe in assuming that you try to help him feel less anxious about these concerns?" I asked.

"Continuously," the mother said. "But on mornings when snow or rain is predicted, he's in his anxious mode and he's beyond reason. In fact, that's when he's most likely to have one of his meltdowns."

"How does that happen?" I asked.

"Well," the mother took a deep breath, "he gets himself very worked up over the weather and he gets going on the power outage thing and gets so upset and preoccupied that he can't be reasoned with. We try to reassure him, but that seems to make it worse. Eventually, he's crying and screaming and totally irrational. That about cover it?" she asked her husband.

"Oh, I think that sums it up pretty well," he replied. "He's really a nervous wreck. And we're at a loss for how to help him."

"And all because of the weather," I pondered aloud. "How long do the meltdowns last?"

"Well, eventually he runs out of gas," said the mother. "But at his worst, he can go on for several hours."

"How's he do in school—you know, on sunny days?" I asked.

"He gets a lot of academic help," the mother replied. "But he likes his teachers and he's always liked going to school. Less so, of course, on cloudy days."

"His teachers love him," the father said. "In fact, most adults do. But he's very concrete and not very good at taking other people's perspective. He's sort of oblivious to how he comes across. He does have a few kids he plays with, though."

"He's really a very sweet kid," interjected the mother. "We just haven't figured out how to help him with the weather thing."

Later in the session, I met alone with Anthony.

"I understand you have some concerns about the weather," I said.

"Yes," he replied. "When it snows, it ruins my whole day."

"Really? How come?"

"If there's too much snow, the power could go off."

"What would happen if the power went off?"

"It would be very bad. We'd be very cold. We couldn't cook our food."

"Hmmm. That *would* be bad. Is there anything *good* about when it snows?"

"Like what?" he asked, looking puzzled.

"I don't know," I replied. "It's kinda pretty."

"It's not so pretty when tree branches start falling on power lines."

"I guess you've got a point there. Does the power stay off for long?" I asked.

"I heard someone say it went off for three or four days once."

"That's a long time. What would your parents do if the power went off?"

"I don't know."

"Doesn't your house have a generator?" I asked.

"Yes."

"Couldn't your parents turn the generator on?"

"Yes. But it could run out of gas."

"Hmmm . . . I suppose it could at that. What would your parents do about that?" I asked.

"I don't know."

"Really? What do you think most people would do if their generator ran out of gas?"

"I don't know."

"Could they get more gas?"

"Yes. But the gas station can't pump gas if there's no power."

"What would your parents do about that?"

"I don't know."

The look on Anthony's face when he said "I don't know" was very convincing. What seemed clear was that Anthony had some very definite ideas about potential weather disasters, but was in the dark about ways people deal with such disasters and stay calm about them.

His parents came back into the office.

"Isn't he great?" asked the father.

"So what are we going to do about the whole weather thing?" asked the mother.

"Well, to be perfectly honest, I'm not sure just yet," I replied. "I need to spend a little more time with Anthony to get a better sense of his way of thinking. I also need to get a better handle on why standard logic—you know, your reassurance and reasoning—aren't having the desired effect. And I'll need a better sense of the specific factors that lead to his meltdowns. But, to be honest, it seems like he lacks some pretty critical thinking skills. I suspect I'll end up trying to give you a roadmap for helping him think his way through his anxiety, in hopes that he'll eventually be able to use the road map on his own."

"You'd think all our reasoning would have rubbed off on him by now," the mother said.

"Indeed," I said. "It sounds like you've tried very hard."

"Is this his nonverbal learning disability, or his sensory stuff, or his anxiety, or what?" asked the father.

"Well, my bet is that the whole package is coming into play in one way or another," I said.

"Is there any hope?" asked the mother.

"I'm always hopeful," I replied.

Danny

I first met with Danny and his mother when he was in the fifth grade. His mother and father had divorced amicably when Danny was seven and still considered themselves "co-parents." Danny and his younger sister stayed with the father and his fiancée every weekend. The mother described Danny as very bright (testing showed him to be in the superior range for general cognitive ability with no learning disabilities); perfectionistic; moody; irritable; and, as fate would have it, strikingly inflexible and easily frustrated. The mother was especially concerned about Danny's "rage attacks," which had occurred several times a week since Danny was a toddler. During such episodes, he would become verbally abusive and physically aggressive. These episodes were especially likely when things didn't go exactly as Danny had anticipated. He'd never had a rage attack at school. The mother was also worried about how these attacks were affecting Danny's sister, who, at times, seemed scared of her older brother and, at others, seemed to take some pleasure in instigating him.

Danny had seen numerous mental health professionals over the years; like many inflexible-explosive children, he'd accumulated a fairly impressive number of psychiatric diagnoses, including ADHD, oppositional-defiant disorder, obsessive-compulsive disorder (OCD), depression, and bipolar disorder. His family physician had medicated Danny with Ritalin several years previously, but Danny had remained moody, rigid, and explosive. The psychiatrist who diagnosed Danny with OCD had subsequently prescribed an antidepressant, but this medication caused Danny to become significantly more agitated and hyperactive.

"Danny can be in what seems to be a perfectly pleasant mood and then—bang!—something doesn't go quite the way he thought it would, and he's cursing and hitting," his mother reported. "I don't know what to do. The other day he and I were in the car together and I took a wrong turn. Danny suddenly became very agitated that it was taking us longer to get where we were going than it should have. All of a sudden, I had a ten-year-old kid punching me! In the car! While I'm driving! It's insanity!"

"I'm tired of people telling me this behavior is occurring because I'm a single parent. My ex-husband is still very much involved in Danny's life, and there hasn't been any of the back-stabbing that occurs with some divorces. Anyway, these explosions started way before there were problems in our marriage, although, I must admit, he's a lot more explosive when he's with me than he is when he's with his father."

When I met with Danny, he seemed genuinely contrite over the behavior his mother had described. He said he'd been trying very hard not to be physically or verbally aggressive but didn't seem to be able to help himself.

At the beginning of one of next sessions, the mother told me about Danny's biggest meltdown of the week. "Yesterday, I told him he had to come in from playing basketball to eat dinner. He whined a little, but I insisted. Next thing I know, his face is red, he's calling me every name in the book, he's accusing me of ruining his life, and I'm hiding behind a door trying to shield myself from getting kicked. I was petrified. So was his sister. And it's not the first time.

"Twenty minutes later, he was sorry. But this is just ridiculous," said the mother. "I'm sick of being hit, and it's just impossible to reason with him once he gets going."

"What did you do once he'd calmed down?" I asked.

"I punished him for swearing at me and trying to kick me," replied the mother. "I feel he needs to be disciplined for that kind of behavior."

"I can understand you feeling that way. Tell me, have you always punished him when he's acted like that?" I asked.

"You bet," the mother said. "I'm not willing to just let that kind of disrespect slide."

"What happens when you punish him?" I asked.

"He goes nuts," she said. "It's horrible."

"But despite all the punishing, he's still very verbally and physically aggressive, yes?"

"That's why I'm here," the mother smiled through gritted teeth.

"Well," I said, "I'm all in favor of punishment when it's productive—you know, when it's effective at changing a child's behavior. But I'm not real keen on punishment just for the sake of punishment."

"What, I should let him *get away* with what he does?" demanded the mother.

"Don't get me wrong," I said. "The behavior has to stop. But, based on what you've been telling me, 'not letting him get away with it' hasn't changed his behavior at all."

The mother pondered this observation for a moment.

"I think I figured that eventually the message would get through if I just kept plugging away," she explained. "I never stopped to think that maybe the message would never get through."

"Oh, I suspect Danny knows you don't like his behavior," I said. "In fact, I'm reasonably certain he even knows how you'd like him to behave."

"Then why doesn't he?" the mother demanded.

"Now that I've met with Danny a few times, I get the feeling he's generally in a pretty unhappy mood. I know he's not crazy about coming here, but is that his mood most of the time?" I asked.

"Absolutely," replied the mother. "We call him 'Grumpy.' He doesn't seem to enjoy himself very much . . . and he's very uptight. Everything seems to bother him."

"What an unpleasant existence," I said. "And it has very unpleasant implications for everyone around him."

"You can say that again," sighed the mother. "But what does that have to do with his being explosive and angry and trying to hurt me?"

"Well, if we view him as grumpy and irritable, rather than as disrespectful and oppositional, then I think our approach to dealing with him might look a lot different," I said.

"I don't understand what you mean," said the mother.

"What I mean is that kids who are grumpy and irritable often don't need more discipline," I said. "I've yet to see discipline be especially useful at helping a kid be less irritable and agitated."

"I still don't understand how being irritable is an excuse for his being so disrespectful and angry towards me," said the mother.

"Well, it's more of an explanation than an excuse," I replied. "But when people go through the day in an irritable, cranky mood, they experience every request or change or inconvenience as yet another demand for an expenditure of energy. If you think about it, over the course of a day or week, a person's energy for dealing with these requests and changes and inconveniences starts to wane. Often the event that sends an irritable, cranky person over the edge isn't necessarily the biggest; rather, it's the one that happened after he'd expended his last ounce of energy.

"Think of times you've been tired after a long day at work," I continued. "Those are probably the times when you're least adaptable and least flexible and when very minor things are likely to set you off. I think Danny is in that state of mind fairly continuously."

"There's no way I'm going to tell him he's allowed to hit me just because he's irritable," said the mother.

"Oh, I'm not saying you should allow him to hit you," I said. "The hitting has got to stop. But to get the hitting and swearing and tantrums to stop, I think we need to focus on things you can do *before* he explodes, rather than on what you can do *after* he's exploded. And we need to focus on all the ingredients that are fueling his inflexibility and explosiveness. From what I've seen so far, helping him with his mood will be high on the list."

Eric

I first met with Eric and his parents when Eric was eleven years old. He was described as a bright, verbal, anxious, irritable eleven year old who was already medicated with an antidepressant, which was being prescribed to help him be less anxious and moody. Previous testing had shown Eric's verbal skills to be markedly better developed than his nonverbal skills. His parents told me that Eric had difficulty in math and with tasks that required writing. From what I was hearing, Eric's inflexibility and explosiveness seemed to be fueled by the combination of mood issues and a nonverbal learning disability. I came to know Eric as a remarkably literal, black-and-white thinker who was particularly inflexible around issues of morality.

During one of our early sessions, Eric's mother told me about an episode that had occurred the previous weekend. It seemed that Eric had been in Harvard Square with some of his friends.

Harvard Square is an exciting, stimulating cluster of shops and interesting people near the Harvard campus. On weekends there are lots of entertainers—musicians, magicians, face-painters—and the area bustles with activity. Eric, his friends, and a few dozen other onlookers had stopped to watch a juggler perform. Every so often, an onlooker would drop money into the open guitar case lying on the ground next to the juggler. While the assembled people were enjoying the show, Eric noticed that the juggler didn't have a permit to be performing in Harvard Square (all performers in Harvard Square are supposed to obtain a permit from the police). Eric locked on to the notion that this was wrong. "All entertainers are supposed to have permits," he thought. "This juggler is breaking the law." During the next several minutes, Eric became increasingly agitated and less rational as he obsessed over the "crime" he was witnessing. He could think of only one thing to do: report the juggler to the police, which he promptly did. When Eric arrived with a policeman in tow, his friends were mortified (even the policeman seemed a little dumbfounded). "Why did you report the guy to the police?" the friends demanded as the policeman was telling the juggler the show was over. Eric was aware that his friends thought he'd done something off-base, but he couldn't figure out what they were so miffed about.

After his mother recounted this episode, Eric still seemed pretty clueless about why his friends were so upset with him. I decided to see if it was possible to get Eric to see the "gray" in a hypothetical situation.

"Eric, is it ever OK to speed in a car? Are there any situations in which it's acceptable to go over the speed limit?"

There was dead silence for the next five minutes. As Eric contemplated this question, I found myself thinking of the courageous but overwhelmed Tandy computer I had used in graduate school. Whenever I tried to pull up a file on this computer, it made promising "searching" noises while I sat on the edge of my seat and prayed. Most of the time, after much searching, my computer would ultimately find the file I'd requested. But about one out of every twenty times, after much searching, it would flash a message saying something to the effect of "Unable to locate file." I watched Eric search his brain's "files" and thought, "I wonder if the information he needs to answer this question is even in his head."

Finally, after a long search of his brain's hard drive, Eric had at last pulled up a file. "It's OK to speed in a car if it's an emergency," he announced.

My expression didn't change, but inside I was jumping with glee. Eric *did* seem to have the capacity to see the grays! The problem, of course, was that most real-life situations were more complex and demanded instantaneous flexibility. I thought, "If it takes him that long to think about this question in the safe, pleasant atmosphere of my office, he's in for some rough sledding when he's required to think quickly in Harvard Square." Still, it was a start.

In a later session, I witnessed one of Eric's meltdowns firsthand. Eric's parents wanted to discuss the possibility of Eric doing a few more chores around the house. As the discussion dragged on, Eric became increasingly agitated. He began to teeter on the edge of a meltdown, and I told him I thought it might be best for him to chill out for a while in the waiting area outside my office. He refused; unfortunately, he'd slipped slightly beyond the point of reason. His computer was crashing. His face turned red. He started yelling at his parents. He banged his chair into the ground. He stalked around the room.

He was on the verge of tears. All because his parents wanted him to do one or two chores around the house. And then I noticed something fascinating: what he was saying was making no sense whatsoever.

"You guys do *not* have the right to be asking me to do these chores!" he shouted at his parents, sounding every bit like a spoiled brat. "I won't do them! I'll make your lives miserable! I hate you! Both of you! I always have! I'd like to do these chores! They're perfectly reasonable requests! You guys should be making me do these things! If you were good parents, you'd force me to do them!" Eric was becoming strikingly disorganized before our very eyes. He was becoming less and less rational.

"Eric, you're not making any sense," said the father. "Come on, calm down and let's talk about this rationally." But Eric was too far gone and nothing any of us said got him back. Eventually the meltdown ran out of gas and, exhausted, he started to cry.

Like Casey, Helen, and Anthony, Eric tended to have difficulty thinking clearly and became quite disorganized in the midst of frustration. And, like Helen, he was especially prone to frustration when his parents insisted that he shift from his agenda to their agenda. The goal of therapy was to help Eric's parents serve as his "surrogate frontal lobe" to help him think through situations that required him to move beyond hard-and-fast rules so that, eventually, he'd be able to think through such situations on his own.

Mitchell

Mitchell was a fifteen-year-old ninth grader when I met him and his parents. I met first with his mother, a law professor, and father, a practicing lawyer, and was told that Mitchell was extremely unhappy about having been brought to my office that day, for he greatly distrusted mental health professionals. I was also told that Mitchell had been diagnosed with both Tourette's disorder and bipolar disorder, but was refusing all medication except an anti-hypertensive, which he was taking to control his tics. The parents reported that Mitchell, their youngest child (the others were already living away from home), was extremely bright and very eccentric, but was repeating the ninth grade because of a very rough time he'd had at a local prep school the year before.

"This is a classic case of wasted potential," said the father. "We were devastated by what happened last year."

"What happened?" I asked.

"He just plain bombed out of prep school," said the father. "Here's a kid with an IQ in the 140s, and he's not making it at one of the area's top prep schools. He practically had a nervous breakdown over it. He had to be hospitalized for a week because he tried to slit his wrist."

"That sounds very serious and very scary. How is he now?" I asked.

"Lousy," said the mother. "He has no self-esteem left . . . he's lost all faith in himself. And he doesn't seem to be able to complete any schoolwork at all anymore. We think he's depressed."

"Where's he going to school now?" I asked.

"Our local high school," the mother replied. "They're very nice there and everything, but we don't think he's being challenged by the work, bright as he is."

"Of course, there's more to doing well in school besides smarts," I said. "Can I take a look at the testing you had done?"

I examined the psychoeducational evaluation that had been performed when Mitchell was in the seventh grade. The report documented a twenty-five-point discrepancy between his exceptional verbal skills and average nonverbal skills, difficulty on tasks sensitive to distractibility, very slow processing speed, and below-average written language skills. But the examiner had concluded that Mitchell had no difficulties that would interfere with his learning.

"This is an interesting report," I said.

"How's that?" asked the father.

"Well, it may give us some clues as to why Mitchell might be struggling to live up to everyone's expectations in school," I said.

"We were told he had no learning problems," the mother said.

"I think that was probably inaccurate," I said. I then explained the potential ramifications of some of the evaluation findings. As we talked, it became clearer that Mitchell was indeed struggling most on tasks involving a lot of writing, problem solving, rapid processing, and sustained effort. "That's something we're going to have to take a closer look at," I said.

"Of course, he's still very bright," said the father.

"There are some areas in which he is clearly quite bright," I said. "And some areas that may be making it very hard for him to show how bright he is. My bet is that he finds that disparity quite frustrating."

"Oh, he's frustrated, all right," said the mother. "We all are."

After a while, I invited Mitchell to come into the office. He refused to meet with me alone, so his parents remained in the room.

"I'm sick of mental health professionals," Mitchell announced from the outset.

"How come?" I asked.

"Never had much use for them . . . none of them has ever done me any good," Mitchell answered.

"Don't be rude, Mitchell," his father intoned.

"SHUT UP, FATHER!" Mitchell boomed. "HE WASN'T TALKING TO YOU!"

The storm passed quickly. "It sounds like you've been through quite a bit in the past two years," I said.

"WHAT DID YOU TELL HIM?!" Mitchell boomed at his parents.

"We told him about the trouble you had in prep school," the mother answered, "and about your being suicidal, and about how we don't . . ."

"ENOUGH!" Mitchell screamed. "I don't know this man from Adam, and you've already told him my life story! And I wouldn't have been suicidal if I hadn't been on about eighty-seven different medications at the time!"

"What were you taking back then?" I asked.

"I don't know," Mitchell said, rubbing hard on his forehead. "*You* tell him, mother!"

"I think he's been on about every psychiatric drug known to mankind," said the mother. "Lithium, Prozac . . ."

"STOP EXAGGERATING, MOTHER!" Mitchell boomed.

"Mitchell, don't be rude to your mother," said the father.

"If you don't stop telling me not to be rude, I'm leaving!" Mitchell screamed.

Once again, the storm quickly subsided.

"What medicines are you taking now?" I asked.

"Just something for my tics," Mitchell replied. "And don't even think about telling me to take something else! Let's just get off this topic!"

"He doesn't even take his tic medication all the time," said the mother. "That's why he still tics so much."

"MOTHER, STOP!" Mitchell boomed. "I don't care about the tics! Leave me alone about them!"

"It's just that . . ." the mother began speaking again.

"MOTHER, NO!" Mitchell boomed. His mother stopped.

"Mitchell, are you suicidal now?" I asked.

"NO! And if you ask me that again, I'm leaving!"

"He still doesn't feel very good about himself, though," the father said.

"I FEEL JUST FINE!" Mitchell boomed. "*You're* the ones who need a psychologist, not me!" Mitchell turned to me. "Can you do something about *them*?"

The father chuckled at this question.

"WHAT'S SO FUNNY?!" Mitchell boomed.

"If I might interrupt," I said, "I know you didn't want to be here today, and I can understand why you might not have much faith in yet another mental health professional. But I'm interested . . . what is it you'd like me to do about your parents?"

"Tell them to leave me alone," he growled. "I'm fine."

"Yes, he's got everything under complete control," the father said sarcastically.

"PLEASE!" Mitchell boomed.

"If I told them to leave you alone, do you think they would?" I asked.

"No." He glared at his parents. "I don't."

"Is it fair," I said, speaking carefully, "to say that your inter-actions with your parents are very frustrating for you?"

Mitchell turned to his parents. "You've found another genius," he said. "We need to pay money and waste our time on this guy telling us the obvious?"

"Mitchell!" said the father. "Don't be rude!"

"STOP TELLING ME WHAT TO DO!" Mitchell boomed.

"I appreciate your looking out for me," I said to the father. "But I actually want to hear what Mitchell has to say." I looked back at Mitchell. "I don't think I can get them to leave you alone without you being here."

"I don't think you can get them to leave me alone *with* me being here," Mitchell said. Then he paused for a moment. "How often do I have to come?" he asked.

"Well, to start, I'd like you to come every other week," I said. "I'd like your parents to come every week. Is that rea-sonable?"

"Fine!" he said. "Can we leave now?"

"I'd like to spend a few more minutes with your parents. But you can wait outside if you'd like." Mitchell left the office.

"Well, that's promising," said the mother. I couldn't tell if she was being sarcastic.

"We've got a lot of work to do," I said. "We've got a kid who's very easily frustrated, who's been diagnosed with Tourette's disorder and bipolar disorder, who's tried to kill himself once . . ."

"Twice," interjected the mother. "He tried twice in the same year."

"Twice," I continued, "who's got very high expectations

academically but some significant learning issues getting in the way, who isn't satisfactorily medicated at the moment, and who has no faith in the mental health profession."

The parents listened intently. "Where do we start?" the mother asked.

"Well, I need more information about a lot of things. But one thing is certain: We're not going to get anywhere unless I can establish a relationship with him. And we're going to have to make life at home a lot less tense and acrimonious so there's a least one domain where he's not frustrated to the max."

"Oh, would you say there's some tension in our family?" the father said sarcastically.

"A little bit." I smiled.

"So we come back next week?" asked the mother.

"You do," I said.

I hope that reading about these children gives you a better sense about what inflexibility-explosiveness can look like, how it can affect interactions with family members and other people, and how it "feels" for a child to be inflexible-explosive. These stories may also have provided a few hints about where this book is heading in terms of how to help a child be more flexible and handle frustration more adaptively. In the next chapter, I'll take a closer look at why the standard motivational approach that mental health professionals often recommend for reducing noncompliance and explosiveness in children may not be well matched to the needs of your child. Then, in later chapters, I'll talk about what you can do instead.

5

The Truth About Consequences

"You know, first we thought Amy was just a willful, spoiled kid," one father recalled. "Here were all these mental health professionals telling us that if we were simply firmer and more consistent with her, things would get better. Of course, Amy's grandparents added their two cents; they were constantly telling my wife and me that we were giving in too much. So we did the whole sticker chart and time-out routine for a long time. It makes me shudder to think of how much time that poor kid spent in time-out. But we were told the lessons we were trying to teach her would sink in eventually. Sometimes she wouldn't stay in the corner, and she'd try to kick us and bite us when we tried to hold her there. When we'd confine her to her room, she'd become destructive. Time-outs and rewards didn't seem to mean anything to her when she was upset. We couldn't figure out what we were doing wrong.

"So we went from doctor to doctor looking for answers. One doctor said Amy's tantrums were just her way of getting our attention and told us to ignore the tantrums and give her lots of attention for good behaviors. But ignoring her didn't help her calm down when she was frustrated about something. I don't care what the experts say, you can't just ignore your kid while she's being destructive and violent.

"Another doctor—this was around when she was eight years old—told us Amy had a lot of anger and rage. Amy spent the next year in play therapy, with this therapist trying to figure out what she was so angry about. He sort of ignored us when we told him Amy wasn't angry all the time, only when things didn't go exactly the way she thought they would. He never did uncover anything that accounted for her anger.

"The last person we went to told us Amy's tantrums were an expression of her 'emerging will and sense of self' and we should let her express her emotions as much as possible. So we went through a few months of letting Amy 'express her sense of self' before my wife and I looked at each other and said, 'This is insanity!' In the meantime, we're still trying to figure out how to live with a kid like this.

"We've done everything we were told to do. We paid a big price—and I'm not just talking about money—listening to different professionals and trying strategies that weren't on target. And we became convinced that if the strategies weren't working, it must be our fault."

Psychology and psychiatry are imprecise sciences, and different mental health professionals have different theories and interpretations of inflexible-explosive behavior in children. As you now know, children may exhibit such behavior for any of a variety of reasons, so there's no right or wrong way to explain it and no one-size-fits-all approach to changing it. The key is to find explanations and interventions that are well matched to individual children and their families. In theory, this is a great idea. In practice, something often gets lost in the translation.

Probably the most recommended and widely used approach to understanding and changing the behavior of inflexible-explosive children is what can generically be referred to as the standard behavior management approach. There are a few central beliefs associated with this approach. The first is that somewhere along the line, noncompliant children have learned that their tantrums, explosions, and destructiveness bring them attention or help them get their way by coercing (or convincing) their parents to "give in." This belief often gives rise to the notion that such behavior is planned, intentional, purposeful, and under the child's conscious control ("He's so manipulative! He knows exactly what buttons to push!"), which, in turn, often causes adults to take the behavior very personally ("Why is he doing this to me?"). A corollary to the belief that such behavior is learned is that the child has been poorly taught ("What that kid needs is parents who are willing to give him a good kick in the pants."). Parents who become convinced of this often blame themselves for their child's inflexible-explosive behavior ("We must be doing something wrong . . . nothing we do seems to work with this kid."). Finally, if you believe that such behavior is learned and the result of poor teaching, then it follows that it can also be unlearned with better and more convincing teaching.

Often, this re-teaching and unlearning process includes (1) providing the child with lots of positive attention to reduce the desirability of negative attention; (2) teaching parents to issue fewer and clearer commands; (3) teaching the child that compliance is expected and enforced on all parental commands and that he must comply quickly because his parents are only going to issue a command once or twice; (4) delivering consequences—rewards, such as allowance money and special privileges, and punishments, such as time-outs and the loss of privileges—contingent upon the child's successful or unsuccessful fulfillment of specific target behaviors (such as complying with adults' commands, doing homework, getting ready for school); and (5) teaching the child that his parents won't back down in the face of tantrums. This approach isn't magic; it merely formalizes practices that have always been important cornerstones of effective parenting: being clear about how a child should and should not behave, consistently insisting on appropriate behavior, and motivating the child to perform such behavior.

Some parents and their children benefit enormously from such formality, find that these procedures give some needed structure and organization to family discipline, and end up sticking with the program for a long time. Other parents benefit mostly from what they learn in behavior management courses about their counterproductive parenting habits. Such parents may not stick with a formal behavior management program for long but still change some fundamental aspects of their approach to parenting and therefore become more effective at teaching and motivating their children.

But for other parents, implementing a behavior management program is a significant departure from their natural style or philosophy of parenting. So, although they understand the logic of behavior management procedures, they neither stick with the program nor make fundamental changes in their parenting behavior. Many such parents may embark on a behavior management program with an initial burst of enthusiasm, energy, and vigilance, but become less enthusiastic, energetic, and vigilant over time. These parents often return to their old ways of doing things, and their child's tantrums and outbursts eventually return as well. Thus, one reason behavior management procedures may not be effective for some children is that their parents fail to implement such procedures correctly or consistently.

But there's another reason, and the second explanation is central to the rationale for this book: Children who are developmentally compromised in the skills of flexibility and frustration tolerance may lack the capacity to (a) manage the emotions associated with frustration

Motivational strategies don't make the impossible possible; they make the possible more possible.

well enough to think clearly in the midst of frustration or (b) shift immediately and consistently from their agenda to their parents' agenda, even when faced with very meaningful consequences. And none of us can consistently exhibit behaviors of which we are incapable, no matter how enticing the reward or how aversive the punishment.

In other words, if the Chicago Bulls offered me Michael Jordan's salary to play basketball like Michael Jordan, I would be extremely motivated (yes, I could probably think of a few things to do with $30 million), but I would still have very mediocre basketball skills. Oh, maybe I'd be able to sink an *occasional* great shot, but—and you'll have to take my word on this, having never seen me play basketball—that definitely wouldn't mean I'd be able to sink great shots consistently. If I was then punished for failing to play basketball like Michael Jordan, I'd start to become frustrated and would probably begin to wonder what was the matter with me (and with the people who had unrealistic expectations of me).

Consequences can be very useful in two specific ways: as an instrument of *learning* or as an instrument of *motivation*. But the vast majority of the inflexible-explosive children with whom I work are already well aware of the behaviors adults like and dislike, so applying consequences to teach the child that adults don't like it when he explodes makes little sense, because he already knows. And—hold on to your hat—the vast majority of inflexible-explosive children with whom I work are already motivated not to make themselves and those around them miserable, so consequences aren't necessary for the purpose of additional motivation. So what do we make of a child who already *knows* inflexibility and explosiveness are undesirable and is already *motivated* to be less inflexible and explosive? That if the child *could* be less inflexible and explosive, he most assuredly *would*.

Why might the use of consequences be ineffective in trying to help such children explode less often? By definition, a consequence is an event that occurs after the fact—in other words, on the back end. For a consequence to achieve its desired effect—that is, for a consequence to make it less likely that a child will explode the next time he's frustrated—you have to have faith that the consequence you administered on the back end the last time (i.e., following the last explosion) is going to be accessible and meaningful to the child on the front end the next time he becomes frustrated.

If a child becomes cognitively debilitated in the midst of frustration, he may have enormous difficulty recalling or fully appreciating how much he disliked the consequences you applied the last time (or even the last 50 times) he behaved inappropriately in the midst of frustration. In other words, what you've been doing on the back end hasn't been helping your child control his emotions or think clearly on the front end the next time. In fact, those consequences you've been administering may actually be heightening his emotional arousal and making it that much harder for him to think rationally.

Consequences can be very effective if a child is in a state of mind to appreciate their meaning, but don't work nearly so well if a child is not able to maintain such a state of mind.

Let's go back and take a closer look at what happened when Amy's parents were instructed on how to implement behavior management procedures. First, the parents were taught how to

For a consequence to achieve its desired effect—that is, for a consequence to make it less likely that a child will explode the next time he's frustrated—you have to have faith that the consequence you administered on the back end the last time (i.e., following the last explosion) is going to be accessible and meaningful to the child on the front end the next time he becomes frustrated.

give directions in a way that made it easier for Amy to comply and were encouraged to "catch Amy being good" (with verbal praise, hugs, and the like) every time she complied. The next week, she and her parents were asked to identify a variety of meaningful rewards that could be earned in exchange for compliance, and the parents were helped to design a "currency" system—in her case, a point system—as a way of keeping track of the percentage of times Amy complied with their requests. The points were to be exchanged periodically for the rewards, each of which had a price tag. The next week, the parents were taught the proper way of implementing the time-out procedure when Amy did not comply. The training was now complete. By the third week, Amy was receiving a specified number of points every time she complied with a parental request and was confined to time-out and lost points when she did not comply. Amy was now, most assuredly, very motivated to comply (assuming, of course, that she wasn't motivated in the first place).

The following scenario ensued. The parents would give directions. Amy would become frustrated. The parents would remind her of the consequences for not obeying and of the necessity for immediate compliance. Rather than helping Amy immediately access the file in her brain that contained the critical information ("If you do what they're asking, you'll earn points; if you don't, you'll get a time-out"), her parents' warning would actually cause Amy to become *more* frustrated and agitated, her thinking increasingly disorganized and irrational, and her control over her words and actions greatly reduced. In other words, vapor lock would commence. In accordance with their training, Amy's parents would interpret her increased intensity and failure to respond to their commands as an example of coercive noncompliance and would warn her of an impending time-out. The result: meltdown.

Amy, now bereft of any semblance of coherence or rationality, would begin screaming and lashing out. Her parents, safe in the belief that the tantrum was merely an attempt to manipulate them into giving in, would stick with their training and try to get Amy into time-out, an action that would intensify her meltdown and deepen her incoherence. Amy would resist being placed in time-out. Her parents would try to restrain her physically in time-out (many therapists no longer recommend this practice, but Amy's therapist wasn't one of them) or confine her to her room until she calmed down. The struggle to keep Amy in time-out or confine her to her room would further intensify her meltdown. She would try to hit, kick, bite, scratch, and spit on her parents. Once in her room—when her parents were actually able to get her there and keep her there—she would try to destroy whatever "destructibles" were handy.

Eventually, meaning somewhere in the range of ten minutes to two hours, Amy would become completely exhausted and start to cry or go to sleep. Coherence would be restored. Her exhausted parents would be frustrated and angry and would hope that what they just did to their daughter—and endured themselves—was eventually going to pay off in the form of improved compliance. When Amy would finally emerge from her room, she would be remorseful. The parents, once again in accordance with their training, would, in a firm tone, reissue the direction that started the whole episode in the first place.

In subsequent sessions with their therapist, the parents were commended for their efforts and reassured that Amy would eventually learn that she had to comply with their requests. They were reminded that Amy's destructive, assaultive behavior was an attempt to coerce them into relenting and were encouraged not to give in. They were told that their daughter's ultimate remorse was an attempt to manipulate them. The therapist recommended that they stick with the program. For months. And months. Even though things weren't improving appreciably.

What's the matter with this picture? Amy lacked two critical ingredients necessary for the success of the behavior management program:

1. She was apparently not *capable* of quickly shifting

> *Consequences can be very effective if a child is in a state of mind to appreciate their meaning, but don't work nearly so well if a child is not able to maintain such a state of mind.*

gears—from Agenda A (her agenda) to Agenda B (her parents' agenda)—in response to her parents' commands.

2. She was apparently not *capable* of remaining relatively calm, coherent, and organized when frustrated by her parents' commands, so she could gain access to her knowledge that (a) compliance with parents' commands is what children are supposed to do; (b) if she complied, she would be rewarded; and (c) if she did not comply, she would be placed in time-out. Consequences can be very effective if a child is in a state of mind to appreciate their meaning, but don't work nearly so well if a child is not able to maintain such a state of mind.

Her parents, on the advice of a well-intentioned mental health professional, had conceived of Amy's difficulties as motivational in nature and thus were trying to motivate their daughter to exhibit behaviors of which she was incapable. Given the multiple pathways to inflexible-explosive behavior, was poor motivation really the best explanation for Amy's difficulties? Was Amy's noncompliance truly planned, purposeful, intentional, and under her conscious control? Are the terms *oppositional, noncompliant, manipulative, coercive*, and so forth, really the best ways to describe Amy? Are her parents truly lousy teachers? Is more and better discipline the answer to a difficult temperament? To difficulties related to mood or anxiety? To deficits in executive functions, social skills, language processing, nonverbal skills, and sensory integration?

This seems like a good time to point out that there are some less familiar but important considerations emanating from the more contemporary variants of the behavior management approach that I believe are critical to the process of helping a child be less inflexible and explosive. These considerations include being cognizant of the events, called "antecedents," that precede or fuel inflexible-explosive episodes; being aware of situational factors that may fuel such episodes; paying attention to what's going on (or not going on) inside a child's head that may be related to such episodes; progressively training the various skills that such a child may be lacking; and being aware of the possible neurobiochemical underpinnings of such behavior. As you'll see, these often-neglected principles are important facets of the alternative approach described in this book.

What I've learned over the years is that some children become so overwhelmed so quickly by their frustration that their capacity to maintain coherence in the midst of frustration is severely compromised. I've seen that these children are also compromised in their ability to gain access to information

"We're encouraging people to become involved in their own rescue."

they've stored from previous experiences and think things through so as to formulate a well-organized, reasoned response to frustrating situations. And, as you've read, I've come to believe that the inflexibility and explosiveness evidenced by these children often have a neurobiochemical basis. Meaningful, immediate, consistent consequences may *not* be "just what the doctor ordered" for these children.

In the cartoon on the previous page, a child is showing every sign of drowning. You could assume that the child was simply pretending to be drowning as a means of seeking your attention, in which case the appropriate response would be to ignore him. If you were right, ignoring him would probably get him to stop pretending to be drowning. Of course, if you were wrong, he'd drown. You could also assume that the child was simply not motivated not to drown, in which case you might swim out to him, hold up a dollar bill, and yell "SWIM!" If you were right, motivating him would probably get him to start swimming. Of course, if you were wrong, he'd drown.

Your child is drowning in a sea of frustration and inflexibility. You are the lifeguard. If your child could swim, he would. It's time for Plan B.

Question: "Aren't flexibility and frustration tolerance critical skills? Doesn't my child have to change?"

Answer: "Flexibility and frustration tolerance are critical skills, and there may be some ways to teach your child how to be more flexible. But you may not be getting anywhere—or doing any productive teaching—by engaging in frequent battles with him whenever you try to force him to be more flexible."

Question: "But if I don't teach my child how to be flexible, how will he learn?"

Answer: "If he's going to learn to be more flexible— and I'm optimistic that he can—it's not going to happen by your being a role model for inflexibility."

Question: "But it worked for me; I'm just raising my kids the same way I was raised."

Answer: "The way you were raised may have worked for you—and it seems to be working for your other children—but it's clearly not working as well for your inflexible-explosive child."

Question: "Don't I need to set a precedent now so my child knows who's boss and doesn't think he can always get his way?"

Answer: "Your inflexible-explosive child probably already knows you are the boss. During vapor lock, your child is in a different sphere and the question of 'who's the boss?' doesn't really enter his 'thoughts.' In fact, if you're trying too hard to show your child who's the boss, you may actually be fueling his meltdowns and setting the stage for an adversarial pattern of parent-child interactions. And my sense is that little or no learning takes place for your child during meltdowns because he's basically incoherent. Teaching a child who's boss is easy; understanding and responding to a child's deficits in *the areas of flexibility and frustration tolerance is a lot harder."*

Question: "But aren't most kids a lot more flexible than mine?"

Answer: "Bingo."

Marvin's mother began to cry. "I can't take this anymore," she said, wiping her eyes. Her husband looked on helplessly, holding back tears of his own. "I'm so worried about him . . . Marvin can be so wonderful sometimes . . . but the minute something doesn't go his way, he goes crazy on us. And I'm tired of getting hit by an eight year old."

You met Marvin—a child diagnosed with ADHD, ODD, OCD, depression, and Tourette's disorder—in Chapter 1. His parents had come to the conclusion that rewards and punishments were not the answer to Marvin's inflexibility and explosiveness, but they had continued trying to "motivate" compliant behavior because they weren't sure what else to do.

"Are we all on the same page here about Marvin's behavior?" I asked in one early session.

"What do you mean?" asked his mother.

"Are we all convinced that Marvin isn't doing what he's doing for attention, or to be manipulative, to coerce you into giving in, or to yank your chains?" I asked. "In other words, are we ready to leave the motivational explanation for his difficulties behind us?"

"Absolutely," said the father. "You've helped us understand that there are a lot of different factors—his chronic irritability, inflexibility, impulsivity, tics—that are making it very hard for him to deal well with frustration."

"But you're still using strategies that are intended to motivate compliance," I said. "If we don't think his problem is motivational, I'm not sure why we'd think motivational strategies would be the best way to help him."

"So I'm not supposed to punish him when he hits me?" asked the mother.

"Do you have any faith that punishment makes it any less likely that he'll refrain from hitting you the next time he's frustrated?" I asked.

She thought for a moment. "No," she replied. "Punishing him certainly hasn't gotten us anywhere so far."

"That's for sure," said the father. "In fact, it's probably made things worse in some ways."

"Punishment is a back-end response to Marvin's difficulties," I said. "It's something you do once he's already fallen apart. But I don't have a lot of faith that anything you do on the back end is going to make much difference. In fact, as best I can tell, it's merely made everybody more frustrated and produced a lot of adversarial interactions. I think we need to focus our efforts on the front end to try to keep Marvin from falling apart in the first place."

"I don't understand," said the mother. "It sounds like you're telling us not to respond at all."

"Oh, I want you to respond all right," I said. "But at different points in time—in other words, before and during vapor lock and at the crossroads, rather than during and after meltdowns—and in a very different way. In fact, the things I think you should be doing are very different from simply responding to Marvin's meltdowns with punishments."

"What should we be trying to do?" asked the father.

"Our first goal is to do a better job of anticipating situations that will be frustrating to Marvin and to be much more judicious about the frustrations we choose for him to deal with," I said. "Our second goal is to help Marvin stay coherent when he gets frustrated so he can think rationally. If we can keep him coherent, we might be able to start working on our third goal, which is to help him think things through when he becomes frustrated, so he doesn't end up hitting you and calling you names. Rather than punishing him and teaching him who's boss, you'll instead be trying to help him with some of the things he's really struggling with."

6

Corrective Lenses

By now you should have a much better sense of why it's crucial for you to understand your child's inflexibility and explosiveness, the factors that may contribute to his difficulties, and why an approach aimed solely at teaching and motivating compliant behavior may not be well-suited to your child's needs. Of course, you still don't have the details on the most important issues: What should you do instead? How do we help a child who—due to a difficult temperament, deficits in executive skills, hyperactivity and impulsivity, depressed or unstable mood, anxiety, language or nonverbal impairments, or deficits in social skills—lacks the capacity to respond adaptively to life's demands for flexibility and frustration tolerance? What might we do differently? As it turns out, there are some things that are quite helpful to many of the children, parents, and teachers with whom I work.

The approach I encourage is comprised of two basic avenues. The first avenue involves the creation of what I call a "user-friendlier environment"—an environment in which your child's deficits in the areas of flexibility and frustration tolerance are less of a handicap. A user-friendlier environment can help set the stage for you and your child to begin working together to deal more effectively with his inflexibility and explosiveness. Coming to a clearer understanding of your child's difficulties is the most important first step down this avenue. By demonstrating to your child that you understand how debilitated he becomes in situations requiring flexibility and a tolerance for frustration, you'll help him maintain coherence in the midst of these situations so he can think through and discuss potential solutions.

A user-friendlier environment is also intended to help you (1) be more realistic about which frustrations your child can actually handle and more open to eliminating unimportant, unnecessary frustrations, thereby greatly reducing the opportunities for vapor lock and meltdowns; (2) think more clearly when your child is in the midst of vapor lock and understand that you—not your child—determine whether a situation develops into a full-fledged meltdown, at least initially; (3) be more attuned to the situations that routinely cause your child the greatest frustration; (4) move away from an adversarial relationship with your child while maintaining your role as an authority figure; and (5) not take your child's inflexible-explosive episodes so personally. In other words, creating a user-friendlier environment should contribute to some very fundamental changes in your relationship with your child. This chapter—and several that follow—elaborates on the user-friendlier theme (this theme is extended to the school environment in Chapter 12).

> By demonstrating to your child that you understand how debilitated he becomes in situations requiring flexibility and a tolerance for frustration, you'll help him maintain coherence in the midst of these situations so he can think through and discuss potential solutions.

The second avenue involves addressing your child's difficulties in a more direct way so he doesn't require a user-friendlier environment forever. This is discussed in Chapters 7, 8, and 9.

Many parents accept the idea that their child has compromised skills in the domains of flexibility and frustration tolerance but want to jump right into addressing their child's difficulties directly. Unfortunately, the direct approach is usually not the ideal place to start. Few of us learn best in an environment we experience as tense, hostile, and adversarial, and your child is no exception. So the first avenue is the optimal starting point because it actually sets the stage for helping your child become increasingly receptive to new learning. Yes, this is a departure from the "throw 'em right into the water" approach, but it seems to work much better for a lot of children.

Take, for example, people who are visually impaired. Most of us don't operate on the assumption that visually challenged people are pretending to have trouble seeing so we'll pay attention to them. And isn't it nice that, when they first report their visual difficulties to their eye doctors ("Doc, I think I'm having trouble seeing"), the doctors don't typically dismiss the difficulties and say something along the lines of, "Well, if you really *wanted* to see, you'd see. . . . Looks to me like you're going to have to hit rock bottom before you start to see." No, eye doctors usually do something very similar to what I'm recommending you do for your inflexible-explosive child: evaluate and understand the (visual) problem thoroughly and apply a treatment (corrective lenses) that makes life more livable and is well-matched to his specific needs.

The components of a user-friendlier environment described next share a critical common ingredient: They emphasize responding to your child *before* he's at his worst, rather than on responding when or after he's at his worst. As you know, I have little faith that back-end interventions will have much impact on your child the next time he becomes frustrated. In other words, the best thing adults can do to reduce meltdowns is to make sure they don't happen in the first place.

- **A user-friendlier environment is one in which all the adults who interact with the child have a clear understanding of his unique difficulties, including the specific factors that fuel his inflexibility-explosiveness.**

If you're a child who has trouble thinking through different options for dealing with frustrating situations or who rapidly becomes overwhelmed by the emotions associated with frustration, it can be calming to be in the presence of an adult who knows you well, has a clear sense of what's going on, and feels empowered to act as a "tour" guide to help you navigate through a frustrating episode. As you've already read, when children are stuck in the red haze of inflexibility and frustration, they respond a lot better if they perceive adults as potential helpers, rather than as enemies. In contrast, adults who don't have a clear understanding of what's going on— or who have unenlightened, unrealistic expectations—may unwittingly place additional obstacles in the child's path. I have a simple equation to describe what can happen when inflexible-explosive children are interacting with similarly inflexible partners:

When children are stuck in the red haze of inflexibility and frustration, they respond a lot better if they perceive adults as potential helpers, rather than as enemies.

$$\textbf{inflexibility + inflexibility = meltdown}$$

One child with whom I was working had been melting down far less frequently at home and school, and his parents and teachers and I had started thinking we were on easy street—until his physical education teacher, whom we had neglected to enlighten, demanded that the child wear a sweatshirt outside on a fifty-five-degree day. After about three minutes of what might best be called "reciprocal inflexibility," the child put his fist through a window. The point here is that it's user-friendlier for moms and dads and principals and teachers and coaches to be on the same wavelength and to have a common set of expectations so a child who has trouble adapting quickly in the first place doesn't have to figure out which wavelength and expectations are in effect at any given moment. Moreover, achieving an in-depth, accurate understanding of the precise factors underlying a child's difficulties is critical to designing interventions that are well matched to his needs.

A comprehensive assessment is critical to achieving a clear understanding of these precise factors. Given the various factors which could be underlying a child's difficulties—and the importance of matching treatment "ingredients" to the needs of each individual child—it's hard to imagine embarking on the difficult task of helping your child without the fullest possible understanding of his difficulties. Indeed, the failure to achieve a full understanding of a child's difficulties lies at the core of many counterproductive interventions. Achieving such a full understanding often requires professional assistance, and your impressions and knowledge of your child will be an essential part of the process. My general recommendation is that you have your child evaluated by a competent child psychologist or neuropsychologist. You don't want to leave any stone unturned. Here are the components that should be integral parts of such an assessment (the sequence is less important, as long as all the components are included).

Information about your child's *developmental, school, and treatment history* is crucial and is typically obtained through interviews with a child's parents. The assessor will want to know about your child's pre-natal history, early development and attachment, whether your child's difficulties with inflexibility and low frustration tolerance are longstanding; whether your child has a history of difficult temperament or developmental delays; whether there is a history of abuse or trauma; and the types of treatment, if any, your child has received for these difficulties. Information you can provide about the *psychiatric history* of family members (parents, grandparents, siblings, and so forth) can provide what may best be described as a historical backdrop to your child's difficulties, along with diagnostic clues. Although arriving at a diagnosis is not the primary goal of the evaluation, the assessor should also obtain information about your child's past and current behavior during a *diagnostic interview*, covering all significant childhood psychiatric diagnostic categories including ADHD, ODD, OCD, PDD, mood and other anxiety disorders, and social functioning. The *situational aspects* of your child's inflexibility-explosiveness—with whom, in what settings, under what circumstances, and at what times of the day meltdowns routinely occur—should also be assessed. The assessor should ask you to complete *behavior checklists* to determine the degree to which your child's behavior differs from that of other children of the same age and gender. Finally,

> The failure to achieve a full understanding of a child's difficulties lies at the core of many counterproductive interventions.

your understanding of and reactions to your child's inflexible-explosive behavior should also be informally assessed.

The assessment process should also include an interview with your child, to assess his understanding of and views about his difficulties. Your child's *emotional functioning* should be formally or informally assessed as well. The assessor will also want to get a good sense of *family dynamics and interactions* (as you'll read later, there are ways in which family members communicate with each other that can actually set the stage for meltdowns). To do so, the assessor may want to include siblings, grandparents, and other important family members in the process.

Information about your child's functioning at *school* and in other relevant settings is also essential. Toward this end, the assessor should ask teachers and other adults who have extensive contact with your child to complete *behavior checklists*, so as to obtain different points of view regarding his behavior and to assess further the situations in which inflexible-explosive behavior does and does not occur. If such behavior occurs with frequency at school, teachers and other school staff should be interviewed in the same manner as parents.

Formal psychoeducational testing should be performed to obtain crucial information regarding other factors which may be fueling your child's difficulties. Such an evaluation should include an assessment of your child's *general cognitive functioning*, to gain a sense of his general abilities and identify unevenness in verbal versus nonverbal skills; *achievement skills*, to determine the presence of additional learning disabilities in academic skill areas such as reading, mathematics, and writing; and *executive, language processing, motor, and sensory integration skills.*

Don't forget, the reason you're putting your child and yourself through all this is that it's hard to know how to help your child until everyone—parents, other family members, teachers, soccer coaches, and mental health professionals—has a much clearer understanding of the factors that are fueling his inflexibility and explosiveness. An evaluation aimed solely at determining whether your child qualifies for special education services is unlikely to produce this comprehensive understanding.

It's time for another car analogy. Let's say the engine in my car began making a lot of strange noises, and I decided to take it to a mechanic. The mechanic wouldn't have a precise idea of what parts of my engine needed fixing until he fully assessed the range of problems that might cause it to make strange noises. If my mechanic *automatically* assumed that strange engine noises were *always* accounted for by, say, a bad belt, it's likely I'd leave his shop with a brand-new belt. But, given the range of alternative explanations, there's a good chance my car would still be making strange noises. In other words, the problem probably wouldn't be fixed until it was well assessed and well understood to begin with.

Don't make the mistake of thinking that having a mental health professional bestow a formal diagnosis is all you need to achieve a complete understanding of your child's difficulties. In other words, knowing that your child "has ADHD" or "is depressed" or "has PDD" doesn't tell you a whole lot about the precise difficulties your child is experiencing, what he needs help with, or what kind of help he needs. I'm much more interested in working toward a consensus about the specific problem behaviors a child is exhibiting, identifying the precise difficulties in thinking skills that are preventing a child from dealing adaptively with frustration, determining where and when problematic behaviors are being exhibited and what factors seem to be fueling them, and—on the basis of this comprehensive understanding—bringing to bear the different treatments that seem appropriate to the child's needs.

- In a user-friendlier environment, parenting goals must be judiciously prioritized, with an emphasis on reducing the overall demands for flexibility and frustration tolerance being placed on the inflexible-explosive child.

Your child has proven beyond a doubt that he can't handle all the frustrations presently on his radar screen. If you clear his radar screen of many unnecessary frustrations—in other words, reduce the opportunities for vapor lock and melt-downs—your child's global level of frustration should decrease and he may be able to more successfully handle the frustrations that remain. Another user-friendlier development: Your own global level of frustration should decrease correspondingly. Also, if your child is melting down less often, the general level of tension and hostility in your family should diminish, thereby facilitating improved parent-child interactions. These improved interactions can set the stage for—hold on to your hat—actual discussions in the midst of frustrating situations instead of meltdowns. But we're not there yet.

While many parents and teachers can appreciate the wisdom of reducing the overall demands for flexibility and frustration tolerance being placed on their child, they often need help understanding how to do it. They want reassurance that the child will not come to view them as "pushovers." Don't forget: Most inflexible-explosive kids are quite clear about who's the boss when they're in a rational state of mind. So Job 1 is to make sure they stay coherent and rational even when they are frustrated, and judicious prioritizing of when and on what issues adult authority is asserted can go a long way. Chapter 7 provides a thorough description of what I've come to call "basket thinking," an enhanced form of picking your battles, so I won't elaborate on the mechanics of prioritizing here.

- A user-friendlier environment is one in which adults try to identify—*in advance*—specific situations that may routinely lead to inflexible-explosive episodes.

There's no question that some episodes seem to come out of the blue, but most are actually predictable. And if they're predictable, you'll be taken by surprise a lot less often and can try to prepare yourself and your child in advance or avoid the situation altogether. Just don't expect advance preparation to work all the time because it won't.

Some parents find it useful to keep an informal record of their child's meltdowns for a few consecutive weeks to try to determine whether there's some sort of predictable pattern. What types of situations seem to contribute to vapor lock and meltdowns in your child? Waking up and getting out of bed in the morning? Getting ready for school? Doing homework? Getting ready for bed at night? Boredom? Shifting from one activity to another? Being in the company of certain individuals? Being hungry just before dinner? Being surprised by a sudden change in plans or in some aspect of the environment? When a social interaction requires an appreciation of the gray in a situation? When a situation has become too complex for him to sort through? When his Ritalin wears off? Are there certain topics, sounds, or articles of clothing that seem to induce meltdowns fairly regularly? Which of these situations can we alter? Which ones can we prepare for in advance? What situations can we avoid altogether, so as to reduce the child's frustration? Which ones can't be altered, prepared for, or avoided? We've got a lot to learn about your child!

· **In a user-friendlier environment, adults "read" the warning signals and take quick action when these signals are present.**

As you've already read, it's the rare child who, as frustration is kicking in, states in a calm, coherent manner, "Uh, folks, this situation is beginning to cause me intense frustration, and I'm reasonably certain that my capacity for rational thought is rapidly diminishing. So I'm wondering if we might begin considering some alternative course of action, so I don't lose it completely." Most of the time, the child provides a less articulate but still meaningful indication that vapor lock has commenced and an altered state of mind has set in. Some children will say, "I'm tired" or "I'm hungry"; others will say, "I can't do this right now!" or "I'm bored" or "I don't feel right" or, in the case of a child you already know, "I was going to have those three waffles tomorrow morning!" Still others may blurt out "I hate you!" or "Screw you!" Others won't say anything but their nonverbals—body language, sudden crankiness, whining, irritability, restlessness, a sudden loss of energy for handling routine tasks or activities (even ones that are normally pleasurable) or unexpectedly intense response to routine requests—are a dead giveaway. These are the signs that your child is moving toward the edge.

At least initially, the burden for recognition of these signs falls on the adults who are interacting with the child. It's critical to read these early warning signs and take action while there's still some coherence to work with to prevent these hints from turning into something much bigger and uglier. A former lifeguard I know, Brian Blanchard, put it this way: "Lifeguards who watch the water closely don't have to jump in and rescue people very often."

What should you do if you read some of the early warning signs? If it's very early in a vapor-lock sequence, there's a chance that the combination of empathy and logical persuasion will work, with empathy being the more important of the two ingredients. Empathy can be an effective way to maintain your child's capacity for rational thought, which, of course, is the main goal. Jumping straight into logical persuasion may not maintain your child's capacity for much of anything except a meltdown.

Mother [calling upstairs]: Addie, it's time to go to the picnic.

Addie [no response].

Mother [walking upstairs]: Come on, Addie, this is our big family reunion; there's going to be lots of people there, and I don't want to be late.

Addie [from under the bedcovers]: I'm not going.

Mother [at the door of Addie's bedroom]: Addie, why are you back in bed? It's almost one o'clock.

Addie [hiding her face]: I don't want to go.

Mother [thinking to herself]:

A. We're in vapor lock; my next response is critical.

B. I wonder what's going on with Addie?

C. I'd better take some time to find out, even if it means being a little late to the reunion.

D. What is it about going to the reunion that might be causing Addie to behave this way?

E. Well, she's not very good at dealing with big crowds, she won't know many people there, and she's not very good at organizing an adaptive response to things that are making her uncomfortable.

Mother [gently]: Addie, how come you don't want to go to the reunion?

Addie: I don't know; I just don't want to.

Mother: Hmm . . . let's think about this; there are going to be a lot of people there, and you won't know that many of them."

Addie: And I don't know who I'll play with.

Mother: I was thinking that might be troubling you. Let's think about this a second. There are some people you will know—Uncle Dave, Aunt Julie,

*cousins Fay and Debbie—you always like playing
with cousin Fay.*

Addie: Cousin Fay will be there?

*Mother: She's probably there already. But I'll tell you
what. If you want, for the first few minutes we're there,
why don't me and you stick together until you find
someone you want to play with.*

Addie: OK.

Empathy can help a child hang in there, and a coherent child
has a much better chance of responding to logical persuasion
than an incoherent one. Nonetheless, for severely inflexible-
explosive children, I tend to think of empathy and logical persuasion as a fairly low-odds intervention, at least early on;
after a few months of living in a user-friendlier environment,
this approach has a better chance.

Aside from empathy and logic, there are a few other quick
interventions that may also be useful when the early warning
signs of vapor lock are apparent. One of my favorites is distraction. With distraction, you're redirecting your child into some
other activity so the inflexibility and frustration associated with
a current activity are diminished. Naturally, distractions should
be enjoyable to your child and require minimal brain energy
(thinking and processing) from him. Distractions that meet
these criteria have a chance. Of course, humor is probably my
favorite distraction—that is, humor that isn't at the child's
expense and that helps him be a little less intense about whatever seems to be causing him frustration at the moment.

Another quick intervention is what I call "downshifting." In the same way that you wouldn't downshift from fifth gear (Agenda A) to reverse (Agenda B) in one easy step in a car (unless you wanted to tear up your transmission), you shouldn't try the same thing with an inflexible-explosive child (unless you want to tear up his). What you should do instead is to try to shift the car (child) from fifth gear to fourth, fourth to third, third to second, and second to first; put on the brakes; and finally put the car (child) into reverse—in gradual steps. All the while, listen closely to the sound of the car's (child's) "engine," so you can maintain a good feel for how close you are to having the transmission blow.

Continuing with the car theme, the following story was told to me by the mother of a very concrete, language-impaired ten-year-old girl with whom I'd begun working:

Lydia's parents had a few family friends over to their house for a get-together. At one point, Lydia's mother and some of her friends decided to go for a drive to the shopping mall, and Lydia was excited about being asked to go with them. Lydia eagerly ran over to her father and asked him for the keys to the car. The father, who on occasion permitted Lydia to steer the car while seated in his lap, was engaged in conversation with one of the friends, and, with barely a second thought, gave Lydia the keys to the car.

When the mother and her friends came out to the car, Lydia, smiling and firmly planted in the driver's seat, proclaimed, "I'm driving!"

The mother's friends laughed, thinking that this behavior was adorable. Which, of course, it would have been had Lydia not been dead serious.

"OK, honey, slide over so I can drive," said her mother.

"I'm driving!" insisted Lydia, her smile a bit less certain.

The mother recognized that vapor lock had commenced, but her embarrassment and desire to get to the mall kept her from reacting as she later wished she had.

"Lydia, move over!" the mother demanded, moving her daughter closer to the edge of a full-blown meltdown (but no closer to the passenger seat).

"I'm driving and I'm not moving over!" insisted Lydia, no longer smiling. The mother's friends began to murmur. Not good.

"Lydia, I'm going to count to three, and then you'd better be in the passenger seat!" insisted the mother.

Commence meltdown. A scene ensued in which the mother tried to drag Lydia from the car and Lydia clung to the steering wheel for dear life. Eventually the father joined the commotion and was able to pry Lydia loose. Lydia was subsequently confined to her room, where she spent the next forty-five minutes screaming and destroying her belongings. The guests left (still murmuring). The mother and her friends never made it to the shopping mall.

Downshifting might have had a chance with Lydia in this situation. In our next session, the parents assured me that Lydia's legs didn't come close to reaching the gas pedals and that she didn't know how to get the key into the ignition, so safety had not been the mother's primary concern. The mother felt she'd overreacted because of the time pressure involved, but agreed that enduring forty-five minutes of Lydia's screaming and throwing toys was far more unpleasant and far less efficient than spending a few minutes helping her daughter downshift.

"The first thing I should have done is tell her how great it was that she'd gotten her ready for us. That probably would have gotten her from fifth gear to fourth gear. She's usually more receptive when we empathize with her first. Then I should have asked her to show us how she would drive the car and to show us the different equipment she would use. That probably would have gotten her from fourth gear to third. Then I could have told her that she could sit in my lap and show everyone how we drive around the driveway—that might have gotten us from third gear to second. I suppose once I had let her show everyone how well she can drive, she would have slid right over to the passenger seat and we would have gone on our merry way."

The father tried to comfort his wife. "Well, I didn't exactly jump in and act like 'Mr. Reasonable' either. I think we both should have been more worried about understanding what was going on in Lydia's head than about what our friends were thinking."

Empathy and logical persuasion, distraction and humor, and downshifting may be useful early in the vapor-lock sequence, but they may be useless if a child's incoherence deepens, thereby requiring a quick shift to the basket thinking described in the next chapter. What this means, of course, is that reading your child must continue past the point of merely recognizing the onset of vapor lock; it's important to continue reading to gauge the effect of your attempts to help your child stay coherent.

By the way, one reason why ignoring isn't particularly effective for these children during vapor lock and meltdowns is that it doesn't provide them with the roadmap they need to help them find safe passage out of their frustrated state. What they need to help them find their way is a coherent adult.

- In a user-friendlier environment, adults can interpret incoherent behaviors for what they really are: incoherent behaviors.

Accurately interpreting incoherent behaviors is very hard to do. Nonetheless, during meltdowns, all bets are off on what kind of mental debris might come out of a child's mouth. When inflexible-explosive kids scream "Screw you!" or "I hate you!" or "I wish I was dead!" in the midst of vapor lock or meltdowns, they often mean "My capacity for rational thought is rapidly diminishing or is already completely gone!" If you immediately punish the child for saying "Screw you!" because it's offensive and disrespectful—which it most certainly is—you've taught another lesson on the importance of respect (a principle to which your child may have no trouble adhering when he's coherent), but you've also thrown fuel on the meltdown fire, all of which may prove fairly meaningless the next time the child is frustrated. If you read the "Screw you!" as "My capacity for rational thought is rapidly diminishing" and use any of the various strategies described in this and the next three chapters to provide the child with a roadmap for dealing with his frustration, you'll probably avoid a full-fledged meltdown and may actually get in some good teaching, role modeling, and relationship-building. It's your choice.

- In a user-friendlier environment, adults can also understand the manner in which they may be fueling a child's inflexibility-explosiveness.

Adults may dwell on certain issues so long or so often that they practically invite meltdowns. They may try so hard to be a good influence that they try to change everything about a child all at once. They may ignore warning signs. They may have short fuses themselves. They may stick with counterproductive strategies and endure countless meltdowns in anticipation of some long-term gain. They may be stressed and frustrated about work, finances, schedules, and so forth. Their response to their inflexible-explosive child may be driven by the example they're trying to set for their other children. In other words, there are many ways an adult may fuel a child's inflexibility-explosiveness by creating a distinctly user-*un*friendly environment. Many of these issues are discussed in greater detail later.

- In a user-friendlier environment, adults try to use a more accurate "common language" to describe various aspects of the child's inflexibility-explosiveness.

As you already know, I don't find a lot of the terminology commonly used to describe these children to be particularly useful, and neither do the children with whom I work. Tell a child he's bratty, manipulative, attention seeking, stubborn, controlling, and angry long enough, and an unfortunate thing may happen: He'll start to believe you. I find it more useful to talk to such children about being "easily frustrated"; how they have trouble "thinking clearly" when they're frustrated; things their parents can do to help them "stay calmer," "think things through," and "consider their options" when in the midst of frustration; the importance of recognizing the "early warning signs" of "vapor lock" and the circumstances that may lead to "meltdowns"; and the necessity of "working things out" and "problem solving." As you might imagine, children tend to be more receptive to being helped when this terminology is used. "Talking the talk" will make more sense as you progress through the next few chapters.

· **That vision thing.**

In some important ways, inflexible-explosive children are not what most parents hope for. Their difficulty adapting to curves in the road and extreme responses make life very difficult for them and those who must interact with them. They can affect family members and family life in potent, adverse ways. They can make parents question whether there's anything that's actually pleasurable and rewarding about being a parent. Yet, I've found that, when we can start helping these children around the obstacles blocking their paths, they can be remarkably rewarding to have around. These are sweet, engaging, intelligent, interesting, curious, imaginative, creative, and sensitive children. But feeling good about them and helping them and you move beyond their difficulties require a change in vision. If you were hoping for the standard, compliant, easygoing child, it's not in the cards. One of the things I hope will happen as you continue reading this book is that you will form a more realistic vision of who your child is and what you can hope to create, both in your child and your relationship with him.

*

Remember Marvin from Chapters 1 and 4? In one early session, I had told his parents that once the user-friendlier environment kicked in I felt certain they'd discover they had a sweet son. I was confident in saying this because I'd seen clear signs of a great child underneath all the irritability, inflexibility, impulsivity, and explosiveness. The parents wanted to believe me, but they were skeptical. We saw a reduction in meltdowns and an improvement in parent-child interactions over the course of a few months. And, after trials of several types of medication, one finally started having the desired effect. Marvin became less moody and more malleable. He was less reactive and explosive. Little things didn't bother him as much. He became much more receptive to talking about and working on his difficulties.

Marvin's mother arrived for one of the next sessions in tears. I thought he'd had some sort of backslide.

"What happened?" I asked, expecting the worst.

"Oh, nothing . . . nothing bad anyway," she said in between sniffles. "It's just that you turned out to be right."

"Right about what?" I asked.

"Remember when you told us that underneath all his difficulties Marvin was really a very sweet kid? Well . . . you were right. He still has his moments, and we know things won't ever be easy. But we're finally enjoying him . . . we're seeing what a great kid he is . . . and that's something we weren't sure would ever happen."

DRAMA IN REAL LIFE
SHIFTING GEARS, EXHIBIT A

April is a sixth-grade girl who managed to live her first eleven years of life without a diagnosis. Although she tended to be mildly impulsive, absentminded, and disorganized, she did well in school academically and behaviorally. Her behavior at home was a different story altogether. At home, April was prone to frequent, intense meltdowns during which she would scream and insist that her demands be met. Although she was neither physically aggressive nor prone to swearing during her meltdowns, her mother found April's inflexibility and low frustration tolerance difficult to deal with. The mother and daughter often ended up in shouting matches over even the most trivial issues.

In one early session, the mother recounted one of the more memorable episodes of the week. "April was doing a report on Colombia in school and decided the night before she was to give the report that she wanted me to cook a traditional Colombian dish for her class. When I told her I didn't know how to cook any Colombian dishes, she went berserk on me. I finally started screaming back at her. Can you imagine?"

"Yes, I can imagine," I replied. "From what I gather, you and April have been screaming at each other for a long time now."

"I can't stand it," said the mother.

"Based on what you've described, it sounds like April is usually a very sweet, well-intentioned child," I said.

"Not a mean bone in her body," said the mother.

"And yet, there are times when she gets something in her head and can't seem to get it out," I said.

"Exactly," said the mother. "But what's the matter with her? Why does she start screaming over the smallest thing?"

"Probably because she can't think of anything else to do," I replied.

"She can't think of anything else to do?" the mother asked.

"That's right," I said. "She gets it in her head that she wants you to cook a Colombian dish for her class and then she's totally at a loss when you tell her you don't know how. She can't configure a way out of the dilemma. So she just keeps repeating the same request over and over."

"That's exactly what she does!" said the mother.

"The more she repeats the same request, the more aggravated you both become until you're finally screaming at each other," I said. "The problem is, you telling her you can't cook a Colombian dish doesn't help her solve the problem."

"What should I do instead?" asked the mother.

"Help her think," I said. "When she's stuck like that—when she's show-ing you she can't shift gears—she's telling you she can't think of a way out of the situation on her own. She needs you to help her think things through. Your challenge is to make sure she stays rational while you're trying to help her. Just remember, the closer to meltdown she gets, the harder it will be to help her think. The more aggravated you get—the more you raise your voice—the closer to meltdown she moves."

"Does this have a name?" the mother asked.

"I just call it inflexibility-explosiveness," I said. "I think that pretty much describes what's going on."

"You know," the mother said sheepishly, "I think I might be inflexible-explosive myself."

"Is that so?" I replied. "I'm glad you're sitting down, because I have some very bad news for you."

"What's that?" asked the mother.

"I have more faith in your ability to help April be more flexible than I do in her ability to help you," I said.

"I had a feeling you were going to say that," said the mother.

"Luckily," I said, "I expect the help we provide to April to be very useful for you, too."

DRAMA IN REAL LIFE
A TRIP TO THE EYE DOCTOR

Craig is a four-year-old boy with a two-year-old brother, a mother, a father, and an extensive collection of toy firefighting equipment (fire helmet, fire trucks, and so forth) that he carries with him at all times. His parents brought Craig to see me because he was melting down literally dozens of times every day.

The first thing I noticed about Craig was that he was very reluctant to part with his large bag of toy firefighter equipment.

"He thinks he's a firefighter," said his father.

"He must have quite an imagination," I said.

"No, I mean he *really* thinks he's a firefighter," the father insisted.

When, in our first meeting, the father volunteered to take Craig and his brother to the cafeteria so I could obtain additional information about Craig from his mother, Craig adamantly refused to leave his fire-fighting equipment behind.

"Craig, it will be right here when you come back," I reassured him.

"There could be a fire while I'm gone," he responded, looking very concerned.

"Are you really a firefighter, Craig?" I asked.

"Yep," he responded.

"That's not just pretend?" I asked.

"Nope," he replied. He left my office with his large bag of fire-fighting equipment slung over his shoulder.

I learned more about Craig in several subsequent sessions with his parents. He insisted on wearing the same pair of pants every day. He spent much time lining up his toys. Unexpected changes and new or unpredictable situations were very difficult for him to handle. He tended to overreact to loud noises and the way things smell. He was in an irritable mood a lot of the time. He was very hyperactive and impulsive. His grandparents thought his parents were doing a lousy job of raising him. We focused most of our energy on trying to identify the specific situations that led to meltdowns so as to achieve a clearer understanding of the factors that seemed to set him off.

"His brother is the cause of 75 percent of his meltdowns," the mother insisted after closely observing Craig for a week. "Craig will be playing quietly with his toys, and when his brother tries to join in, Craig will literally try to strangle him."

"What is it about having his brother join in that is so difficult for Craig?" I asked.

"Isn't that sort of a normal sibling thing?" asked the father.

"Not wanting to share your toys with your brother isn't terribly unusual," I agreed. "But trying to strangle your brother every time he tries to join in would be considered a bit extreme."

"I think he's still upset about his brother being born," the mother said.

"Having a new sibling can be a major adjustment," I agreed. "Particularly for a child like Craig who likes things to be 'just so.' But we aren't getting rid of his brother any time soon, so we'd better figure out why it's so difficult for Craig when his brother tries to play with him. My sense is that when Craig is playing with his toys, he has a very set plan in his mind about what each toy is supposed to be doing and when. When his brother intrudes, Craig has a lot of trouble—much more so than most kids—adjusting to the interruption of his plan. He's at a loss for what to do next. Then it gets ugly."

"What makes him act that way?" asked the mother.

"Well, a variety of things we already know about Craig could be contributing factors," I replied. "His hyperactivity, poor impulse control, and irritability could certainly be coming into play. Some other factors may be relevant as well. We've discussed the diagnosis of Asperger's disorder previously. We'll get a more precise handle on things as time goes on, and it's likely that I'll refer you for some testing. Suffice to say, though, that the reason Craig likes the world to be a very predictable place is that he deals very poorly with situations that are unpredictable for him or that disrupt his game plan."

The parents confirmed this description with their recounting of a trip to the county fair during the ensuing week.

"We had a rough Sunday," said the mother. "We took him to the fair, and when we got there, he wanted me to carry his fire equipment for him. I told him I wasn't about to carry his bag of fire equipment for him, and he went crazy."

"What happened next?" I asked.

"I carried the bag for him," said the father. "I could see that he was completely out-of-sorts just being at the fair. Y'know, he'd never been to the fair before, and there's all these people and all these things he's never seen before. I figured that if having his fire equipment with him made it easier for him to handle the fair, it wasn't that big a deal."

"Do you think he should have done that?" asked the wife. "Give in like that?"

"I'm not sure I would characterize what your husband did as giving in," I replied.

"Well, he carried the fire equipment, didn't he?" the wife said.

"He did, that's true," I replied. "But there might be another way to interpret your husband's behavior. He recognized the warning signs that Craig was out-of-sorts, had a pretty good sense about why Craig was out-of-sorts, and decided that making Craig leave his bag of fire-fighting equipment in the car was not a high priority right now. At this stage of the game, that all sounds pretty user-friendly."

"So we'll be carrying Craig's fire equipment for him the rest of our lives," the mother said.

"I doubt it," I said. "Making the world user-friendlier for Craig now should set the stage for us to understand him better and teach him how to better handle things that are hard for him. Meltdowns don't help us achieve either goal."

"I'm not sure we should have even gone to the fair in the first place," the father said.

"Well, helping you better anticipate situations Craig can't handle will also be an extremely user-friendly development," I said. "When did you first begin to think that the fair might be difficult for Craig to handle?"

"When I opened the door to get him out of the car and I saw the look on his face," the father replied. "Looking back, there are a lot of things about the fair that I don't think he can handle yet. An ordinary kid might have handled it fine... Craig's a different story."

"We disagree a lot on how to handle those types of situations," said the mother. "I'm much more inclined to force the issue compared to my husband. Seems to me my husband is always doing exactly what Craig wants him to."

"Seems to me you're always causing unnecessary meltdowns," the father responded.

"Once we have a better understanding of Craig's difficulties—and I think we're moving toward such an understanding already—I suspect it will be much easier for you guys to agree on which issues to force and which issues to let go. And, most importantly, you'll agree on what type of help your son needs and how you can go about providing it."

Before we move on to basket thinking, a brief summary of this chapter may be useful.

- The approach described in this book is comprised of two basic avenues. In this chapter, an important component of the first avenue—creating user-friendlier environments—was discussed. Creating a user-friendlier environment can set the stage for you and your child to begin working together to deal more effectively with his inflexibility and explosiveness. You're creating a user-friendlier environment now so as to set the stage for not needing a user-friendlier environment later.

- First and foremost, a user-friendlier environment should help you respond to your child before he's at his worst, rather than when or after he's at his worst. Here are the specific components:

    1. Making sure all the adults who interact with your child have a clear understanding of his unique difficulties, including the specific factors that fuel his inflexibility-explosiveness.
    2. Reducing the overall demands for flexibility and frustration tolerance that are being placed on your child, by judiciously establishing priorities among your parenting goals.
    3. Identifying—in advance—specific situations that may routinely lead to inflexible-explosive episodes.
    4. Reading the warning signals and taking quick action when these signals are present.
    5. Interpreting incoherent behaviors for what they really are: incoherent behaviors.
    6. Understanding the manner in which you and other adults may be fueling your child's inflexibility-explosiveness.
    7. Using a more accurate common language to describe various aspects of your child's inflexibility-explosiveness.
    8. Coming to a more realistic vision of who your child is and what

you can hope to create, both in your child and your relationship
with your child.

· Probably the most important part of creating a user-friendlier environment is achieving a clear understanding of the factors fueling your
child's difficulties. Interventions that are initiated before such an
understanding has been achieved are often counterproductive.

7

Basket Case

One of the most important aspects of my work with inflex-ible-explosive children and their families is repetition. Old habits die hard and old interaction patterns are hard to break, so repetition is a crucial ingredient for keeping things moving in the right direction. Toward this end, here are some of the critical points we want to keep fresh:

· Flexibility and tolerance for frustration are skills. Because of any of a variety of factors, your child is predisposed to have difficulty respond-ing to the world in an adaptable, flexible manner.

· Because inept parenting, poor motivation, attention-seeking, and the lack of appreciation for who's boss may not be the best explanations for your child's difficulties, standard parenting practices and motiva-tional programs may be mismatched to his needs. Your child may require a different approach.

· How you perceive and understand your child's inflexibility-explosiveness is directly related to how you'll ultimately respond to it. If you respond to the child in an inflexible, angry manner, then you will increase the likelihood of meltdowns, fuel adversarial parent-child interactions, and reduce the likelihood of improving your child's inflexibility and explosiveness.

· As you've probably already discovered, it's unlikely that the meltdowns you've been inducing and enduring have taught your child anything productive or led to any meaningful positive change in his behavior.

· I am more optimistic about your ability to respond differently to your child's inflexibility than I am about your child's ability to radically improve his capacity to be flexible, at least initially.

· If you create a user-friendlier environment and concentrate more on the front end (before and during vapor lock and crossroads) than the back end (during and after meltdowns), interactions between you and the child should improve. Once things begin to improve a little, he should become more receptive to, and have a greater capacity to benefit from, more direct methods for increasing his flexibility and frustration tolerance.

The last chapter reviewed some of the important components of creating a user-friendlier environment, including adjusting your parenting priorities to reduce the overall demands for flexibility and frustration tolerance being placed on your child, identifying specific situations that may routinely lead to inflexible-explosive episodes, reading the warning signals of vapor lock so you can take quick action before your child melts down completely, and accurately interpreting the mental debris flowing out of your child's mouth during meltdowns. You also read about some strategies that may be helpful in the early phases of vapor lock. Let's now turn to a simple framework for helping you incorporate many of these components.

In this framework, there are three goals critical to helping your child:

A. Maintaining adults as authority figures.
B. Teaching your child the skills of flexibility and frustration tolerance.
C. Being cognizant of your child's limitations.

A lot of adults (including authors of popular parenting books!) believe that the first goal—maintaining adults as authority figures—is the most important goal. I don't. You see, while I believe that it's important for children to know that adults are authority figures, I don't believe that such knowledge goes very far as it relates to helping inflexible-explosive children respond more adaptively to frustration. If what these children really needed was simply more authority, they'd all be fixed by now!

The second goal—teaching the child the skills of flexibility and frustration tolerance—is the most important goal, for it emphasizes the actual factors that are fueling the child's difficulties. These children are going to need some specialized help learning, practicing, and performing the thinking skills that are critical to handling the frustrations and curves in the road that come their way. They've proven that, in the absence of such help, they continue to respond to such frustrations and curves in the road in a strikingly maladaptive fashion that reflects the utter absence of such thinking skills.

The third goal—being cognizant of your child's limitations—is also critical. An awareness of what your child can and can't do will help you make intelligent decisions about how to reduce your child's general level of frustration so you can start training those critical thinking skills.

Now picture three baskets in a row: Basket A, Basket B, and Basket C. Basket A contains those important behaviors that are worth inducing and enduring a meltdown over. Basket A helps us achieve Goal A: maintaining adults as authority figures. Basket B contains those behaviors that are important but aren't worth inducing and enduring a meltdown over. It's on Basket B behaviors that you'll work toward achieving Goal B: teaching your child the skills of flexibility and frustration tolerance. In other words, Basket B is the roadmap basket. Finally, Basket C contains unimportant behaviors that aren't worth even saying anything about anymore. In other words, these behaviors are off the radar screen. Basket C helps us achieve Goal C: being cognizant of your child's limitations. Let's take a closer look inside each of these baskets.

Basket A

As a rule of thumb, the instant you say "No," "You must," or "You can't" to your child, you're in Basket A.

Safety is always in Basket A. In other words, unsafe behaviors—defined as those that could be harmful to your child, other people, animals, or property—are not negotiable and are worth inducing and enduring meltdowns over. Of course, just because you're willing to induce and endure a meltdown to ensure safety doesn't mean a meltdown is your goal. If your child engages in an unsafe behavior—hitting, kicking, throwing things, destroying property, and the like—you're taking the least intense, least physical, least antagonistic route to restoring safety and coherence.

For many inflexible-explosive children, safety is the only behavior placed in Basket A early on. The good news is that through the combination of a user-friendlier environment and the baskets (and sometimes medication), the majority of inflexible-explosive children are able to stay safe even when they become frustrated.

The following litmus test should be applied to any behaviors being considered for placement in Basket A:

1. The issue must be important enough to induce and endure meltdowns over.
2. Your child must be capable of successfully exhibiting the desired behavior on a fairly consistent basis.
3. You must be willing and able to enforce your wishes.

If a behavior doesn't pass the Basket A litmus test, it doesn't belong in Basket A. It doesn't matter how much you *wish* the behavior was in Basket A. And even if the behavior is very important, it doesn't go into Basket A unless it passes the rest of the Basket A litmus test.

A few other important points about Basket A. First, simply placing safety in Basket A doesn't guarantee that your child will be safe. You still have to put an enormous amount of hard work into identifying the factors that are causing your child to be unsafe and applying the interventions that are necessary for him to be safer. Putting safety in Basket A simply means that you're willing to induce and endure a meltdown so as to enforce safety. The other baskets—especially Basket C—are actually more essential to the creation of a safe environment, something you'll understand more clearly by the end of this chapter. Second, Basket A doesn't train your child how to think in the midst of frustration; it simply teaches him that you are an authority figure.

How will your child know a behavior is in Basket A? You'll say, "Johnny, I can see that you're very frustrated right now—unfortunately, this is not an issue we can discuss."

Why are there very few behaviors in Basket A? Because reducing the frequency and intensity of meltdowns is a very high priority. And because teaching your child who's boss hasn't helped him be any more flexible or deal any more adaptively with frustration. Parents of inflexible-explosive children must constantly decide whether a given expectation is worth the price of a major, destructive, labor-intensive meltdown. Is a messy bedroom important or undesirable enough to induce and endure a meltdown? An unmade bed? Unbrushed teeth? Incomplete homework? Bad manners? Eating unhealthy foods? Destruction of property? Swearing?

If you want to restore some level of sanity to your household and start helping your child be more flexible and less explosive, then for now—and maybe for quite some time—reducing the frequency of your child's meltdowns will have to rank higher on your list of parenting priorities than a lot of other priorities. Thus, on many issues, you'll purposely choose to avert a meltdown and consciously decide that family peace, improving your relationship with your child, and setting the stage for helping your child be more flexible and handle frustration more adaptively are higher priorities than a bed being made or a room being cleaned or homework being done. As you already know, your other option is to continue routinely inducing and enduring meltdowns in the hope that such meltdowns will lead to a productive outcome. As you also know, my sense is that if inducing meltdowns hasn't been a useful teaching tool for the past two to ten years, inducing several hundred more meltdowns for another year probably won't be either. This theme definitely takes some getting used to. Don't stop reading yet.

If you've been bothered by the nagging feeling that averting meltdowns means you'll have little authority over your child, take heart: you're an authority figure in Basket B, too—just a different kind of authority figure.

Most inflexible-explosive children are already convinced of your status as an authority figure; the problem is that, once vapor lock commences, they have trouble acting on this knowledge.

Basket B

Basket B is the most important basket because it helps you achieve Goal B: teaching your child the skills of flexibility and frustration tolerance. Basket B contains behaviors that you've decided are important but over which you are not willing to induce a meltdown. What do you do instead? Help him think. Create a roadmap. Communicate. Problem-solve. Work it out.

Now, according to many popular books on parenting difficult children, parents should never work things out with a child. According to the book you're reading right now, working things out can be an extremely effective way to help your child learn skills he clearly lacks: engaging in give-and-take with another person, staying calm in the midst of frustration, taking another's perspective, coming up with alternative ways to solve a problem, resolving disagreements in a mutually satisfactory manner, and so forth.

Many inflexible-explosive children are quite limited in the ability to engage in the give-and-take required to reach solutions that are mutually satisfactory. So we've got a lot of teaching and modeling to do. Working out disagreements is hard for many parents, too; although most figured they'd eventually have to start working things out with their child once he reached adolescence, they never envisioned the necessity of collaborative problem solving with a six year old. Of course, there are many things parents never envisioned before they discovered they had an inflexible-explosive child.

Here's how it often sounds when we're trying to teach a child how to work things out, with appropriate modifications depending on the child's age:

Me: Johnny, do you know what a solution is?

Johnny [age seven]: Sorta.

Me: What's a solution?

Johnny [brief pause]: It's like an idea.

Me: Well, that's actually pretty close. A solution is a way to work things out when you're having a disagreement with someone. Now, I'm not going to tell you that you should never disagree, because people disagree with each other a lot. I am saying you have to disagree well. In other words, I want you to disagree better than you do now. I want to help you get better at working things out with people when you disagree with them. A

*solution makes everybody happy because it means
people were able to solve a problem without fighting.*

Johnny: Yeah.

Me: So, should we try one?

Johnny: One what?

Me: A problem. You know, to see if you can do it.

Johnny: OK.

*Me: If I wanted to go skating at two o'clock and you
wanted to go skating at four o'clock, and we really
wanted to go together, what would a good solution be?
(Don't forget, Johnny's not very good at this yet, and he's
probably a pretty impulsive problem-solver, so I don't
expect much from him at this point.)*

Johnny: TWO O'CLOCK!!!

*Me: We could go at two o'clock, but then I'd be very
happy and you'd be very unhappy, so it wouldn't be a
very good way to work it out. Can you think of a way to
make me a little happy and you a little happy?*

Johnny: FOUR O'CLOCK!!!

*Me: Well, we could go at four o'clock but then you'd be
very happy and I'd be very unhappy, so it wouldn't be a*

very good way to solve the problem. Can you think of a
good way to work this out?

Johnny [brief pause]: Nope.

Me: Well, what's in the middle of two and four o'clock?

Johnny: Three o'clock.

Me: So do you think three o'clock would make you a
little happy and me a little happy?

The child often looks to his parents for approval of this
high-stakes deal.

"Would it?" he might ask. The parents, surprised that the
child is even participating in this discussion, vigorously
nod their approval.

Me: I think that would be a good way to work it out. OK,
let's try a harder one. Let's say I wanted to go to the
shopping mall this weekend and you wanted to go
to the movies this weekend, and we really wanted to
do something together. What would be a good way to
solve this problem?

Johnny: We could go to a shopping mall that has movie
theatres.

Me: That would work. What if there was no such
shopping mall?

Johnny: We could go to the movies on Saturday and to the shopping mall on Sunday . . . or we could go to the shopping mall on Saturday and to the movies on Sunday. Right?

Me: Those would be great solutions, Johnny. I think you've got the hang of it.

I'll then turn to the parent(s) and say: By the way, he can't do this yet.

Parent: But he just did!

Me: Yes, he did just show us that he can work things out. But he can't do it yet in the midst of frustration. He's going to need a ton of help from you, especially with two things: thinking clearly in the midst of frustration and staying calm enough to do it. Johnny, this week when you and your mom or dad disagree about something, they'll let you know whether they're willing to work things out. If they are, try to think of good ideas. Just remember, your parents have the final say on any solution, so try to come up with ideas that you think your parents will like. If your first idea doesn't work, keep coming up with ideas until you and your mom or dad find a solution you all can agree on.

Because inflexible-explosive children have difficulty thinking rationally during vapor lock and usually require some practice thinking about how to work things out, getting good at generating solutions may take longer than you'd think and may require additional practice at calmer times. Some have a hard time generating solutions on their own initially. What this means is that, early on, you may have to provide suggestions for a lot of the solutions. You don't want to provide suggestions forever, though, because eventually you want your child to be able to generate different solutions on his own.

How will a child know a behavior is in Basket B? There are a few key steps. The first is *empathy*. I think of empathy as the "access code" to your child's brain (similar to the code you must enter to get money from an automated bank machine). Empathy signals to your child that you understand what he wants, that you think it's a legitimate desire (it usually is), and that you are his advocate rather than his adversary. Thus, empathy is a great way to keep the child from instantaneously overreacting to the frustration that just landed on his radar screen. The second step is the *invitation*. This is where you're inviting your child to solve the problem with you...together. The invitation can be as simple as saying "Let's think of how we can work that out."

Some children—especially those who are very disorganized—may need you to frame the disagreement for them so they know what it is they're trying to work out. That would sound like this: "Johnny, you want to go sailing today—which is a great idea—and your brother wants to go hiking—which is also a thing we like to do. Let's think of how we can work this out."

As this dialogue suggests, it's often appropriate to bring siblings into the problem-solving mix after a while. The siblings will need to be trained how to work things out, too, of course, but they'll appreciate the eventual absence of screaming and the fact that their needs are being taken into account.

What does it look like when Basket B is executed well? Here's an example straight out of my office. It was my initial meeting with a mother and her very articulate but very explosive four-year-old daughter, Emily. I met first with the mother, who described Emily's intense inflexibility and ferocious meltdowns. I then invited the little girl into my office while her mother waited outside.

"Can you think of something your mother and you have disagreed about lately?" I asked Emily in the course of our conversation.

After a brief pause, Emily said, "Yes . . . she poked a hole in my chicken pot pie."

"She poked a hole in your chicken pot pie?" I asked. "Why did she do that?"

"She wanted to see if it was too hot in the middle for me to eat," Emily responded.

"Well, that sounds reasonable," I said. "What's the problem with your mom poking a hole in your chicken pot pie?"

Emily, with a very serious look on her face, responded, "If you poke a hole in the chicken pot pie, the crust will get wet . . . and the crust is supposed to be crusty."

I hid my smile. "Hmmm. That wouldn't be too good. Emily, your mom doesn't want you to burn your tongue on the chicken pot pie, and you don't want the crust to get wet. Can you think of a way for you two to work that out?"

Emily contemplated this conundrum for about 20 seconds, and then responded, "Well, she could take a spatula . . . and she could lift off the crust of my chicken pot pie . . . and she could lay it on the side . . . and I could eat the crust first . . . and by the time I was through eating the crust, the insides would have cooled down enough so my mother wouldn't have to stick her stupid finger into my food."

I thought to myself, "Emily's mother has got to hear this." So I excused myself, raced out to the waiting room, and gleefully invited the mother back into my office. She thought I had uncovered some deep-rooted psychological issue, and was therefore full of expectation when she sat back down in my office and asked, "So, what have you both been talking about?"

"Pot pies," I replied.

The mother's face turned ashen. "I haven't made that for dinner lately," she said.

"Emily has come up with a very interesting solution to the pot pie problem," I said. "Go ahead, Emily, tell your mom your idea."

As Emily described the solution to the pot pie problem, her mother's mouth slowly dropped wide open. Why was her mother so stunned? Because she never knew her daughter to be capable of such problem solving. And why did she not know her daughter was capable of such problem solving? Because she'd never given her the chance to demonstrate such skills. Moral of the story: When you knee-jerk things into Basket A, you slam the door on Basket B. And if you slam the door on Basket B, you close yourself off to some very useful information, the opportunity to give your child practice at problem solving, and the chance to do some relationship-building.

What does Basket B look like outside my office? Another relatively straightforward example:

Parent: Sally, it's time to come inside.

Sally [vapor lock]: I want to stay outside and play a little longer.

Parent: Uhm . . .

Sally [deeper vapor lock]: You always make me come in before everyone else! It's not fair! I hate . . .

Parent: Whoa! Slow down! I don't really think this is one to get all upset about. I may actually be willing to talk about this if you could chill a little.

Sally [more coherent]: Everyone else gets to stay out longer than me.

Parent: Yes, I can see why you'd want to stay outside— you're having a lot of fun. Let's think about this for a second. I want you to come in right now and you want to stay out longer. How much longer do you want to stay out?

Sally: Twenty minutes!

Parent: Hmm. Sounds like we definitely need to work that out. You want to stay outside twenty more minutes and I was thinking more like ten extra minutes. Can you think of a good solution?

Sally: No! Ten minutes isn't enough!

*Parent: Now, don't go getting yourself all worked up
again . . . I told you I'd be willing to work this out. But we
have to figure this out. Let's try to think of a good way to
work this out.*

Sally: I can't do this! I can't think!

*Parent: Well, fifteen minutes is in between ten and
twenty . . . would fifteen minutes be a good solution?*

Sally: Okay, yes! Fine!

*Parent: Before you go running off, I just want to
remind you that in fifteen minutes I expect you to
come in with no problem at all. Are we on the same
page?*

Sally: Yes! Geez!

Don't make the mistake of thinking that Basket B is magical—the fact is, Basket B is very hard work. For many children, the hard work of staying calm and thinking in the midst of frustration demanded by Basket B can be almost as upsetting and arousing as the hard work demanded by Basket A. And it doesn't always go as easily as suggested by the examples above. Here's what I mean:

Mother: Davis, it's time to go to your swim lesson.

*Davis (playing with Legos at the kitchen table): I'm not
going. I hate swim lessons.*

Mother (placing the request in Basket B): Davis, we have a problem, because your brother has a swim lesson, too, and I can't leave you home alone.

Davis: I don't care! I'm not going!

Mother: We need to find a way to work this out. You don't want to go to your swim lesson, but I need to take . . .

Davis, slamming his fist on the table, red-faced: HOW MANY TIMES DO I HAVE TO TELL YOU?! I HATE SWIMMING! I'M NOT GOING! GET AWAY FROM ME!

Mother: Davis, I didn't say you had to go to your swim lesson. I said we have to find a way to work this out. That's different.

Davis: I'm sick of working things out. IF YOU DON'T SHUT UP, I'M GOING TO KILL YOU!

Davis' brother: Mom, I'm gonna be late for my swim lesson!

Mother, to brother: Alden, let's me and you go get my purse . . . I think it's in my bedroom.

Mother, upon returning, to Davis: Davis, I'm not going to make you go to your swim lesson. Can you take the

*Legos with you and you can work on your Legos while
your brother is at his swim lesson?*

Davis: The pieces will break apart. I don't want to go.

*Mother: I understand that you don't want to go. But I
can't leave you home alone. The only way I can think of
to work this out is for you to come with me and bring
the Legos along.*

Davis: (no response)

Mother: What do you think?

Alden: I'm going to be late!

Davis, to his brother: SHUT UP, JERK!

Alden: No, you shut up!

*Mother, to Alden: Alden, I want you to go wait for me by
the front door. Now!*

Alden: He told me to shut up!

*Mother: I heard what he told you. It wasn't very nice.
Now go wait for me by the front door.*

*Mother, to Davis: Davis, the only way I can think of to
work this out is for you to bring the Legos with you*

while your brother is at his swim lesson. If you can think of other solutions, I'm happy to listen.

Davis (starting to pack up his Legos): I'm not taking a swim lesson, so don't try to make me. Look! I told you the Legos were going to break apart!

Mother: Let's think of how we can transport the Legos so they don't fall apart. Thanks for trying to work this out.

Davis: I wasn't trying to work it out.

Mother: Well, you did a good job anyway.

Obviously, there's a lot more to Basket B than just avoiding meltdowns on important issues. It's in Basket B where, over time, you're helping your child develop skills that he may be sorely lacking, including hanging in in the midst of frustration; generating alternative solutions; and thinking things through. It's also in Basket B where your child recognizes that you're able to help him learn these things. But skillful execution of Basket B is an art, and it takes time to get good at it. More guidance on Basket B is provided later in this chapter.

Basket C

Basket C contains those goals and behaviors that may once have seemed a high priority but have since been downgraded considerably. Basket C is very full—that is, full of behaviors you're going to forget about completely, at least for now. Basket C is important to the goal of safety because it contains many behaviors that will no longer cause meltdowns. So Basket C helps us achieve Goal C—being cognizant of your child's limitations—and should help you reduce your child's global level of frustration, which should pay dividends the next time he does become frustrated.

The idea is that if a behavior is in Basket C, you don't even mention it anymore, let alone induce meltdowns over it. Which behaviors should be in Basket C? A lot of them, but the specifics depend on you and your child. A few more stories might be instructive. One mother thought it was imperative for her inflexible-explosive daughter to wear gloves while she was snow skiing. Each week the mother and daughter happily arrived at the ski lodge. Each week the child melted down when the mother demanded that she put her gloves on. Each week, after thirty to forty-five minutes of lunacy, the mother would carry her daughter, kicking and screaming, out to the car and drive home.

"Why doesn't she want to wear the gloves?" I asked in one early session.

"She hates the way they feel," the mother replied.

"Will she wear them if her hands get cold?" I asked.

"Yes, but I want her to wear them all the time," replied the mother.

"You want her to wear the gloves so badly that you're willing to endure a thirty- to forty-five minute meltdown and a kid who kicks you and screams at you and embarrasses you and ends up not doing any skiing?"

"Well, I think it's important that she wear gloves, don't you?" the mother asked.

Actually, no. The gloves belonged in Basket C. It took awhile to convince the mother of this logic, but the daughter wound up doing a lot more skiing, a lot less melting down, and she never did let her hands get frostbitten.

Another child was remarkably particular about what foods he was willing to eat: certain cereals for breakfast and pizza for dinner. His parents were quite determined—as evidenced by their relentless badgering (badgering is a half-hearted form of Basket A)—that he have a balanced diet, but weren't willing or able to force lima beans down their son's throat. This example of reciprocal inflexibility led to at least two meltdowns a day, at breakfast and dinner. Except in extreme cases, such as bona fide eating disorders, issues associated with diabetes, and so forth, I have what can best be described as a Basket C mentality toward these picky-eating inflexible-explosive children: They won't starve. And, indeed, this child wasn't starving. We placed "eating a variety of foods" in Basket C, reduced meltdowns, improved communication, went after our higher priorities, and eventually were able to put food variety into Basket B. The child is now eating a somewhat wider range of foods, and he actually goes to the supermarket with his mother to make his own selections.

A mother found that her moody, impulsive, hyperactive six-year-old son, Eduardo, routinely melted down when she brought him to the supermarket. Eduardo melted down in other situations as well, of course, but none as predictably as the supermarket. Maybe it was the over-stimulation, maybe it was the fact that he had very inflexible ideas about the foods he wanted his mother to buy (most of which were not at the top of his mother's list). Whatever the reason, no matter what the mother tried—preparing him in advance for trips, rewarding him for good behavior and punishing him for inappropriate behavior, making shorter trips, having Grandma accompany them, trying to steer him around the aisles where meltdowns seemed to occur most often, agreeing that he could select one or two of the foods on his list—he still routinely melted down when she brought him to the supermarket. The mother finally came to the conclusion that mastery of the demands of the supermarket—staying next to the shopping cart, not demanding the purchase of every high-sugar cereal on the shelves, being patient in the checkout line—simply wasn't going to improve at that point in her son's development. She decided he'd be much better off if she started going to the supermarket without Eduardo (Basket C).

Mother: But he can't avoid supermarkets forever, right?

Me: Right. Luckily, going to the supermarket is not critical to Eduardo's existence right now.

Mother: When should I try taking him into supermarkets again?

Me: When it becomes more important, and you think he can do it.

Mother: It's not always easy for my mother to watch him for me.

Me: I know. But it's even harder—and a lot more detrimental to your relationship with your son—to have him melting down every time you take him to the supermarket.

There's a world of difference between "giving in" and placing a behavior in Basket C. Giving in is when you decide a behavior is in Basket A and then, because your child has made your life miserable over this basket placement, you capitulate to his wishes. When you place a behavior in Basket C, you're deciding ahead of time that the behavior is neither important enough to induce and endure a meltdown over nor important enough to try to problem-solve.

Who decides what basket a behavior is in? You. Who decides whether an acceptable solution has been reached? You. Who decides whether a child is actually capable of following through on a potential solution? You. Who's still in charge? You.

*

Now you've got a basic, user-friendly framework that helps *you* decide what *you* want to happen before or when your child enters vapor lock. Basket A helps you ensure safety and maintain your role as an authority figure. Basket B helps your child maintain coherence in the midst of frustration; think through mutually satisfactory solutions; learn how to problem solve; and view you as a helper, rather than as an enemy. Basket C helps remove many unnecessary frustrations from your child's radar screen. From now on, before or when your child enters vapor lock, and before you respond, your first step is to ask yourself a simple question:

"Is this behavior in Basket A, B, or C?"

If your answer is Basket A, you'll say, "Johnny, I can see that you're very frustrated right now—unfortunately, this is not an issue we can discuss." If the behavior doesn't pass the Basket A litmus test, it's not in Basket A. If your answer is Basket B, you'll do the empathy/invitation thing and say something like, "Johnny, I can understand that it's hard for you to turn off the TV in the middle of a show. Let's find a

way to work this out!" and you'll embark on a process of trying to work things out and teach your child how to be more
flexible and to deal with frustration more adaptively. If the
behavior is in Basket C, you let it go.

Many parents are skeptical when this framework is first
described, so let's make sure you're crystal clear about what
we're trying to accomplish here. Your frustration over your
child's difficulty adhering to your parenting agenda, combined
with (1) your child's own frustration over his difficulties
adhering to this agenda and (2) his difficulty dealing with frustration adaptively, has led to (3) communication patterns that
can best be described as unhelpful and (4) a child who can best
be described as inflexible-explosive. To deal effectively with
this set of circumstances, we need to prioritize a reduction in
meltdowns, temporarily suspend much of your parenting
agenda, reduce frustration all the way around, and work
toward a more adaptive pattern of communication to set the
stage for the development of skills your child lacks. This
won't happen overnight, and it won't be easy. But you've been
working very hard already. Let's just make sure your hard
work is getting you somewhere.

What you're doing is judiciously choosing when, where,
and especially over what issues he has a meltdown. In so
doing, you're exerting more control—not less—over his
behavior than before. In other words, starting now it is
you—not your child—who becomes the primary determi-
nant of whether or not he has a meltdown. So, instead of
feeling like you have absolutely no control over your child,
you'll start finding that you actually have a great deal of control. By replacing your fear of meltdowns with a sense of
empowerment over when and under what circumstances

meltdowns occur, you're putting yourself in a much better mind-set for responding to vapor lock calmly and rationally, thereby helping your child respond to vapor lock calmly and rationally.

Simply put, your role in all of this is **"surrogate frontal lobe."** Your child has trouble thinking clearly in the midst of frustration and staying calm enough to do it. He's proven to you that sage wisdom delivered *after* a meltdown doesn't do him much good the *next* time he enters vapor lock. He needs sage wisdom when vapor lock first kicks in. He needs a surrogate frontal lobe: someone to help him do the thinking he can't do for himself yet in the midst of frustration; to help him stay calm enough to think about how to solve the problem that induced vapor lock; to think of different solutions; to think about the outcomes of each possible solution; to think of different ways to respond to an unexpected turn of events; to understand the "big picture"; to come up with a plan for delaying something he wants "right now" until a little later. You're elected.

Will he need a surrogate frontal lobe forever? No. As soon as he can start responding to frustration adaptively on his own, he'll let you know.

By the way, so far we've talked about Basket B as if it can only be applied during vapor lock (I call this the "In the Moment" form of Basket B). There's another time at which being a surrogate frontal lobe can be productive: "Outside the Moment." Let's say you've noticed your child is having difficulty getting ready for school in the morning and that this causes reliable meltdowns on a daily basis. I suppose you could have a Basket B discussion one morning while your child is in the midst of being frustrated over having difficulty getting ready for school, but it would probably be more productive to have the discussion "Outside the Moment" (i.e., at some opportune moment when the pressure is off). Here's what that might sound like:

Parent: *"Joey, I noticed that our mornings haven't been going so well lately."*

Joey: *"Yeah...so?"*

Parent: *"What I mean is that mornings are very hard for us. But it would be nice if we could find a way not to fight about it."*

Joey: *"Uh-huh."*

Parent: *"In other words, maybe we could talk about what's so hard for us in the morning...then maybe we could figure out what to do about it."*

Let's look at some more examples of what basket thinking looks like when it goes well. Then we'll turn our attention to circumstances in which things don't go quite as well.

DRAMA IN REAL LIFE
BASKET WEAVING

I'd been working with Anthony (from Chapter 4) for about a month, and his parents and I had come to the conclusion that his difficulty thinking through solutions to potential weather disasters was only the tip of the proverbial iceberg. Anthony had difficulty thinking clearly in all sorts of situations, driven by his anxiety, disorganization, and concrete style of thinking. We began using the baskets framework to help his parents clarify Anthony's true capabilities; identify their priorities; help Anthony hang in, so he could think more clearly when he was frustrated; remove UFOs (unnecessary frustrating objects) from his radar screen; and intervene primarily on the front end, rather than the back end.

"Tell me about these baskets my wife's been talking about," said the father, who had missed the previous session.

"The baskets help you and your wife decide which situations are important enough to have meltdowns over—those are in what we call Basket A—which ones to remove from Anthony's radar screen altogether—those go in Basket C—and those on which it might be best to help Anthony learn to think things through when he's stuck—that's Basket B."

"So what should we put in Basket A?" asked the father.

"That's up to you and your wife," I said. "Safety is always in Basket A."

"What do you mean by safety?" the father asked.

"Hurting people—you, his sister—or destroying property," I said.

"He's more likely to destroy property than to hurt one of us," said the mother. "In fact, his sister handles him better than we do."

"Anything else in Basket A?" asked the father.

"Well, to help you decide, let's think about the Basket A litmus test. First, a behavior has to be important. Second, Anthony has to be capable of performing it consistently. Third, you guys have to be willing and able to enforce it. And fourth, it has to be worth inducing and enduring a meltdown over. My sense is that, for Anthony, going to school is also in Basket A."

The parents agreed.

"What about Basket C?" asked the father.

"We've started putting a ton of things in Basket C already," said the mother. "We decided that his learning to tie his shoes could be taken off his radar screen for now, so we've been giving him a lot more help with that and some other things he gets frustrated about in the morning."

"Good," I said. "What else?"

"We've pretty much concluded that his doing a lot of his own writing is in Basket C for now, too," said the father. "We've been struggling to help him write for years, and he still clearly needs our help."

"That's fine," I said. "It sounds like you get the idea about Basket C. So let's think about Basket B."

"I had a few Basket B items this week," the mother said. "The other day he started freaking out when I told him to brush his teeth. I always thought it was because he just didn't want to do it. But I did the Basket B thing—I said to him, 'We want you to brush your teeth and you don't want to brush your teeth, so we need to discuss how to work this out.' "

"What'd he say?" I asked.

"He said, 'Who says I don't want to brush my teeth?' " replied the mother. "I said, 'Because you always go nuts when I tell you it's time to brush your teeth.' He eventually told me the reason he didn't like to brush his teeth was because he had trouble putting the toothpaste on the toothbrush. You'd think I would have figured that out, with all his troubles with motor skills. So I asked him if he had any ideas about how we could solve the problem. It was actually his idea that I put the toothpaste on his toothbrush. Then he brushed with no problem."

"Fabulous," I said. "Isn't it great how he was able to come up with the solution once you were able to help him stay coherent and tell you what was the matter? Not every child can do that this early in the process."

"So let me make sure I've got this straight," said the father. "He has trouble knowing what's bothering him and figuring out what to do. We help him get better at it, so he can eventually do it on his own. Some things he just has to do—like go to school—and others we don't care about anymore. Right?"

"Right," I said.

"So who's going to help him do this when he's twenty-five years old?" asked the father.

"Hopefully, you guys and his teachers will do such a great job of training him, he won't need this kind of help when he's twenty-five," I said.

"This is hard work, isn't it?" asked the mother.

"It's very hard work," I said. "But you're working hard already. Let's make sure you have something to show for all that hard work."

"How did he get this way?" asked the father.

"Anthony loves predictability. And I think the reason he likes predictability so much is that he deals quite poorly with unpredictability, which requires a lot more flexibility and thinking. Our goal is to help Anthony get better at being flexible and thinking things through, so he can deal better with the unpredictable events that pop up in his life."

"How are the baskets different from what we're doing already?" asked the father. "When Anthony gets upset, I wait till he calms down and then I talk to him about how he could have handled the situation better. You don't think that's helping?"

"It might well be helping," I said. "But given that Anthony has a lot of trouble remembering a lot of the things he learns, I'm concerned that he doesn't seem to recall the things you've taught him the next time he becomes upset. I think the things we're trying to teach him are more likely to stick if your help is given when he needs it the most—in the early stages of his being stuck. Then he'll experience what it's like to figure out what he's anxious or upset about, how to think of solutions to problems, and how good you are at helping him. Ultimately—with lots of practice—I'm hopeful he'll start doing some of the calming, figuring out, and problem solving on his own."

DRAMA IN REAL LIFE

MICKEY, MINNIE . . . MELTDOWN?

Remember Casey from Chapter 4? He and his parents and sister took a trip to Disney World, and their first day went wonderfully. They were a pretty tired*, hungry* crew as they left the Magic Kingdom on their way back to their hotel* (the asterisks designate well-known vapor lock fuelers: fatigue, hunger, and transitions). Of course, this scenario had graver implications for Casey than for his sister. Just after they'd gotten outside the gates, Casey uttered the following, ominous request:

"I want cotton candy."

"You can't have cotton candy because we're not going back into the park to look for it," said the father instinctively. (Don't forget, saying "No," "You must," or "You can't" automatically means you're in Basket A.)

Casey stopped dead in his tracks. "I want cotton candy!" he said loudly. Commence vapor lock.

The parents exchanged quick glances. They'd become pretty good at making quick "basket" decisions and went through their mental basket checklist quickly. This was not a safety issue, nor were any of their other few Basket A issues involved. Nonetheless, going back into the park for cotton candy would have been extremely inconvenient, and they did want Casey to eat a good dinner. Basket B or C?

"Look, Casey, we're all tired . . ." The mother tried the empathy and logical persuasion route and hoped Casey still had a few coherent brain cells available. "Let's just go back to the hotel and get something to eat."

Casey was stuck. "I want cotton candy!" he said, moving closer to the edge of the cliff. Commence crossroads.

The parents exchanged glances again and decided to try Basket B. "I think we need to find a way to work this out, Casey," the father said calmly. "You want cotton candy, and we want to get back to the hotel to get something to eat. Can you think of a good solution?"

"No!" Casey pouted, crossing his arms, still on the edge.

"Well, let's think about this for a second," said the father, crouching down next to, but not touching, his son. "We could look for someone selling cotton candy on the way back to the hotel . . . or we could buy you something to snack on besides cotton candy. Can you think of something else you'd like to eat on the way home besides cotton candy?"

"I want cotton candy," whined Casey, but his tone suggested slightly greater coherence.

"Well, I don't want to go back into the park, but I'm happy to look for someone selling cotton candy on the way home," said the father. Casey started walking toward the car again.

"Can I have cotton candy, too?" asked Casey's sister.

The mother bit her lip. "We'll get something we can all share," she said.

Once in the car, the family spent the next ten minutes with their faces glued to the windows, scanning the horizon for potential cotton candy vendors. Casey's coherence slowly returned. There was one small problem, of course: They hadn't yet stumbled across any stores that might be selling cotton candy. Nonetheless, with Casey's coherence restored, the father felt Casey might be able to handle the bad news without falling apart.

"I don't think we're going to find cotton candy, folks," he said, pulling the car into a McDonald's. "But let's see what kinds of snacks we can find at this McDonald's. Maybe some french fries."

"I want a Coke, too!" announced Casey.

"No, we're going to have to pass on the Coke right now," said the father, carefully reading his son's response. "You and your sister must have Coke coming out your ears by now. Let's hurry up and get something good."

Casey rushed into the McDonald's, ate his fries, forgot about the Coke, and wound up eating a decent dinner back at the hotel.

Had the parents decided that cotton candy was a Basket A issue, they would likely have endured a long meltdown. Had they decided it was a

Basket C issue, they would have gone back into the park for cotton candy. By deciding the issue was in Basket B, they averted a meltdown on an important issue, and their son still ate some of what they wanted him to eat. It was their choice to make. They were in control of whether, and under what circumstance, they induced and endured a meltdown.

DRAMA IN REAL LIFE

SITTING ON THE REGISTER IS NOT IN BASKET A

Remember Helen, the girl who wanted macaroni and cheese instead of chili? One of the most difficult times of the day in Helen's family is when she has to sit down and do her homework.

One night, Helen had somehow decided that she wanted to do her homework sitting atop the "register" in the kitchen. (I grew up in Florida, so Helen's parents had to explain to me that a "register" is a heating vent on the floor.) Helen's parents objected to her doing her homework sitting atop the register. This minor issue had the potential to totally disrupt Helen's completion of her homework by inducing a prolonged meltdown.

"Helen, you can't do your homework sitting on the register," said the father.

"I want to," whined Helen. Commence vapor lock.

"Helen, I want you to come over to the kitchen table and do your homework," commanded the father.

"I want to sit here!" Helen whined with a little more fervor. Commence crossroads.

Basket A, Basket B, or Basket C? Although the father felt strongly that Helen should do her homework at the kitchen table, he nonetheless quickly decided this was a Basket B issue (ideally he would have decided this at the first sign of vapor lock).

"Helen, we need to find some way to work this out. I don't want you doing your homework sitting on the register, and you seem to really want to do your homework sitting on the register. Can you come up with a solution so that I'm happy and you're happy?"

"No, I want to sit here." Helen pouted.

"Come on, Helen, let's find a way for us both to be happy," the father encouraged.

"How 'bout I do my homework on the register tonight and at the kitchen table tomorrow night?" volunteered Helen, coherence kicking in.

"Well, that's an idea, but it wouldn't make me happy," said the father. "Can you think of some other way for us both to be happy?"

"No, that's it!" Helen responded.

"Come on, I think we can do it together," the father said, gently pulling Helen away from the cliff. "How about you do your math homework on the register—as long as it doesn't take more than fifteen minutes—and your reading homework at the table."

"Uhm." Helen pondered this idea for a few moments. "OK."

"So if your math doesn't take longer than fifteen minutes, you can do your math on the register and your reading at the table. But at the fifteen-minute mark or when it comes time to do your reading, I don't want a big fuss."

"OK," said Helen, returning to her math assignment.

"You did a very nice job of working things out," said the father.

Homework done. Problem-solving skills reinforced. Relationship strengthened. And no meltdown.

In one of our next sessions, the father needed a little reassurance. "I'm afraid we're teaching her that she never has to listen to us, and I don't think that bodes well for the future."

"What, she never does what you tell her to now?" I asked.

"No, she actually does what we ask quite often," he replied. "I'm worried that she'll think that all she has to do is start to throw a fit to get what she wants."

"You've been doing the baskets for a few months now. Is she melting down less or more?" I asked.

"A lot less." The father smiled.

"Is she more or less compliant with Basket A issues?" I asked.

"More," said the father.

"Are you getting better compliance with things that aren't even in Basket A?"

"Yes, absolutely," the father replied.

"Are you yelling a lot less?"

"Yes."

"How are you and Helen getting along lately?" I asked.

"It's a lot better."

"Do you think that when she's in vapor lock, she's starting to be able to view you as a helper rather than as the enemy?"

"Yes, I think so," the father replied. "You know, Helen was always a very affectionate kid. But we were battling so much that, up until a few weeks ago, when I'd get home from work she'd barely even acknowledge my presence. For the past two weeks, when I get home from work, she jumps up from whatever she's doing and gives me a big hug."

"I think we're doing OK," I said.

"But what about the real world?" the father asked.

"What about it?" I asked.

"The real world doesn't have baskets in it or people who always try to understand," he said.

"I don't expect that your fighting with her a lot will help her live in the real world. On the other hand, I do expect that helping her stay calm enough to think clearly in the midst of frustration will be very helpful to her in the real world. If you think about what the real world demands from us, it's a whole lot more resolving disputes and disagreements than it is blind adherence to authority."

Are there times when things don't go this well? Absolutely. Can the baskets be implemented in ways that diminish their effectiveness? Positively. Described below are a variety of the ways in which I've seen the baskets framework applied incorrectly. The truth is, it's rare for the baskets to be implemented perfectly early on. So chin up . . . you'll get good at it.

PATTERN #1: PUTTING A BEHAVIOR IN BASKET A THAT HAS NO BUSINESS BEING IN BASKET A

A mother was very upset that her son had punched her as they argued over whether he could eat five chocolate chip cookies. She was understandably very upset over having been hit. Her story told me we still had more work to do on achieving safety. But her story also told me we had more work to do on her basket placement skills.

"Hitting is in Basket A, right?" the mother asked.

"Right," I responded.

"So what should I have done when he hit me?" she asked.

"Well, I'm more concerned about what it was that he hit you over," I said.

"I don't understand what you mean," the mother responded. "Hitting is safety and safety is always in Basket A."

"True enough," I said. "But what basket is chocolate chip cookies in?"

The mother paused. "I didn't want him to have more chocolate chip cookies."

"So you told him he couldn't have any more, yes?" I asked.

"Right," said the mother.

"So it was in Basket A and worth a meltdown," I summarized.

"Well . . . I don't know that it was worth a meltdown," said the mother.

"Then it wasn't in Basket A," I said.

"So what should I do about the hitting?" the mother asked.

"For starters, let's not put things in Basket A that don't belong there," I said. "Remember, the instant you say 'No,' 'You can't,' or 'You must' to your son, you're in Basket A. If you act like you're in Basket A when you really don't mean to be, you'll deprive yourself of the tension-reducing benefits of Basket C and the training of thinking skills that goes on in Basket B."

"So you're saying if I'd put the chocolate chip cookies into Basket B or C, I wouldn't have gotten hit," said the mother.

"That's right," I said. "Now that doesn't mean his hitting you isn't serious. It just means that the baskets—executed properly—can make your household a much safer place."

Early in treatment I often ask the parents of an inflexible-explosive child to give me a written list of the behavioral priorities their child is not meeting on a consistent basis. It's not unusual for me to be greeted with a long list. I typically inform the parents that their priorities are going to need some serious pruning. If you overburden your child with a lengthy list of priorities—even if they're all ones you're willing and able to enforce—you'll actually increase the number of opportunities for meltdowns, but you most assuredly won't increase the likelihood that your priorities will be met. It follows that if you reduce the number of priorities to a number that is more realistic—by temporarily suspending your desire for, and apparent willingness to induce meltdowns over, things like good manners, clean rooms, completed homework, and so forth—you'll simultaneously reduce the opportunities for vapor lock and meltdowns, lower the general level of family tension, and quite possibly get better compliance on the demands you actually do keep in Basket A. Once the number of meltdowns begins to decline—and not a moment before—you may be able to begin slowly expanding your list of undesirable and important behaviors again.

The truth is, even parents of ordinary children can't intervene every single time they see their child engaged in an undesirable behavior; they understand that they have to let some behaviors slide without correction, fully appreciative of the old "pick your battles" adage. This formula applies to your child as well—just more so.

The parents of another child with whom I was working had decided they wanted him to reduce his sugar intake because they thought his consumption of soda and candy adversely affected his mood and behavior. This would have been fine, I suppose, except for two significant problems: The child had no interest in reducing his sugar intake and, worse yet, he was consuming most of his sugar outside the home, making this issue virtually impossible to enforce. Unfortunately, the parents had skipped past the Basket A litmus test and had been jumping on the child's case for alleged sugar consumption whenever he came home from being with his friends. This practice induced meltdowns with predictable regularity. I was able to convince the parents that since they could not enforce this issue, sugar consumption should be placed in either Basket B or C, but absolutely not in Basket A. Their son ended up consuming no more or less sugar as a result of their moving this issue to a different basket, but he melted down about a dozen fewer times each week.

What else may end up in Basket A besides safety? Some inflexible-explosive children refuse to go to school, have great difficulty getting there on time, or skip out once they do manage to get there. These school-related issues often find their way into Basket A. The trouble is, these problems don't typically occur out of the blue. In other words, when children feel that school is a place where they can experience success, they are generally willing to go there, get there on time, and stay put. It's when things aren't going well—either at school or in other areas of children's lives—that these problems tend to arise. So I usually hold off on placing these problems in Basket A until I've had a chance to assess and address what's not going so well. Once the problems are fixed, I often don't need to place "going to school" in Basket A because the child is now willing and able to go.

Difficulty getting going in the morning and settling down in the evening are common in children with ADHD and mood disorders. Lots of inflexible-explosive children are still revved at 9 P.M. when you wish they'd start fading. At 10 P.M., some are just beginning to work on the homework you couldn't force them to do earlier in the day. Others are so overtired at night that their moods have begun to deteriorate. The next morning they're dead to the world or, at best, extremely agitated the minute they manage to get their eyes open.

Sometimes medication can resolve these difficulties, sometimes not. Frequently, the best we can do nonmedically in the morning is to make sure that demands are sharply reduced so the child needs only to get dressed (sometimes with help) and get out the door (perhaps with a banana planted firmly in his hand on his way out). There are lots of other perfectly reasonable priorities that may present unnecessary roadblocks to a child whose brain hasn't clicked on yet in the morning, such as eating breakfast, brushing teeth, combing hair, taking out the trash, walking the dog, and packing the backpack. Many of these priorities ultimately end up in Basket B or C, which means dropping the priority completely, permitting the child to delay its execution until later (for instance, taking a shower after school), or performing certain tasks for him (he may never learn to pack his backpack himself, but that's probably not going to keep him from getting into Harvard.) The best we can usually do nonmedically at night is to enforce getting the child to stay in his bedroom at a designated time.

My view on homework is a little controversial because, at least initially, I'm not enthusiastic about putting the completion of homework into Basket A. In other words, I often find that I can make a major dent in the frequency and intensity of meltdowns by throwing homework out of Basket A. In the case of severely explosive children, sometimes we simply decide that the child won't be doing much homework for a while until we can get the explosions under control. In less severe cases, I usually find that something—a learning disability, ADHD, etc.—is interfering with a child's ability to complete assigned homework. Once that "something" is satisfactorily addressed, homework completion is no longer a major issue. More on homework later.

Swearing is not a Basket A issue, as excruciating as it is to listen to. Once we give these children a new language to express their frustration, the swearing usually begins to subside. I often ask adults what *they* do when they become frustrated and have found swearing to be a remarkably popular response—which begs the question of why we would expect children to respond more adaptively to frustration than we do ourselves. I say more about swearing in later chapters.

PATTERN #2: OVERDOING BASKET C

For just about every inflexible-explosive child, Basket C is very full early in treatment. But some families place so much emphasis on Basket C that they wind up neglecting Basket B. Remember, if you neglect Basket B, you're not training any thinking skills.

PATTERN #3: NEGLECTING BASKET B

If you're only doing Baskets A and C, you're just picking your battles. Things might be a little better, because you're not fighting over the things in Basket C. But only Basket B trains lacking thinking skills, and your child's long-term prognosis depends on his learning to think in the midst of frustration and stay calm enough to be able to do it. Neither Basket A nor C trains lacking thinking skills.

PATTERN #4: BELIEVING A CHILD IS SUDDENLY CAPABLE OF WORKING THINGS OUT JUST BECAUSE YOU'RE NOW WILLING TO DO SO

Many children are able to start working things out once their parents set the stage for it, but others may need additional training. Such children may need to see you come up with possible solutions for a while until they catch on. Situations that have a clear middle-of-the-road solution (for example, going to the movies at 3 o'clock instead of 2 or 4) are the easiest to train on. You can get more complicated as time goes on.

Some families reap immediate benefits from Basket B. For

other families, Basket B can feel like slogging through mud, at least initially. But Basket B has been very hard work for just about every family I've worked with. Don't forget, you were working hard before you started implementing this approach, and had little to show for it—now we're making sure your hard work gets you somewhere and leads to durable changes in the way you and your child think and interact.

PATTERN #5: ACTING LIKE YOU'RE IN BASKET A WHEN YOU REALLY MEANT TO BE IN BASKET B OR C

Adults have this interesting little tendency to act like something is in Basket A even when it's not. If you start off sounding like you're in Basket A when you're really in Basket B or C, you're taking ten steps backward from the get-go.

A ten-year-old boy with whom I was working went to summer camp for two months. I anticipated that he and his parents would be very happy when they came in for their first session after he came home from camp. But what walked into my office was three livid people.

"What's up?" I asked no one in particular once the three were assembled in my office.

With his last dying breath of coherence, the boy seethed, "They won't give me my money."

"What money?" I asked.

With his next last dying breath of coherence, the boy growled, "They put two months of allowance into the camp canteen so I'd have money to spend at camp. I didn't spend all of the money they put into the canteen. NOW I WANT MY MONEY BACK!"

Though this sounded reasonable, I turned to the father and asked, "What do you think?"

He replied, "Over my dead body."

I thought, "What basket would 'Over my dead body' be in?" I quickly concluded that the father was in Basket A. Because I don't like to undermine parents in front of their children, I briefly tried to let the father know, through non-verbal facial expressions, that he might consider a different basket. The father missed my signals, however, and the boy melted down in my office. For the next ten minutes, the scene in my office was quite unpleasant. I was finally able to convince the boy to leave my office, whereupon I looked at the father and asked the million-dollar question:

"That's in Basket A?"

"What makes you think that?" he responded, a little puzzled.

"Well, if it had been in Basket B you would have tried to work it out, and if it had been in Basket C you would have dropped it," I said. "You said, 'Over my dead body,' which sounded like a 'No' to me."

"Oh, I don't care if he gets the money," replied the father. "I just don't like the tone he was using."

Time for a little basket re-tuning. If a behavior is in Basket B, it has to look, smell, taste, feel, and sound like it's in Basket B right off the bat.

PATTERN #6: USING BASKET B AS A LAST RESORT

Technically, you're deciding what basket a given issue is being placed in on the front end. Thus, if you've decided an issue is in Basket B, you're beginning the process of working things out immediately.

In practice, I've seen many parents use Basket B as a last resort, which, of course, misses the whole point (and doesn't work very well, either). It looks like this:

Parent: You can't have ice cream for dessert. (Sounds like a "no," "you must," or "you can't" to me, which tells me we're in Basket A.)

Child: Why not?

Parent: You've had enough ice cream the past few days. Plus, I don't like the way you talked to me this afternoon.

Child: What are you talking about! What happened this afternoon?! I want ice cream!

Parent: Well, you can't have any, so you might as well pipe down.

Child, moving toward parent with fist raised: Try to stop me!

Parent: Don't even think about it!

Child: Stop me, you pig!

Parent: OK, let's try to work this out!

Too little, too late, and too bad. Basket B starts on the front end, not the back end. Basket B is an act of parental mastery and empowerment, not an act of desperation.

PATTERN #7: THE UNILATERAL SOLUTION

"Unilateral solution" refers to instances in which you express a willingness to work things out with your child but then dictate the terms. I've seen a lot of parents try to apply unilateral solutions with their inflexible-explosive children, with unpleasant results. An example might help.

A mother of a nine-year-old inflexible-explosive boy named Chuck arrived at my office for an appointment one April day and was extremely exasperated. "What's up?" I asked.

"He just melted down in the car," she responded.

"Over what?"

"He wants caps for his cap gun," she replied. "Can you imagine? A meltdown over caps?"

"I can imagine," I said. "Why did he melt down over caps?"

"He wants them today," she said, "and I don't have time to buy them today."

"So you don't object to his having caps for his cap gun," I said.

"No, he can have all the caps he wants," she said. "I even tried to work things out with him!"

"Really, what was the solution?" I asked expectantly.

"I told him I'd buy him the caps in June," she said.

"June?" I asked. "But what was the solution?"

"June," she said. "I told him he could have the caps in June."

"Where did you come up with June?" I asked.

"I don't know, it just came to me," she said.

"Uhm, I think that might be a unilateral solution," I said.

"What do you mean?" she asked.

"Well, he wants his caps today, and you said he could have them in June, and you never really worked it out together," I said. "You never budged off of June."

"What would a good solution have been?" the mother asked.

"Well, let's get Chuck in here and see," I said.

Chuck came into the office. "I understand you want caps for your cap gun," I said.

"Yeah, but she won't get them for me 'til June," he groused.

"I think your mom might be willing to work on a solution to that problem," I said.

"That *was* the solution!" Chuck complained.

"No, I think your mom might *really* be willing to work that out," I said. "Chuck, you want to buy caps today and your mom wants to buy them for you in June. Can you think of a way to work that out?"

Chuck became a little agitated. "I can't think of a way to work it out!" he said, squirming on the couch.

"If you need my help figuring it out, I'm happy to assist," I said. "Can you think of any ideas?"

"NO!" Chuck screamed. "How 'bout May?" he pleaded in desperation.

"May would be a very good solution," I said. Chuck quickly calmed. Then, knowing full well what his response would be, I asked, "When in May?"

Without missing a beat, Chuck said, "May first."

I looked at the mother. "How would May first be for you?"

The mother pulled out her date-book, leafed through to May 1st, and said, "May first would be a fine day to buy caps."

❖

What if a Basket B discussion is going poorly? Some children will tolerate delaying the discussion until things have calmed down enough to make an agreement more likely. In rare instances—almost always early in treatment—it's necessary to jettison a Basket B issue into Basket C. Remember, if you've decided that a behavior doesn't belong in Basket A, you've already decided that the behavior is not worth a meltdown. Just because you can't find a solution doesn't mean you're now willing to induce and endure a meltdown. As you and your child get better at working things out, you won't have to jettison things into Basket C anymore.

I've met many parents who have trouble sorting things through themselves when their child enters vapor lock. Fortunately, some children will tolerate the uncertainty of a delayed basket decision for a few minutes while their parent sorts through his or her own thoughts. In other words, it's not always critical that a basket placement be made immediately. If you think you can maintain your child's coherence while you buy time, you can say something like, "I haven't decided yet whether that's negotiable or not—you'll have to wait a few minutes so I can decide." Some children can handle a brief delay, others a longer delay, some no delay at all. And some of those who can't tolerate a delay eventually can once the user-friendlier environment takes hold. If you're really having trouble deciding which basket you're in, default into Basket B.

Other parents feel the need to delay a basket decision because they'd prefer not to have such a dialogue in the car, supermarket, or shopping mall (places where their capacity to deal with their child's worst—if it happens—is compromised). When vapor lock sets in, these parents do a quick "probability estimate" of the likelihood they'll be able to deal successfully with a given issue under the current circumstances. If they aren't optimistic, they try to delay.

A mother came in for a session one night hoarse from all the screaming she'd been doing at her daughter on the drive to my office.

"What were you screaming about?" I asked.

"Alycia was very upset that we're going to have to change our plans for her birthday," she replied.

"That must have been very upsetting to her. But why all the screaming?" I asked.

"Because it was foggy out, and I'm not the best at driving at night to begin with, and I've got a frustrated daughter sobbing in the backseat telling me I don't love her," she replied.

"What did you do?" I asked.

"I screamed at her," said the mother. "And now I'm sitting here really mad at myself for doing it. I guess I get a little worked up when she gets worked up."

"What was your goal when she started getting upset?" I asked.

"I have no idea," replied the mother. "I just wanted to get past the problem, be done with it."

"That's an interesting goal," I said. "Because you have a daughter who's not very good at just getting past problems and being done with them."

"That's for sure," the mother agreed. "So what should my goal be?"

"I think one important goal is to think about whether the ideal time and place to have a discussion that's going to be frustrating to Alycia is in the car at night when it's foggy. In other words, whether it's at all likely a productive discussion could take place under those conditions. If you decide that scenario probably wouldn't set the stage for the discussion you want to have with her, you could try to delay the discussion until the circumstances are more ideal. Do you think Alycia would have been able to delay the discussion?"

"She still would have cried in the backseat," the mother said.

"Well, we can't keep her from feeling what she legitimately feels about her birthday plans being changed. But we can give more thought to whether delaying the discussion has the potential to lead to a more productive outcome."

The truth is, delay can work in the child's best interests, too, since some inflexible-explosive children are able to think more clearly if the Basket B discussion is delayed.

Even when things do go well as you get good at using the baskets, there's a temptation to become complacent or even to sharply increase the number of priorities in Basket A. A simple word of advice: Don't. In the same way that former alcoholics try to take things one day at a time because they know that falling off the wagon is always only one drink away, early on your child is still capable of melting down no matter how good you and he have become at working things out. It's like driving a car, in that you're always checking the gauges to make sure you have enough fuel, the engine isn't overheating, and you're not exceeding the speed limit. The same thing goes with your inflexible-explosive child: You've got to constantly check the gauges. Just because things are going well right now doesn't mean a problem isn't right around the bend.

Let's summarize the major points of this chapter:

- On the front end—before and during vapor lock and at the cross-roads—you should ask yourself the following question: "*Is this behavior in Basket A, B, or C?*"

- If the answer to this question is "A"—and except for safety, it won't be often—you're willing to induce and endure a meltdown.

- If the answer to this question is "B," you're embarking on the process of negotiating a mutually satisfactory resolution.

- If the answer is "C"—and that's going to happen a lot more than it used to—your lips are sealed.

- Basket A is important because it helps you maintain your status as an authority figure. Basket C is important because it helps you remove low-priority issues from your child's radar screen and helps restore safety. But Basket B is the most important, since it provides a framework for your child to learn to stay coherent in the midst of frustration and think things through.

- Basket B helps you directly address the factors that may be fueling your child's meltdowns. For example, Basket B can help the child with ADHD shift sets more readily and respond to frustration in a less disorganized, impulsive manner. Basket B can help the child with nonverbal learning disability learn to see the "gray" in what seemed like "black-and-white" situations and develop a broader repertoire of response options. Basket B can help the anxious child learn to think more rationally in the midst of anxiety. And Basket B can help the child with language processing difficulties learn a new vocabulary for expressing frustration (more on this in Chapter 9). By assuming the role of "surrogate frontal lobe," you're doing the thinking the child is presently unable to do on his own at times when he needs you the most.

Change can be slow, sometimes very slow, but you've put a lot of time in already. Rather than putting your energy into thinking up better ways to reward and punish your child in the pursuit of improved compliance, you're putting energy into problem solving and communicating for the purposes of rebuilding your relationship and setting the stage for improving the deficient skills underlying your child's inflexibility and low tolerance for frustration.

8

Brain Chemistry

There are some children who will not benefit substantially from the approach described in this book until they've been satisfactorily medicated. You see, while there are some issues the nonmedical approach described thus far addresses more effectively than the medical approach (for example, no medicine has ever taught a child how to think—that's what adults are for), there are some factors medicine addresses better than the nonmedical approach. Addressing such factors can set the stage for achieving many of the goals we're trying to achieve. By contrast, failing to address such factors can make it far more difficult to teach some children how to think in the midst of frustration. My purpose in writing this chapter is not to provide you with all the ins and outs of medical treatment of inflexible-explosive children and adolescents. Such a goal is well beyond the scope of this book and my own expertise. My goal is simply to orient you to some of the medications that might be used, either alone or in combination, to address the various pathways that may contribute to inflexibility and poor response to frustration. Deciding whether to medicate one's child is often difficult; you'll need a lot of information—much more than is provided in this chapter. You may wish to read a book by Dr. Tim Wilens, my colleague at Mass General, called *Straight Talk About Psychiatric Medications for Kids*.

Ultimately, what you'll need most of all is an outstanding child psychiatrist or pediatric psychopharmacologist. You'll want one who:

- Is current on the latest research findings.

- Has a good working knowledge of the potential side effects of medication and their management.

- Is an expert in "combined pharmacotherapy"—the art of utilizing several medications simultaneously.

- Is familiar with and recognizes the potential benefits of non-medical interventions.

- Takes the time to get to know and understand you and your child and to listen to and address your concerns.

- Makes sure you—and your child, depending on what's developmentally appropriate—understand each medication and its anticipated benefits and potential side effects and interactions with other medications.

- Tries to prescribe medications that have the fewest potential side effects and at the lowest possible dose, and slowly moves on to higher doses or other medications with a greater potential for side effects only if the initial medication treatment plan fails to achieve its objectives.

- Monitors your child's progress carefully and continuously over time.

When I hear about children who have had extreme difficulties with medication, it is often because one of the foregoing elements was missing from their treatment.

All medications—aspirin included—have side effects. Fortunately, extremely serious side effects tend to be rare. Of course, regardless of their infrequency, side effects are always worrisome when they happen to your child. Your doctor should help you weigh the anticipated benefits of a medication with the potential risks so you can make educated decisions. Although it's important to have faith in the doctor's expertise, it's equally important that you feel comfortable with the treatment plan he or she proposes, or at least that you're comfortable with the balance between benefits and risks. If you are not comfortable with or confident in the information you've been given, you need more information. If your doctor doesn't have the time to provide you with more information, you need a new doctor. Medical treatment is not something to fear, but it needs to be implemented and monitored competently and compassionately.

Remember, medication alone can not teach your child how to think in the midst of frustration. But medication can open the door to training such thinking. Once an understanding of your child's specific difficulties has been achieved, medications may be considered as a means of addressing one or more of the various issues that may be compromising your child's capacity for flexibility and a tolerance of frustration, including inattention and cognitive inefficiency; hyperactivity-impulsivity; irritable, agitated, or dysphoric mood; extreme mood instability; and anxiety or obsessiveness. As you'll read, some medications address several of these issues at once. Not all the medications described here have been officially approved for use with children, nor have many been studied extensively in use with children and adolescents, especially with regard to their long-term side effects.

Inattention and Cognitive Inefficiency

As you know, inattention and cognitive inefficiency are often seen in children with ADHD and can contribute to inflexibility-explosiveness both by fueling a child's cumulative level of frustration and by hindering a child's capacity to think things through and organize his thoughts. The mainstays of medical treatment for inattention and cognitive inefficiency are the stimulant medications. These agents are thought to increase the levels of the neurotransmitters dopamine and norepinephrine in the brain, either by blocking their re-uptake or stimulating their release. The stimulants, which have been in use for over sixty years, include well-known, well-studied medicines, such as methylphenidate (Ritalin) and dextroamphetamine sulfate (Dexedrine), and other agents, such as a mixture of amphetamine salts called Adderall. Stimulants come in short- and long-acting preparations and are highly effective in improving attention and cognitive efficiency in many children.

In most cases, the side effects associated with stimulants tend to be mild, but they are worth mentioning. Two of the more common side effects are insomnia (especially if a full dose is administered after the mid- to late-afternoon hours) and loss of appetite, which can, over the long term, result in weight loss. In some children, stimulants may unmask or exacerbate existing tics (this circumstance may require adding a second medication to reduce the tics or discontinuing the stimulant medication). Stimulants may increase anxiety and irritability in some children—an undesirable circumstance for inflexible-explosive children. The behavior of some children worsens when stimulant medication wears off (a phenomenon called "rebound"), and this side effect is sometimes addressed by administering a half dose late in the afternoon to ease the child off the medication. Finally, particularly in adolescents, parents need to be aware of the potential for abusing stimulants.

Hyperactivity and Poor Impulse Control

Hyperactivity and poor impulse control can also compromise a child's capacity for flexibility and frustration tolerance. Some children are so hyperactive that they have difficulty adapting to even minor frustrations. Such children can't sit still long enough to participate in a Basket B discussion. And an impulsive cognitive style may hinder a child's capacity to think through options for dealing with frustration. Several classes of medications are used to improve self-regulation in children, and stimulants are, again, often the agents of first choice. However, in some children, untoward side effects, the lack of a positive response to stimulants, or complicating conditions may require consideration of alternative medications for enhancing impulse control and reducing hyperactivity. The tricyclic antidepressants, which include agents such as nortriptyline (Pamelor), desipramine (Norpramin), imipramine (Tofranil), and clomipramine (Anafranil), may be quite useful. An advantage of tricyclic medications is that they provide twenty-four-hour coverage and typically do not interfere with sleep. These agents, especially nortriptyline and desipramine, have also been found to have positive effects on attention span and are the best studied of the antidepressant medications used in the treatment of childhood ADHD.

The side effects of these medications are also worthy of mention. One of the rare, but more serious, side effects of the tricyclic medications is cardiac toxicity, which often necessitates that children medicated with such agents undergo initial and then periodic electrocardiograms. There are a variety of additional potential side effects that may not be well tolerated by children, including dry mouth, weight gain, sedation, lightheadedness, and constipation.

An atypical antidepressant called bupropion (Wellbutrin) has also been used to ameliorate hyperactivity-impulsivity in children with ADHD. The side-effects of bupropion tend to be better tolerated than those of tricyclic medications. Bupropion may also improve mood and reduce irritability and anxiety. Thus, it may be especially useful in children whose ADHD-related concerns are complicated by mood and anxiety issues. Bupropion may increase the risk of seizures; exacerbate tics; cause insomnia, nausea, headache, constipation, tremor, and dry mouth; and initially cause an increase in agitation.

The antihypertensives, including clonidine (Catapres) and guanfacine (Tenex) are also commonly used to reduce hyperactivity and impulsivity, but may be less effective for inattention. Antihypertensives can also be effective at reducing tics and aggression. In addition, because of their sedating effect, antihypertensives have been used to help children sleep at night. However, in some children, this sedation may be a problem during daytime hours, and is sometimes manifested in the form of heightened irritability. In inflexible-explosive children whose difficulties seem fueled by mood issues, this increased irritability is undesirable. Side effects can include headache, dizziness, nausea, constipation, and dry mouth.

Irritable, Agitated, Dysphoric Mood

As you know, mood issues can contribute to inflexibility-explosiveness. Children whose mood is chronically irritable, agitated, or dysphoric often respond to even minor frustrations as if they were major obstacles, in the same way many of us do during transient periods of irritability and agitation. Mood issues in children are often treated with a group of medications called selective serotonin re-uptake inhibitors (SSRI antidepressants), which include agents such as fluoxetine (Prozac), sertraline (Zoloft), paroxetine (Paxil), citalopram (Celexa) and fluvoxamine (Luvox). These medications are newer to the market than the tricyclic medications discussed earlier, and their popularity is owed to their effectiveness in easing a wide range of symptoms, including dysphoric mood and irritability. The SSRI medications are not thought to be useful for treating the core symptoms of ADHD; indeed, in some children, they can actually cause behavioral activation, sometimes to the point of inducing manic behaviors. While the potential side effects associated with the SSRIs are thought to be better tolerated than those associated with tricyclic medications, they are noteworthy. The most troublesome untoward side effects include nausea, weight loss or weight gain, anxiety, nervousness, insomnia, and sweating.

Extreme Mood Instability

The term *mood instability* is often used to describe extreme levels of irritability and agitation and frequent aggressive outbursts. You may recall that some clinicians prefer the terms *bipolar disorder* or *manic-depression* to describe such children; in other circles, "really bad ADHD" or "ADHD with depression" are the labels of choice. Among researchers, these labels are still an issue of some controversy because of the overlap between the symptoms of ADHD and bipolar disorder. Regardless of the label one chooses, in my experience—and the research of my colleagues at Mass General confirms this impression—children with ADHD who also meet the criteria for bipolar disorder exhibit more severe behavior, are more impaired psychosocially, and have poorer long-term outcomes than do those with ADHD alone.

A class of medications called mood stabilizers—which broadly includes medications like lithium carbonate and anti-convulsants, such as carbamazepine (Tegretol), valproic acid (Depakote), and gabapentin (Neurontin)—can be effective at helping such children respond to frustration in a less reactive, volatile, explosive manner. The mood stabilizers may be less effective in children who are predominantly dysphoric. Indeed, because these agents may produce drowsiness or fatigue, they may actually increase irritability in some children. All four provide twenty-four-hour coverage and typically do not affect the sleep of most children. The potential side effects of these agents are worth noting. Lithium can cause sedation, nausea, diarrhea, thirst, increased urination, mild tremor, and weight gain and must be monitored closely and continuously. Valproic acid and carbamazepine may cause sedation, nausea, diarrhea, heartburn, tremor, and weight gain. Valproic acid can also cause liver toxicity, and carbamazepine can be associated with a decrease in white blood cell count and aplastic anemia, so the use of these agents requires periodic blood work. Gabapentin is thought to have milder side effects and does not require periodic blood monitoring. Less traditional agents such as flaxseed oil and fish oil have also been shown to have promising mood stabilizing effects.

In some instances, antipsychotic medications—which include newer medications, such as risperidone (Risperdal) and olanzapine (Zyprexa)—may be used to control extremely aggressive and explosive behavior. These medications have prompted much enthusiasm because they tend to be better tolerated than more traditional antipsychotics. However, these agents have been associated with sedation and weight gain, and may be associated with extrapyramidal symptoms, such as eye-rolling, rigidity in the limbs, fixed facial expression, blank emotions, and involuntary movements. These latter side effects can be quite serious and should be discussed with your doctor.

Anxiety and Obsessiveness

Anxiety can also set the stage for inflexibility-explosiveness, especially when it interferes with a child's capacity to think things through. Several classes of medication may be used to address various forms of anxiety in children, including the SSRI antidepressants, which I discussed earlier; the anxiolytics, which include medications such as buspirone (Buspar); and the benzodiazepines, which include medications such as clonazepam (Klonopin). In addition to helping with anxiety in general, the SSRIs can also be useful in the treatment of obsessive-compulsive disorder (OCD). In my experience, the OCD label is sometimes applied to children who are strikingly inflexible but do not actually satisfy the criteria for the full OCD syndrome. The SSRIs can help such children be more malleable, and this, of course, is a desirable effect in inflexible-explosive children. Clomipramine (Anafranil), one of the tricyclic antidepressants you read about before, is also commonly used to treat true OCD.

I've seen a few of the explosive children with whom I've worked benefit to some degree from taking "natural" or "homeopathic" agents. While I'm quite open to the use of such agents, it's important to note that these agents *do* have a chemical effect on a child's body (we have a tendency to view "natural" agents as somehow more benign), can produce undesirable side effects, often have not been carefully studied (of course, the same can be said about many of the traditional psychiatric medications presently being prescribed for children), and must be taken under the supervision of a qualified professional.

No one wants to see a child medicated unnecessarily, so a conservative approach to medication is appropriate. But it's also worth repeating that in some inflexible-explosive children, medication is an essential—sometimes indispensible—component of treatment. In many instances medications are combined because the child's difficulties can not be satisfactorily improved by a single agent. In other instances, a medication may be added to counteract the undesirable side effects of another medication that is having otherwise beneficial effects.

At the risk of redundancy, it should be clear that the most crucial component in the psychopharmacology picture is a competent, clinically savvy, attentive, available prescribing doctor. But the doctor can't treat your child successfully unless he or she receives accurate information from you and your child's teachers about the effects of the prescribed medications. When all relevant adults work in concert with the doctor, side effects are handled more efficiently and adjustments are made more responsively.

A discreet approach to medication is also recommended. Most children aren't eager for their classmates to know that they're receiving medication for emotional or behavioral purposes. And there's a temptation for parents to keep school personnel in the dark about their child's medication status as well. True to the collaborative spirit required for intervening effectively with inflexible-explosive children, and because the observations and feedback of teachers are often crucial to making appropriate adjustments in medication, I generally encourage parents to keep relevant school personnel in the loop on medications. If there's no way to keep a child's classmates in the dark, it's often necessary to educate the classmates about individual differences (asthma, allergies, diabetes, difficulty concentrating, low frustration tolerance, and the like) that may require medicinal treatment.

Will your child be taking medication the rest of his life? That's hard to predict. In general, the chemical benefits of these agents endure only as long as the medication is taken. Nonetheless, in some children, the behavioral improvements that are facilitated by medication persist even after the medications are discontinued, especially if a child has acquired new compensatory skills. Ultimately, the question of whether a child should remain on medication must be continuously and collaboratively revisited.

Finally, as a practical matter, you may be wondering if a child's compliance with medication is in Basket A. Most of the younger children I work with don't object to taking medication unless they have trouble swallowing pills, and adjustments for this problem are easy to make (for example, some medications come in liquid form, and pills can be crushed and mixed with food). When a child objects strongly to taking medication—and, in my experience, this circumstance is far more common in preadolescents and adolescents—it's usually a sign that the child is objecting to the side effects (drowsiness, dizziness, weight gain, and nausea seem to be at the top of the list), feels stigmatized or embarrassed about having to take medication at school, wants or needs to become a more active participant in discussions about his own care, or has grown tired of being treated like a patient. Whatever the issue, Basket B—where things can be discussed, processed, and negotiated—is where the issue usually lands. In other words, forcing pills down the throat of an inflexible-explosive fourteen-year-old is not a successful long-term strategy, nor is hospitalizing an adolescent who refuses to take his medication (although the latter action is necessary under extreme circumstances). In the vast majority of cases, adolescents are willing to take medication if their concerns are taken into account and adjustments are made in accordance with their needs.

9

Roadmaps

The interventions described in the last three chapters can lead to significant changes in interactions between you and your inflexible-explosive child. Creating a user-friendlier environment should have helped make the world a little less onerous for a child compromised in the skills of flexibility and frustration tolerance, as well as set the stage for you to teach your child how to think in the midst of frustration (and stay calm enough to be able to do it). Achieving a clearer understanding of the factors fueling your child's difficulties is, of course, the most crucial aspect of creating a user-friendlier environment. The baskets framework should have helped you make the hard decisions about the parenting priorities that are worth meltdowns (i.e., safety), the issues which aren't even worth mentioning (at least for the time being), and the issues on which to help you child learn how to handle frustration more adaptively (with you in the role of surrogate frontal lobe). And in some children, medication can be a means of addressing various factors impeding your child's progress in Basket B.

But we may have some fine-tuning to do before Basket B is operating at peak efficiency. Just as medication may be necessary to address some of the issues that may be impeding progress in Basket B, additional skills training may be necessary to address other issues. In this chapter, we'll discuss some of these other issues and ways to go about handling them.

We'll basically be looking at two issues. First, some children lack the skills to recognize that they're frustrated, lack the vocabulary to tell you they're frustrated, or lack the language skills to tell you what they're frustrated about. These lacking skills can make it extremely difficult to open the door to Basket B. Second, some children interpret events around them in an innacurate or distorted fashion, and this can greatly impede the process of collaborative problem solving. Under both circumstances, the children may need a more detailed roadmap to help them navigate frustration more effectively.

What's a roadmap? As described briefly in Chapter 3, a roadmap is a mental script that can provide a child with a way to think more clearly and stay calm in the midst of situations that might otherwise cause him to be irrational or explosive. Like other types of roadmaps (the kind that keep our cars headed in the right direction), roadmaps can help a child stay on track and not get lost in the emotional tide of inflexibility and frustration. Roadmaps require advance planning (many inflexible-explosive children won't ask for directions once they're lost!), and must be simple enough to follow.

As strange as it may seem, some children actually have trouble recognizing that they're frustrated or that they're experiencing other feelings—such as fatigue or hunger—that may lead to frustration. It's hard for a child to figure out what to do about being frustrated if he doesn't realize that's what he is. A user-friendlier environment should give you a good jump-start on helping such a child because you're already reading the early warning signs of frustration and providing the child with feedback about these signs ("Casey, you're starting to look a little frustrated, is there something I can help you with?"). Nonetheless, we want the child eventually to recognize that he's frustrated on his own.

Some children benefit from being helped to recognize the physical reactions that can accompany frustration (such as fatigue, hunger, a hot face, burning ears, dizziness, and head spinning). But even after they recognize the physiologic sensations of frustration, they often need the words to express that frustration. The roadmap? Give them the words! I often teach such children a rudimentary vocabulary for categorizing and labeling their feelings. Often, this vocabulary consists of three feelings: happy, sad, and—of course—frustrated.

But I don't have any faith that simply teaching a child this new vocabulary in my office will facilitate reliable use of the vocabulary outside of my office. So we need adults to provide frequent cues regarding its use. We helped Helen, a child you read about in Chapter 4, learn and practice using her rudimentary vocabulary by having her parents discuss the past day's events with her at bedtime in a very relaxed, user-friendly, nurturing manner. They would ask her what happened during the day that made her "happy," whether anything made her "sad," and whether anything caused her to feel "frustrated." If Helen couldn't remember specific events that fit one of these three categories, her parents would suggest some possibilities. If Helen had difficulty labeling the emotions that were associated with a particular event, her parents would help her. The parents made sure Helen's teacher was also aware of her new vocabulary so that Helen didn't become confused by different terminology. Over the course of several months, Helen began to express her emotions in a much more appropriate manner across an increased number and range of situations. Her vocabulary of emotions slowly became broader and more sophisticated and eventually included such terms as "confused," "disappointed," "excited," "bored," and "annoyed."

As you might imagine, "I'm frustrated" is a lot more palatable to the ears of most parents than "Leave me alone!" or "Screw you!" and makes it a lot easier to be a helper. For the linguistically compromised child, this vocabulary provides a simple language for expressing emotions. For the executively compromised child, it requires minimal processing and imposes an organizational framework. For the child with a nonverbal learning disability, the use of language to express frustration is just what the doctor ordered.

Many children get the basic vocabulary ("I'm frustrated," "I'm very sad right now," "I'm angry with you") down pat but still fall apart because they can't figure out or tell people what's the matter. So while they may recognize that they're frustrated—and may even be able to say "I'm frustrated"— they become cognitively paralyzed the instant they try to think about or describe what it is they're frustrated about. The roadmap? Give them the words to articulate their frustration with expressions like, "That's bothering me," "I don't know how to do that," "I don't know what to do," "I'm scared," "I don't feel right," "I need a break," "I can't talk about that right now," and "I need some help." Of course, you'll need to remind your child of his new vocabulary and respond in a way that encourages its continued use.

Mother: Jackson, how was your day at school?

Jackson: DON'T ASK ME THAT QUESTION?!!! SHUT UP!!!

Mother: Sounds like you can't talk about that right now.

Jackson: I CAN'T TALK ABOUT THAT RIGHT NOW!

Mother: Great, maybe you'll be able to talk about it later.

Some children take slowly to their new vocabulary and continue to express frustration in ways (*"No! I can't do that right now!"*) that still require enlightened interpretation and a gentle reminder (*"Boy, you sure sound frustrated!"*). In some instances, children begin to verbalize their frustration more adaptively, but adults fail to appreciate the significance of this skill (*"You're frustrated? Just do what you're told, and you won't be frustrated!"*).

Father: We had a few major blowouts this week.

Me: Over what?

Father: I don't like the way Andy speaks to me when I tell him to do things.

Me: Can you give me an example?

Father: Well, this is a pretty common scenario. He's watching TV the other morning, and I tell him he needs to put his shoes on. He tells me to leave him alone.

Me: What did you do?

Father: I screamed at him.

Mother: See, I think the problem was that he usually puts his shoes on after he eats breakfast.

Father: That doesn't give him the right to speak to me that way.

Me [to Andy]: Andy, do you remember saying "Leave me alone" to your father?

Andy: Yes.

Me: What would cause you to tell your father to leave you alone after he'd told you to do something?

Andy: I was mesmerized.

Me: Mesmerized?

Andy: Yes, when I watch TV, I get mesmerized.

Me: So it was hard for you to drag yourself away from the TV to put your shoes on?

Andy: Kinda.

Me: Andy, can you think of other things you say to your parents when they ask you to do something that they don't like?

Andy: Yes. Sometimes I say, "I don't want to."

Father: Sometimes you just yell, "No!"

Mother: Sometimes you say, "I don't have to listen to you" or "You can't tell me what to do."

Me: What's our explanation for why Andy says these things?

Father: I think he's just very disrespectful sometimes.

Me: May I offer a different explanation?

Father: Sure.

Me: Based on what we know about Andy—his poor impulse control, distractibility, difficulty with expressive language—I'm wondering if maybe he isn't that great at shifting gears and at articulating the frustration he feels when he's asked to make such shifts.

Father: You lost me.

Me: Here's what I mean. Andy, what could you have said
to your father when he asked you to stop watching TV
and put your shoes on?

Andy: Good morning?

Me: Hmmm. You could have said that. But what were
you trying to tell your father?

Andy: That I wanted to watch TV longer.

Me: How could you have said that?

Andy: I don't know.

Father: I think I see what you mean. So what should I
have said?

Me: Well, it depends on what you wanted to teach Andy.
I must confess, I can't think of any lesson that would be
best taught by your screaming at him.

Father: I just can't tolerate disrespect. My immediate
reaction is to start screaming.

Me: What I'm saying is that I think Andy has the utmost
respect for you already, particularly in his coherent
moments. Do you agree?

Father: In his coherent moments, yes.

Me: So there must be some other reason Andy speaks to you in a disrespectful manner when you ask him to do things when he's watching TV.

Mother: You're saying he says these things because he doesn't know how to say he's frustrated any better?

Me: Precisely. At least at that moment.

Father: So what should we say to him when he says these things?

Me: Well, there are different ways to do this, but ultimately your goal is to give him a roadmap for using more appropriate words.

Father: Give me an example.

Me: Well, let's take the most recent episode. You told Andy to put his shoes on while he was watching TV. He responded with "Leave me alone." He probably wanted to be left alone, so his words, while disrespectful, were probably right on target. But instead of thinking, "'I will not be spoken to that way!" and getting all heated up, I think you'd be a lot better off thinking, "I bet I can help him say that differently," and giving him different words like, "You'd like to watch TV a few more minutes?"

Andy: I could have told him that Mom always lets me put my shoes on after breakfast.

Me: You could have ... why didn't you?

Andy: I was mesmerized. And he started yelling too fast.

Me: Andy, is there something your mom and dad could do to help you get unmesmerized when they want you to do something while you're watching TV?

Mother: I'll tell you what I do ... I go in and rub his shoulders a little ... that demesmerizes him.

Me: Then he's better able to respond to you in a respectful way?

Mother: Absolutely.

Father: This is going to be very hard.

Me: I know. But think about how hard you're working already. Let's at least make sure you have something to show for all that hard work.

With lots of help from his parents, the manner in which Andy expressed frustration and asked for help became more sophisticated. For example, when he was in "information overload," he began saying things like, "Slow down, I can't keep track." When he became confused, he'd say, "I don't know what to do." When he felt himself becoming frustrated and needed some help, he'd say, "I feel really bad right now." And when he needed some extra time to organize an appropriate response (and avert an inappropriate one), he'd say, "I think I need a minute here." New roadmaps are a beautiful thing.

Don't forget: just as a child with a reading disability won't begin reading overnight, an inflexible-explosive child who has difficulty recognizing, expressing, or describing frustration won't begin using his new vocabulary overnight. This is not a quick fix. But it's also not rocket science. The skills we're training are fairly basic, but they're essential to opening the door to the collaborative problem solving of Basket B.

Swearing in the midst of frustration is often a very clear sign that a child doesn't currently have the thinking or linguistic skills to express frustration adaptively. With this interpretation and explanation of swearing in mind, our main goal is the same: to give the child a new roadmap so as to help him alter his method of delivery and use different words. Responses like, *"I refuse to be spoken to like that!"* or *"Go to your room and come back when you're ready to talk to me the right way!"* would be close to the mark if your child lacked the knowledge that you didn't want to be spoken to that way or wasn't motivated to speak to you the right way. But if the true issue is that your child lacks the thinking or linguistic skills—or coherence—to articulate frustration, these comments are way off the mark.

Mother: *We had a bad incident this week, and I'm not sure I handled it well.*

Me: *Tell me.*

Mother: *Well, I was making pancakes for breakfast. Derrick came into the kitchen and said he didn't want pancakes. I told him that's what was on the menu...*

Me: *Sorry to interrupt, but was eating pancakes in Basket A?*

Mother [smiling]: *No.*

Me: *Just curious. Go on.*

Mother: *So then he called me a "freaking bitch" and ran out of the kitchen. I ran after him and told him he was grounded for a week for calling me a name. He told me to get away from him. I insisted on an immediate apology. He went ballistic for the next half hour.*

Me: *It sounds extremely unpleasant. You mentioned that you wished you'd handled things differently?*

Mother: *First off, since eating pancakes wasn't in Basket A, I could have helped him find something else to eat.*

Me: *True... Baskets B and C can spare him and you a lot of meltdowns. Anything else?*

Mother: *I guess I shouldn't get so upset when he swears at me.*

Me: *It's very hard not to get upset when your son calls you a freaking bitch. But you've been punishing him for calling you names for a very long time, and he still calls you a name every time he gets frustrated. So I don't think he needs any more lessons on the importance of not swearing or any more motivation not to swear. At the* moment, I don't think Derrick is capable of expressing his frustration without swearing. In fact, since we've forbidden hitting—because it's unsafe—my sense is that, at this point, swearing is the only way Derrick has to express his frustration. Now, we've started trying to give him different words to use, but I don't think the new words come to him automatically yet. So I suspect we've got some more swearing to endure. The truth is, each time he swears, he gives us an opportunity to help him find different words.

Mother: So what should I have said?

Me: If eating pancakes was in Basket C, you could have said, "I think what you're saying is that you'd like something else to eat besides pancakes. Let's see if there's something else you'd like." If the issue was in Basket B, you could have said, "I think what you're saying is that you're frustrated about the pancakes—let's talk about that so we can work it out."

Mother: So I blew it, right?

Me: No, you didn't blow it . . . this is really hard. Your understandable knee-jerk instinct is to punish your kid when he swears at you, and I'm asking you to do something different because punishing him hasn't worked. It's hard to do.

Mother: Yes it is.

Me: I think it's worth pointing out that Derrick did something very adaptive in the incident you described.

Mother: He did? What?

Me: Instead of going toe-to-toe with you in the kitchen, he detached himself from the situation. In other words, he left. He went in the other room. That's something he would never have done before. But you followed him.

Mother: I did, didn't I.

Me: So we have some more work to do. But we're getting there.

Don't forget, your child has the potential to become over-whelmed by frustration at any point in the process. So no matter what part of the recognizing-expressing-thinking-through sequence you're trying to train, keeping your child coherent in the midst of frustration is still Job Number One. In other words, don't forget the necessity of continuously reading how your child is responding to your help. If he says—in whatever words he can muster—that he's becoming overwhelmed by the assistance you're giving, believe him. Take a break. Give him some time to collect himself. Try a new tack. Come back to it later.

Not all kids swear when they lack a more adaptive vocabulary. Some instead trip into some very automatic statements that still block access to Basket B, such as "It's not fair!," "You always blame me!," "It's always my fault!,""I never do anything right!," and "I hate you!" These statements have the same detouring effect as swearing, especially if adults decide that the statements are meaningful. In many instances, children deny that they meant what they said once coherence has been restored. In such instances, it is often most useful to interpret the statements in the same way we're interpreting swearing: something the child automatically says in the absence of a more accurate vocabulary. And we'd deal with it in the same way as we're dealing with swearing: by spoon-feeding a new vocabulary.

In some children, these and other statements—"I hate school," "Nobody likes me," "I'm stupid"—are meaningful, because they represent the child's actual interpretation of events. Training a new vocabulary takes on a somewhat different meaning with these children. These "attributions" tend to be very tough to change.

Me: Cindy, how do you like school?

Cindy: I hate school.

Me: You hate school? What is it about school that you hate?

Cindy: I just don't like it.

Me: That's a shame, because you have to spend a lot of time there. But what is it that you don't like?

Cindy: The other kids think I'm stupid.

Me: They do? How so?

Cindy: *They just do.*

Me: *Tell me what you mean by 'stupid.'*

Cindy: *You know ... dumb ... stupid.*

Me: *That must not feel very good to you. What makes you think the other kids think you're stupid? Do they say you're stupid?*

Cindy: *No ... not exactly. I just know they think that.*

Me: *Is there anyone else who makes you feel that you're stupid?*

Cindy: *No.*

Me: *Well, there must be some reason you think the other kids think you're stupid. What made you decide that?*

Cindy: *I sometimes say the wrong answer in class.*

Me: *That can be very embarrassing. Can you remember a time when that happened?*

Cindy: *Well, like last week we were doing math problems on the chalkboard, and my answer was wrong.*

Me: *Did the other kids laugh?*

Cindy: *No ... not really.*

Me: Did someone tease you about putting the wrong answer?

Cindy: No.

Me: Did any of the other kids put the wrong answer?

Cindy: Yes. . . . lots.

Me: Were they stupid when they put the wrong answer?

Cindy: No.

Me: What's different when you put the wrong answer?

Cindy: I don't know. I just know they think I'm stupid.

Me: Hmmm. When you put the wrong answer, you're stupid, but when they put the wrong answer, they're not. I don't get it.

Cindy: Me either.

Me: It's a little confusing because you get really good grades. How can you be stupid if you get really good grades?

Cindy: I don't know.

Me: Maybe you're not stupid.

Cindy: No, I'm stupid. Like sometimes I don't understand what I read right away and I have to go back and read it again.

Me: That happens to me sometimes, too. It's interesting, I don't think I'm stupid because I have to read things twice.

Cindy: That's you.

Me: Does your mom know the other kids think you're stupid?

Cindy: Yes.

Me: What does your mom say about that?

Cindy: She tells me she thinks I'm very smart.

Me: Does that help you think you're not stupid?

Cindy: No.

Me: Is there anything else about school you don't like besides that the other kids think you're stupid?

Cindy: Well, nobody likes me.

Clearly, such inflexible interpretations often defy logic. And in many instances these interpretations contribute to a child's cumulative level of frustration or fuel his frustration at a given moment. Sometimes the hard part is to distinguish such statements from mental debris. In general, when these statements are made only in the context of vapor lock and meltdown, they may simply be a sign that the child is having trouble thinking clearly *at that moment*. If they occur outside the context of vapor lock and meltdown, the statements may reflect something less fleeting.

Entire books have been written on how to "restructure" the inaccurate, maladaptive thoughts of children and adults. The idea is to help the individual recognize the inaccuracy of his existing belief systems and replace the inaccurate thoughts that make up these belief systems with a new roadmap; in other words, a more accurate, adaptive way of thinking. This restructuring usually involves "disconfirming" the individual's old thoughts by presenting—in a user-friendly, low key, systematic manner—evidence that is contrary to these rigid beliefs. With a child who is stuck on the belief that she's stupid, we might have a teacher or parent whisper the following comment in response to a good grade on an assignment: *"I know you sometimes think you're stupid, but I don't think someone who's stupid could have done that well on that task."* In a child who has bona fide weaknesses in one area and strengths in another, a teacher's feedback might be as follows: *"I know you're struggling with reading—and that makes you say you're stupid sometimes—but I've never seen anybody who was so good at math. Looks to me like you're really good in math and still need some help in reading."* With such feedback being presented continuously—and I don't mean just once or twice—we can, over the long haul, sometimes make a dent in a child's inflexible belief system. Parents and teachers do this sort of thing with *all* children. It just takes on a little more urgency and requires more time, patience, and hard work with inflexible-explosive children. But it would be a therapeutic coup for a child who previously summarized her abilities with "I'm stupid" to instead begin saying, "I'm good in math, but I still need help in reading." Then you're ready for the next extension of the roadmap.

DRAMA IN REAL LIFE:
GETTING THERE

"This was a horrendous week," said Danny's mother in our fourth or fifth session.

"It was?" Danny asked, a little surprised.

"Yes, it was!" said the mother emphatically. "I got called every name in the book this week—repeatedly."

"But I didn't hit you, and that's good, right?" said Danny.

"Look Danny, it's fine that you haven't hit me lately," said the mother, "but you're still attacking me with words."

"Like when?" asked Danny.

"Like this morning when I was trying to help you get ready for school on time and you were late for the car pool. You called me a 'bitch' because I told you the car pool was waiting for you in the driveway."

"I'm sorry." Danny slid over on the couch and tried to hug his mother.

"I don't want to be hugged right now." The mother tried to escape her son's grasp. "I'm sick of how I'm being spoken to."

"I won't do it anymore," Danny pleaded. Then he looked at me, tears welling up in his eyes. "Am I going to be like this forever?"

"I doubt it," I said. "But it's obvious we've got more work to do. Tell me"—I looked at the mother—"what did you do when Danny called you a bitch?"

"I got very angry . . . I told him he couldn't speak to me that way . . . and if he was going to speak to me that way, I wasn't going to make him breakfast anymore," she replied.

"Then what happened?" I asked.

"He got more upset," the mother answered. "He screamed something about how the reason he swears so much is because of the way I've raised him."

"What happened next?" I asked.

"We started screaming at each other about how I've raised him," said the mother.

"But that has nothing to do with Danny being late for the car pool," I observed.

"Yes, that's true, but I'm not going to put up with that kind of talk from him," said the mother.

"You've been telling Danny you're not going to put up with that kind of talk from him for a very long time, yes?" I asked.

"Yes, of course I have," she replied.

"Has saying that helped him swear any less?" I asked.

The mother paused. "No."

"Has all the punishing you've done over the years in response to his swearing helped him swear any less?" I asked.

"Not that I've ever noticed," she said. "It just makes him scream even louder."

"Then it may be time to help him find better words to let you know he's frustrated," I said.

"What does that mean?" she asked.

"It means that, at the moment, Danny apparently isn't able to let you know he's frustrated in a way that isn't offensive to you," I said. "So, instead of being offended, or threatening consequences that haven't worked, you'd probably be better off helping him find better words."

"Help him find better words? I've never heard of such a thing," she said. "This is not the universal approach to parenting."

"I'm not sure what you mean by 'universal,'" I said. "But whatever you mean, it's pretty clear that Danny hasn't responded to it very well."

"So what do I do when he starts screaming about how I've raised him?" the mother asked.

"I'm assuming that's just mental debris—the stuff that comes out of Danny's mouth when he's not thinking clearly. Don't forget, there's little to be gained by trying to process mental debris. Talking about it when Danny's frustrated certainly isn't going to achieve anything except to move him closer to a meltdown."

"It's not so easy to ignore him when he says that kind of thing," said the mother.

"I know," I said. "Initially, that's the hardest part. But once Danny figures out that you're able to get past his foul language and accusations and actually help him, I think he'll slowly begin communicating his frustration in a less offensive manner."

"What do you want me to do?" Danny insisted.

"You can try to let your mother know you're frustrated in a way that's less offensive to her," I said.

"I could try that," said Danny. "What should I say instead?"

"Well, what else could you say when you get frustrated?" I asked.

"I could say, 'I'm getting really frustrated!'" Danny suggested.

"That would be excellent," I said.

"What am I supposed to say if he swears at me?" the mother asked.

"Maybe something like, 'I can see you're getting very frustrated,'" I suggested.

"That's queer!" Danny interjected. "She'd sound too much like a psychologist."

"What would sound better to you?" I asked.

"Uhm . . . how 'bout 'Damn, you're frustrated!' " he volunteered.

I looked to the mother for her opinion of this suggestion.

"You know, given what usually comes out of my mouth, that would actually be a major improvement."

"Super," I said.

"So once we've determined he's frustrated, what do I do next?" the mother asked.

"First, let him know you're happy to help," I said. "Then the trick is for Danny to let you know what he's frustrated about."

"Oh, it's usually pretty obvious," said the mother.

"So you're never at a loss for what he's so upset about?" I asked.

"Not usually," said the mother.

"OK," I said, turning to Danny. "Danny, when you're frustrated, do you want your mother's help or do you want her to just leave you alone?"

"Sometimes I want her help and sometimes I want her to leave me alone," he said.

"Hmmm. Are you pretty clear about what you want when you're frustrated?" I asked.

"Sometimes . . . uhm . . . usually . . . I . . . I don't know," he sputtered.

"How good are you at figuring out what would be most helpful to Danny when he's frustrated?" I asked the mother.

The mother paused. "I don't know . . . I've been so caught up in the swearing that I never really considered the possibility that he might need my help."

"He does," I said. "Badly." I turned to Danny again. "Danny, you've got two challenging goals this week. First, I want you to try to let your mother know you're frustrated in a way that isn't offensive to her; like we just rehearsed. Second, try to let her know how she can be most helpful to you when you're frustrated. What do you think?"

"I'll try," he said. "I might slip a few times."

"Danny will not be perfect at this," I said to the mother. "He's going to need your help expressing his frustration in ways that are more appropriate. And if he's receptive to it, he probably could also use some help figuring out how to deal best with the problem that's frustrating him. If he wants to be left alone, leave him alone. What do you think?"

"This is very different for me," she said. "I'll try." She looked at Danny. "I might slip up a little, too."

"Well, I think this is a very good thing for you both to be trying hard at," I said. "And something that's going to take a little getting used to for both of you. Here's the good part: This is the beginning of you guys being able to talk to each other about frustrating things without attacking, swearing, hitting, or making each other feel bad. That's pretty exciting. And I think we're getting there."

Let's summarize what we've been up to in this chapter. You've implemented a user-friendlier environment to help set the stage for more adaptive parent-child interactions; you've been using the baskets framework to help you establish priorities and decide what issues are worth inducing and enduring meltdowns over; and (perhaps) your child's fuse has been lengthened and capacity to think rationally in the midst of frustration has been enhanced through use of medicine. But you may not be finished yet. You may have some additional roadmaps to create so as to address additional thinking skill deficits that may be fueling routine meltdowns in certain situations.

In many instances, inflexible-explosive children need a "roadmap," or "mental script," to help them through situations in which they are prone to have difficulties. The roadmap suggestions presented in this chapter are far from exhaustive, so if your current universe of options isn't getting the job done, seek the guidance of a mental health professional whose universe is wider.

Just in case you hadn't noticed, something we laid the seeds for in Chapter 7 sprang to life in this chapter: Children are becoming active participants in their own treatment. They have begun to assume some ownership of their difficulties and to be involved in working toward solutions. These children can take their problems seriously, can develop at least a basic understanding of the factors underlying these problems, can discuss these problems, can participate in problem solving, and can come to see adults as potential allies—as long as the adults get past the motivational thing, create user-friendlier environments, and try to get a handle on the specific deficits in skills that are preventing these children from responding adaptively. Instead of asking yourself, "What's it going to take to motivate this kid to behave differently?" you've begun to ask, "Why is this so hard for my child? What's getting in his way? How can I help?"

10

Family Matters

An inflexible-explosive child can lay bare many family issues that might never have risen to the surface had the parents been blessed with a less difficult child. But family issues can also complicate or impede the creation of a user-friendlier home environment and implementation of the baskets framework. Maladaptive family communication patterns, for example, can make it a lot harder for family members to discuss important problems productively; in some instances, these communication patterns can actually fuel meltdowns. Sibling issues, never easy to deal with under the best circumstances, are even more troublesome when one of the siblings is inflexible and explosive. Sometimes parents have difficulties of their own—job stresses, financial problems, or marital issues—that may make it hard to devote extra energy to the creation of a user-friendlier household. And sometimes grandparents or other relatives don't make the task easier. We'd better take a closer look at these issues.

Siblings

Even in so-called ordinary families, adversarial interactions between siblings can be considered something of a rite of passage. But adding an inflexible-explosive child to the mix can make typical sibling rivalry look like a walk in the park. For example, though it's not uncommon for "ordinary" siblings to direct their greatest hostility and most savage acts toward each other, these acts can be more intense and traumatizing when they're inflicted—chronically—by an inflexible-explosive child. And though it's not unusual for "ordinary" siblings to complain about preferential treatment and disparities in parental attention and expectations, these issues can be magnified in families with an inflexible-explosive child because he requires such a disproportionate share of the parents' resources. Finally, though many siblings seem to get their thrills by antagonizing or teasing one another, an inflexible-explosive sibling may be considered less capable of responding to such antagonism in an adaptive way; such interactions may therefore have the primary effect of fueling countless meltdowns.

Fortunately, a user-friendlier environment and the baskets framework can improve interactions among siblings. But siblings cannot merely be considered beneficiaries of such interventions; they are also essential to their creation and implementation. Therefore, depending on their ages, it is often useful to help brothers and sisters understand why their inflexible-explosive sibling acts the way he does, why his behavior is so difficult to change, how to interact with him in a way that reduces hostility and minimizes the likelihood of aggression or explosions, and what the parents are actively doing to try to improve things. Brothers and sisters tend to be more receptive if there's an improvement in the general tone of family interactions and if their inflexible-explosive sibling begins to blow up less often and becomes an active participant in making things better.

Nonetheless, this understanding doesn't always prevent siblings from complaining about an apparent double standard between them and their inflexible-explosive brother or sister. Armed with the knowledge that parental attention is never distributed with 100 percent parity and parental priorities are never exactly the same for each child in any family, you should resist responding to this complaint by trying even harder to get your inflexible-explosive child to look like your other children. In all families—yours and everyone else's—*fair does not mean equal*. Even parents in "ordinary" families often find themselves providing one child with more help with homework, having higher academic expectations for one child, or being more nurturing toward another. In your family, you're doing things a little differently for the child who has deficits in the areas of flexibility and frustration tolerance, but you're also doing things differently for the other children, who have difficulties of their own. So when siblings are complaining over disparities in parental expectations, it's an excellent opportunity to do some empathizing and educating.

Sister: How come you don't get mad at Danny when he swears at you? It's not fair!

Mother: I know that it's very hard for you to listen to him swearing. I don't like it very much, either. But in our family we try to help one another and make sure everyone gets what he or she needs. I'm trying to help Danny stay calm when he gets frustrated and to help him think of different words he could use instead of swearing. That's what he needs help with.

Sister: But swearing is bad. You should get mad at him when he swears.

Mother: Well, I don't get mad at you when I'm helping you with your math, right? That's because I don't think getting mad at you would help very much. Remember how I used to get mad at Danny whenever he swore? It didn't work very well, did it? It just made things worse. So I'm doing something now that I think will eventually work better. I think it's starting to work pretty well.

Sister: Will you help me think of different words if I swear?

Mother: Of course I would. Then again, you don't swear very much, which is really good. But if you were to start having trouble with swearing, I would try to help you stay calm and tell you different words, just like I'm doing with Danny. Luckily, I don't think you'll need too much help with that.

Sister: Yes. Math is what I need help with.

Mother: Exactly.

How may basket thinking be applied to interactions between an inflexible-explosive child and his siblings? To begin with, safety is still in Basket A. Issues that don't matter much are still in Basket C. And working things out is still in Basket B. Let's look at a few examples.

Brothers and sisters are often on the receiving end of the aggressive acts of their inflexible-explosive sibling. Thus, in some families, safety is of paramount concern. Because of Basket A, safety is now a very high family priority, and this can reduce the level of aggression dramatically. But in some instances—especially early in treatment—safety can be achieved only through skillful management of the home environment. For example, in some cases, I recommend that parents deprive siblings of the pleasure of one another's company unless they're under adult supervision. In more extreme cases, I'll suggest that it's too risky for siblings to be together at all. In such instances, siblings don't eat dinner together, don't watch television together, don't sleep in the same room together, don't sit together at the same table in a restaurant, don't sit near each other in the car, and so forth. Once parents become more confident that safety can be maintained, the never-together policy may be reconsidered.

> Mother: But Danny's sister loves him so much. I can't imagine depriving them of each other's company.

> Me: I can. Safety is more important than having Danny and his sister be together right now. It's our responsibility to make sure she's safe no matter how much she loves him.

Basket B is still where some essential negotiating, problem-solving, and cooperation skills are trained and practiced, except now these activities are also applied to sibling interactions. Thus, when disputes arise between an inflexible-explosive child and his brother or sister, Basket B is where parents help both parties stay coherent, articulate their concerns, identify the problem to be resolved, and work toward a mutually satisfactory solution. You're not acting as a referee, just as a facilitator of conflict resolution. The brothers and sisters end up feeling good because such disputes are less terrifying; they see that their views are being heard, are involved in the process of negotiating a solution that takes their needs into account, and see that you're able to handle things in an evenhanded manner. The inflexible-explosive child ends up feeling good because you've helped him stay coherent in the midst of frustration, prevented him from committing an aggressive act he'd be sorry for later, helped him negotiate a solution that takes his needs into account, and reinforced your role as helper. Eventually the goal is for them to work out their difficulties without your assistance, but that's probably a long way off. As time goes on, it's often possible to begin having family meetings aimed at processing and resolving general issues, especially if your inflexible-explosive child is able to tolerate such meetings.

Unfortunately, I've seen instances where the behavior of seemingly "angelic" siblings begins to deteriorate just as the behavior of their inflexible-explosive brother or sister begins to improve. This is often a sign that the emotional needs of the siblings require closer examination. In some cases, individual therapy may be necessary for brothers and sisters who have been traumatized by their inflexible-explosive sibling or who may be manifesting other problems that can be traced back to the old family atmosphere.

If you feel that your family needs help working on these issues, a skilled family therapist can be of great assistance. You may also wish to read an excellent book entitled *Siblings without Rivalry*, by Adele Faber and Elaine Mazlish.

Child [to younger brother]: You dumb-ass. I hate you!

Parent: What's going on, fellas?

Child: He wrecked the plane I was building! He always does this! He does it on purpose!

Parent: I know how frustrated you get when he does that.

Child: I hate him! I'm going to break something of his!

Parent: I think we need to think of something better for you to do than that, even though you're very frustrated right now.

Child: No! He wrecks my stuff, so I wreck his!

Parent: Hmm. I bet you can think of better things to do than that. Remember when you used to hit your brother when you were mad at him? You don't do that anymore.

Child: I don't care! He wrecks my stuff, so I wreck his!

Parent: We can think of something better than that. Let's think.

Child: I don't want to think. I get so mad when he does that.

Parent: I know you do. I'm sorry he wrecked your airplane. Let's think of what you did the last time he wrecked something of yours.

Child: I don't remember.

Parent: I do. You asked me to help you rebuild it. And your brother helped. It was fun.

Child: I don't want his help. I hate him.

Parent: You're still very mad at him. What else could you do right now so you're not so mad?

Child: I could go outside and play.

Parent: You could go outside and play if you wanted to. Anything else you'd like to do right now so you're not so mad?

Child: Uhm ... I think I need to drink some juice. Then I want to rebuild my plane. By myself!

Parent: That sounds easy enough. What kind of juice do you want?

Communication Patterns

A family therapist can also help when it comes to making some fundamental changes in how you communicate with your child. Dealing effectively with an inflexible-explosive child is easier (not easy, easier) when patterns of communication between parents and child are adaptive. When these patterns are maladaptive, dealing effectively with such a child is much harder. Many of the patterns depicted below have been described by a host of family therapy theorists and clinicians (for example, Drs. Arthur Robin and Sharon Foster in their book, *Negotiating Parent-Adolescent Conflict*). As you may expect, some of these patterns are more typical of older inflexible-explosive children. But the seeds may be sown early. Although not an exhaustive list, here's a sampling of some of the more common patterns:

Parents and children sometimes get into a vicious cycle of drawing erroneous conclusions about each other's motives or cognitions. I usually refer to this pattern as "speculation"; others have referred to it as "psychologizing" or "mind reading," and it can sound something like this:

Parent: The reason Oscar doesn't listen to us is that he thinks he's so much smarter than we are.

Now, it's not uncommon for people to make inaccurate inferences about one another. Indeed, responding effectively to these inaccuracies—in other words, setting people straight about yourself in a manner they can understand— is a real talent and requires some pretty complex, rapid processing. Of course, in an inflexible-explosive child, the demand for complex, rapid processing presents a small problem—he's not very good at it. So while there are some children who can respond to speculation by making appropriate, corrective statements to set the record straight, an inflexible-explosive child may hear himself being talked about inaccurately and spin straight into vapor lock. This is an undesirable circumstance in and of itself, but it's especially undesirable because whether Oscar thinks he's smarter than his parents probably isn't worth spending much time discussing. In fact, this topic is a red herring that just distracts everyone from the main issue, which is that Oscar and his parents still haven't figured out how to get past his inflexibility and low tolerance for frustration so they can discuss and resolve important issues.

Of course, speculation can be a two-way street. From a child's mouth, it might sound something like this:

Oscar: The only reason you guys get so mad at me so much is because you like pushing me around.

Such statements can have the exact same detouring effect, especially when adults follow the careening child in front of them straight through the flashing lights and detour barriers and right off the cliff:

Mother: Yes, that's exactly right, our main goal in life is to push you around. I can't believe you'd say that, after all we've been through with you.

Oscar: Well, what is your main goal then?

Father: Our main goal is to help you be normal.

Oscar: So now I'm not normal. Thank you very much, loser.

Speculation is always going to be a risky undertaking. So it's time for a user-friendlier rule: Each family member is allowed to comment only on his or her own thoughts and motivations. In other words, you should only speak for yourself, using a lot of "I" statements, such as "I worry about your getting to bed so late" or "I feel very hurt when you say that." If your child does need help articulating his needs or frustrations, your attempts to assist him should be framed tentatively ("Correct me if I'm wrong, but I think what you may be trying to say is . . ." or "Maybe what you're frustrated about is . . .") and should involve an absolute minimum of psychologizing and value judgments. You're also going to need someone to keep conversations on track so they don't swing off the topic. Now, a therapist could be that someone for an hour or two a week. But ultimately, it's going to have to be a family member and, as you may expect, parents are the early frontrunners for this position. In my experience, many of the explosions that occur in interactions with inflexible-explosive children have little to do with the issues that were the main topic of conversation in the first place. When issues are brought up in a way that doesn't elicit defensiveness, most of these children are willing or even eager to talk about important desired topics such as these:

· How they can handle frustration and think things through more adaptively and how you might be able to help.

· How you'd like to start trying to resolve disagreements in a mutually satisfactory manner through civil discussion.

· Things each family member is saying that make another family member defensive and how to communicate with each other in a more productive way.

Of course, it's also critical to listen closely to what the child has to say on these topics; to recognize that it can take the child a long time to spit something out; and to remember that if a child isn't ready to talk about something at a given moment, you probably won't have much luck trying to force the issue. Come back to it later when you've got better odds.

Another maladaptive communication pattern has been called "overgeneralization": the tendency to draw global conclusions in response to isolated events. Here's how it would sound from a parent:

Mother: Billy, maybe you can tell Dr. Greene why you're not doing your homework.

Billy: What are you talking about?! I do my homework every night!

Mother: Your teachers told me you have a few missing assignments this semester.

Billy: So does everybody! What's the big deal? I miss a few assignments, and you're ready to call in the damn cavalry!

Mother: Why do you always give me such a hard time? I just want what's best for you.

Billy: Stay out of my damn business! That's what's best for me!

What a shame, because there may actually be ways in which Billy's mother could be helpful to him with his homework or, at least, get some of the reassurance she was looking for about his compliance with homework assignments. Not by starting the discussion with an overgeneralization, though. While other children are sometimes able to get past their parents' overgeneralizations to address the real issues, inflexible-

explosive children often object almost immediately to statements that overgeneralize reality and may lack the skills to
respond appropriately with information that corrects them.
Phrasing things tentatively should help you overgeneralize
less often and can therefore feel user-friendlier to your child
(*"Oscar, I wonder if we can talk about this without screaming
at each other"* or *"Billy, you'll let me know if there's anything
about your homework I can help you with?"* or *"Myrna, I
don't want to bug you about your homework; can we figure
out some way for me to know if it's actually getting done?"*

In "perfectionism," parents fail to acknowledge the
progress their child has made and demonstrate a tendency to
cling to an old, unmodified vision of the child's capabilities.
Perfectionism is often driven less by the child's lack of
progress and more by the parents' own anxiety. Wherever it's
coming from, perfectionism typically feels very user-
*un*friendly to a child who may actually have been trying hard
to stay on track or who may feel enormously frustrated by his
parents' unrealistic expectations:

*Father: Eric, your mother and I are pretty pleased about
how much better you're doing in school, but you're still
not working as hard as you ought to be.*

Eric: Huh?

*Mother: But that's not what we wanted to talk to you
about. You're staying up too late doing your homework.*

Eric: I get it done don't I?

Father: Yes, apparently you do, but we want you to get it done earlier so you get more sleep.

Eric: I get enough sleep.

Father: We don't think you do. You're very grouchy in the morning, and you have trouble waking up. We want you to do your homework when you get home from school from now on.

Eric: I'm not doing my homework when I get home from school! I need a break when I get home from school! What difference does it make?

Mother: It makes a difference to us. Now, your father and I have already talked this over, so there's no discussion on it. You need to get your homework done when you get home from school.

Eric: No freaking way.

Hmmm. Eric may or may not actually be interested in thinking about how to get his homework done earlier. Probably not. Either way, perfectionism is not a particularly effective way to engage him in a discussion on the topic. The ultimate antidote for perfectionism is perspective: Here's who my child was, here's who he is, and here's who he's likely to be—I should try to stop insisting that he become something he isn't.

Other maladaptive communication patterns include sarcasm, which is either totally lost on or extremely frustrating to inflexible-explosive children, who don't have the patience to figure out that the parent meant the exact opposite of what he or she actually said; put-downs (*Parent: "What's the matter with you?! Why can't you be more like your sister?"*); "ruination," sometimes called "catastrophizing," in which parents greatly overblow the effect of current behavior on a child's future well-being (*Parent: "We've resigned ourselves to the fact that Hector will probably end up in jail some day"*); interrupting (don't forget, the child is probably having trouble sorting through his thoughts in the first place—your interruptions don't help); lecturing (*"How many times do I have to tell you ..."*); dwelling on the past (*"Listen, kid, your duck's been upside down in the water for a long time ... you think I'm gonna get all excited just because you've put together a few good months?"*), and talking through a third person (*"I'm very upset about this, and your father is going to tell you why ... isn't that right, dear?"*). All distinctly user-*un*friendly.

> Over time, the goal is for you to be able to communicate with your inflexible-explosive child in a way that demonstrates to him that you can control yourself during discussions, stay on topic, recognize when discussions aren't going anywhere, get them back on track, and deal more adaptively with things that are frustrating to you both.

Over time, the goal is for you to be able to communicate with your inflexible-explosive child in a way that demonstrates to him that you can control yourself during discussions, stay on topic, recognize when discussions aren't going anywhere, get them back on track, and deal more adaptively with things that are frustrating to you both.

This is very hard to do, and it's made even harder by the fact that you probably have very powerful feelings of your own that influence the way you react to your child. But things can change; you may just need a little help to make them change.

As a parent, you exert enormous influence over family communication patterns. Again, a family therapist can help you establish some basic rules of communicating that can improve interactions dramatically.

Parents

Needless to say, living with an inflexible-explosive child is a lot easier when adults communicate well enough to work as a team in establishing a user-friendlier environment. At the least, the adults need to reach a consensus on what belongs in Baskets A, B, and C. That means seeing eye-to-eye on the child's capabilities and agreeing on what's actually enforceable. If you're unable to reach such a consensus, your child will have to continue to handle two completely different sets of expectations, and we already know that boat won't float.

While an inflexible-explosive child can put pressure on adults' relationships with each other, troubles between a couple can make life with such a child much more difficult to deal with. For partners who aren't even very good at working things out with *each other*, reaching a consensus about the baskets and working things out with a child may be even more challenging. Partners who are drained by their own difficulties often have little left for a labor-intensive inflexible-explosive child. Sometimes one partner feels exhausted and resentful over being the "primary" parent because the other parent spends a lot of time at work. Power struggles that may occur between the adults often affect interactions with the child. And sometimes step-parent issues can enter the mix (Child: *"Stay out of this! You're not my real father!* or Step-father: *"That kid was a problem before I arrived on the scene . . . this is between him and his mother"*). It's very difficult to make a user-friendlier environment work without addressing these issues. Sometimes marital and family therapy are necessary adjuncts.

Many parents feel very de-energized by their own personal difficulties. Some parents are quite bitter over having been dealt an inflexible-explosive hand by the great deck shuffler of children. For one mother, her son's explosions tapped into her own abusive childhood, and it was extremely difficult for her to get past her visceral reaction to her son's raised voice. Another simply felt so drained by being a full-time mother to her three other children that she simply had no energy left for helping her inflexible-explosive son. A father had to get a handle on his own explosiveness before he could help his daughter with hers (he found many of the strategies we were using with his daughter helped him explode less often, too). Another father needed to be medicated for ADHD before he was able to stick to the plan agreed upon in treatment. Yet another father had to come to grips with his excessive drinking and its impact on the whole family before we could press ahead with creating a user-friendlier environment and the baskets framework. It's hard to work on helping your child if you're feeling the tug to put your own house in order first. Take care of yourself. Work hard at creating a support system for yourself. Seek professional help or other forms of support if you need it. These things don't change on their own.

Grandparents

At times it's necessary to bring grandparents into the therapeutic mix. In many families, grandparents or other relatives function as co-parents, taking care of the children while the parents are at work. If the grandparents aren't with the program, the inflexible-explosive child may be spending part of his day in a user-friendlier environment (when he's with his parents) and another part of the day in a user-*un*friendly environment (when he's with grandparents). This isn't an ideal scenario. In such circumstances, the grandparents are an integral part of the family unit and need to be brought into the loop (don't forget, it's important to ensure that all adults who interact with your child understand his unique difficulties). In other instances, the grandparents may not spend much time with the child but never miss an opportunity to remind the parents that what the child really needs is a good kick in the pants. These grandparents need to be brought into the loop as well, although sometimes they simply need to be enlightened about why their ideas probably aren't going to work with their inflexible-explosive grandchild.

DRAMA IN REAL LIFE
RULES OF COMMUNICATING

When Mitchell—the fifteen-year-old ninth grader who was diagnosed with Tourette's disorder and bipolar disorder—and his parents arrived for their second session, I was advised that it had been a difficult week.

"We can't talk to him anymore—about anything—without him going crazy," said his mother.

"THAT'S NOT SO, MOTHER!" Mitchell boomed. "I'm not going to sit here and listen to you exaggerate."

"Why don't you stand then?" the father cracked.

Mitchell paused, reflecting on his father's words. "If you were joking, then you're even less funny than I thought you were," he said. "If you weren't, then you're dumber than I thought you were."

"I'm not the one who flunked out of prep school," the father jabbed back.

"AND I'M NOT THE ONE WHO MADE ME GO TO THAT SCHOOL!" Mitchell boomed.

"Look, I'm really not interested in getting into a pissing contest with you, Mitchell," said the father.

"What do you call what you just did?" the mother chimed in. "Anyway, I don't think Mitchell is ready to face flunking out of prep school yet."

"DON'T SPEAK FOR ME, MOTHER!" Mitchell boomed. "YOU DON'T KNOW WHAT I'M READY TO FACE!"

"Pardon me for interrupting," I said, "but is this the way conversations usually go in this family?"

"Why, do you think we're all lunatics?" asked Mitchell.

"Speak for yourself," said the father.

"Screw you," said Mitchell.

"Well, we're off to a wonderful start, aren't we?" said the mother.

"WE ARE NOT OFF TO A WONDERFUL START, MOTHER!" Mitchell boomed.

"I was being sarcastic," said the mother. "I thought a little humor might lighten things up a bit."

"I'm not amused," Mitchell grumbled.

"Fortunately, we're not here to amuse you," said the father.

"Sorry to interrupt you folks again," I said. "But I'm still wondering if this is a pretty typical conversation."

"Oh, Mitchell would have gotten insulted and stormed out of the room if we were at home," said the mother. "In fact, I'm surprised he's still sitting here now."

"YOU HAVE NO IDEA HOW I FEEL!" boomed Mitchell.

"We've been listening to you telling us how you feel since you were a baby," said the father. "We know more about how you feel than you know."

"ENOUGH!" boomed Mitchell.

"My sentiments exactly," I said. "I think I'll answer my own question. Forgive me for being so direct, but you guys have some not-so-wonderful ways of communicating with one another."

"How do you mean?" asked the mother.

"You're a very sarcastic group," I said. "Which would be fine, I guess, except that when you're sarcastic, I think it makes it very hard for Mitchell to figure out what you mean."

"But he's so smart and we're so dumb," said the father.

Mitchell paused, reflecting on his father's words. "Are you trying to be funny again?" he asked his father.

"You're so smart, figure it out," the father said.

"Uhm," I interrupted. "I'm sure you guys could do this all day, but I don't think it would get us anywhere."

Mitchell chuckled. "He still thinks we're going to accomplish something by coming here," he said into the air.

"I should add that sarcasm isn't the only bad habit," I continued. "The one-upmanship in this family is intense."

"Birds of a feather," the mother chirped.

"What does that mean?" Mitchell demanded.

"It means that the apple didn't fall far from the tree," said the mother.

"Be careful about whose tree you're talking about," said the father. "I don't want any credit for this."

"Oh, I'm afraid you're right in the thick of things," I reassured the father. "I wonder if we could establish a few rules of communicating. I must warn you, I'm not sure you'll have much to say to one another once I tell you these rules."

"Bravo," said Mitchell. "That's music to my ears."

"What kind of rules?" asked the mother.

"Well, it would be a lot more productive if we got rid of a lot of the sarcasm," I said. "It really muddies up the communication waters. And the one-upmanship has got to go."

The ensuing silence was broken by the father. "I don't think he can do it," he said, looking at Mitchell.

Before Mitchell could erupt, I interjected, "That's one-upmanship."

Mitchell's frown turned upside down. "Thank you," he said.

"This is going to be hard," said the father. "And no more sarcasm either?"

"Not if you guys want your son to start talking to you again," I said.

"Where's that team spirit, fellas?" the mother chimed in.

"That's sarcasm," I interjected.

"Ooo, this guy is tough," said the father, turning to his wife. "I don't like coming here anymore." He smiled.

"That's sarcasm, too," I said.

"My husband isn't accustomed to being corrected," said the mother.

"Oh, that reminds me of the last bad habit," I said.

"Oh, God, what did I say?" the mother said, covering her mouth.

"You guys talk for one another a lot," I said, "like you can read one another's minds."

"Well, we know one another very well," said the mother.

"That may be," I said, "but from what I've observed, your speculations about one another are often off-target, and they don't go over very well."

"What'd you call it?" asked the mother.

"Speculation," I said. "Thinking you know what's going on in someone's head. It just gets you guys more agitated with one another."

"No more speculation?" said the mother.

"No more speculation," I confirmed.

"What should we do if someone does one of those three things?" Mitchell asked.

"Just point it out to them without being judgmental," I said. "If someone is sarcastic, just say, 'That's sarcasm.' If someone is one-upping, say 'That's one-upmanship.' And if someone is speculating, say . . ."

" 'That's speculation,' " said Mitchell.

"My, we catch on fast," said the father.

"That's sarcasm," said Mitchell.

11

All Things Considered

We've come a long way in ten chapters. We started by taking a close look at how we conceptualize and interpret inflexible and explosive behavior in children, with particular emphasis on how your interpretations of and explanations for this behavior will greatly influence the ways in which you respond to it and attempt to change it. I encouraged you to try a new explanation on for size; namely, that many of these children are not choosing to be explosive and noncompliant but are delayed in the process of developing the skills that are critical to being flexible and tolerating frustration or have difficulty applying these skills when they are most needed. These difficulties may emanate from a variety of pathways, including difficult temperament; deficits in executive skills, social skills, and sensory integration; mood and anxiety disorders, and impaired language-processing and nonverbal skills. Coming to a clear understanding of the factors that fuel a child's difficulties is the first step in trying to figure out how to help the child overcome them.

We took a closer look at the way adults often respond to inflexible-explosive behavior. I suggested that many of the popular motivational strategies that adults tend to apply to such behavior may not achieve the desired effect; although motivational strategies make the possible more possible, they do not make the impossible possible. In other words, it makes little sense to try to motivate skills of which a child is presently incapable. Doing so has the potential to set the stage for, and then perpetuate, adversarial interactions, which is exactly what we wouldn't want to see happen. My firm belief is that many of these children are *already* motivated; if they could be more flexible and handle frustration more adaptively, they would. They're waiting for us to provide them with the type of help they need.

Next, we began thinking about what that help may actually look like. We started by striving to create a user-friendlier environment, which includes having adults (1) achieve a comprehensive understanding of the factors fueling a child's difficulties and ensure that all adults are on the same wavelength; (2) be much more judicious about the demands for flexibility and tolerance of frustration being placed on the child; (3) identify—in advance—specific situations that may routinely lead to inflexible-explosive episodes; (4) get better at reading the warning signals and take quick action when these signals are present; (5) interpret behaviors that occur during vapor lock and meltdowns for what they really are; (6) understand the manner by which different adults may actually be fueling the child's inflexibility-explosiveness; (7) use a more accurate common language to describe various aspects of the child's inflexibility-explosiveness; and (8) come to a more realistic vision of who the child is and what he can become.

The baskets framework is intended to help you achieve many of these goals. Basket A—which contains behaviors that are high priorities and are worth inducing and enduring meltdowns over—helps you maintain safety and your role as authority figure. Basket B—which contains behaviors that are high priorities but not worth inducing and enduring melt-downs over—helps you teach your child how to resolve conflict in a manner that promotes communication, problem solving, relationship building, and perspective taking. Basket C—which contains all those behaviors that aren't important any more—helps you remove as many unnecessary frustrations as possible from your child's radar screen. The user-friendlier components and the baskets share an important common theme: intervening before the child is at his worst—before and during vapor lock and at the crossroads—rather than after he's already at his worst—during and after melt-downs. We also took a close look at sibling issues and family communication patterns that may impede this process and how they may best be addressed. Though we've come a long way, you probably still have some questions that haven't yet been answered. This chapter is devoted to answering some of the questions I hear most often.

Question: "Isn't this a very passive, permissive approach to parenting?"

No . . . in fact, this is a very active, authoritative approach to parenting. Remember, there is no easy way to parent an inflexible-explosive child. Hard work is a given. Let's just make sure you have something to show for it. The notion that the only thing these kids need is a good kick in the butt is extraordinarily narrow and doesn't do justice to the diverse mechanisms that may underlie the child's difficulties. There simply is no one-size-fits-all approach to intervention for this population.

Question: "How much progress should I expect from my child, and how fast? When should I stop doing the whole user-friendlier environment and baskets thing?"

Children and parents vary widely in terms of how quickly they respond to this approach. The first goal is to take the fuel out of the fire as quickly as possible; in other words, for there to be a fairly immediate decrease in unsafe behaviors, an increase in stability, and a dramatic shift in the way parents respond to and communicate with their children. Some families are able to achieve this in a few weeks, others take several months, and yet others longer still. Some children continue to have occasional, residual unsafe episodes for a few months, but such episodes are often far less intense and fizzle out a lot faster.

As you know, once parents and children are communicating more adaptively and starting to feel better about each other, the stage is set for work on the skills that will help the child handle frustration more adaptively. The timing of this process varies from child to child and family to family as well. Dealing with frustration is a continuous learning process even for those of us who aren't children anymore. So we're basically looking for slow, steady progress in the child's capacity for empathy and perspective taking; improvements in the child's ability to anticipate, recognize, express, and think through solutions to frustrating situations independently; a longer fuse; less frequent vapor lock; and fewer total meltdowns. Reductions in swearing and lying often take longer, but I still expect slow, steady progress in these domains, too.

Many parents want to know when they can get back to their old way of doing things. My question is, Why would you want to? A lot of parents begin to use the approach described in this book thinking that eventually they'll be able to put lots of things into Basket A. In reality, as parents and children get better at communicating, negotiating, and problem solving; as parents get better at creating a user-friendlier environment and implementing the baskets; and as the relationship between parents and child steadily improves, the importance of Basket A actually *diminishes*. Many families I've been working with for three or four months hardly ever mention Basket A anymore.

Question: "So does using this approach mean that rewards and punishments are completely out of the picture?"

Not necessarily. But my hope is that by now, you have a very realistic sense of what the motivational approach can and can't help you achieve and an awareness of the special care required when using rewards and punishments with an inflexible-explosive child. The real question is this: Will additional motivation enhance your child's performance at any point along the way? The answer: maybe.

The first thing I'd want to be convinced of is that the child would actually benefit from additional motivation. If so, consequences are still in the running. If not, hold off.

Second, I'd want to be sure that the motivational strategies are worth their potential price. My rule of thumb is that motivational strategies should be applied only to behaviors that are in Basket A. Since you're willing to induce and endure meltdowns only over behaviors that are in Basket A—and meltdowns are likely to occur if your child loses or fails to obtain a privilege or is punished—you should use motivational strategies only for Basket A behaviors. For example, a few of the children I've worked with have earned and lost privileges contingent upon having a safe day. Was I hopeful that a little added reminding and motivating would be helpful? Yes. Did I think incentives would be the primary reason the child would start behaving in a safer manner? No, I thought the user-friendlier environment, baskets, and new thinking skills would be the primary reasons the child would start behaving more safely.

Third, I'd want parents to be certain that they're willing and able to enforce whatever consequences are being applied. If so, keep going. If not, do not pass go. Consequences that can't be enforced aren't consequences at all; they just detract from your credibility, which is something we're trying to avoid.

Finally, I'd want you to have faith that a consequence administered on the back end of one inflexible-explosive episode is going to be accessible and meaningful to your child the next time he's frustrated. In other words, I'd want you to be confident that the next time your child enters vapor lock, he could navigate his way through the following thought process: "The last time I got frustrated I broke a lamp and my mom grounded me for a week. I don't want that to happen again. So I'd better think of a better way to handle my frustration this time. Let me think of what the possibilities are." If you're not confident of your child's ability to benefit from consequences in this manner, then consequences may be of limited benefit.

Mother: So I'm not supposed to punish my kid anymore?

Me: Tell me about the last time you punished him.

Mother: The other day I told him to turn off the TV and do his homework. He called me a witch, so I took away TV for three days.

Me: Is that a punishment you're able to enforce?

Mother: Enforce? Not really . . . in fact, he was watching TV the very next day.

Me: What did you do then?

Mother: What could I do? There really aren't any punishments I can enforce anymore.

Me: I guess you shouldn't be punishing much then.

Mother: I shouldn't be punishing much? Then what should I do?

Me: I think if we make some fundamental changes in the way you two interact, he'll end up swearing at you a lot less and you won't have much cause to punish him anymore. By leading with punishment—in other words, by having punishment be your primary way of responding to behavior you don't like—you end up cutting off communication the instant there's a disagreement or something happens that you don't like.

*You also end up making yourself the target of his
frustration, rather than whatever it was that was
frustrating him in the first place. There's not much sense
in putting yourself in that position. And since you can't
enforce your punishments anyway, you end up feeling
ineffective and disempowered.*

Once communication between parents and children
improves, I sometimes encourage the parents to involve the
children in discussing whether a punishment is warranted for
a certain inappropriate behavior and what that punishment
should be. Children are often much harder on themselves
than adults would be, so I don't usually worry about whether
the punishment they come up with will be stiff enough.
Enforcement of agreed-upon punishments can be a problem:
Sometimes children agree that a certain punishment is appropriate (for example, an earlier bedtime) and then melt down
when the punishment is invoked. This may be a sign that they
aren't quite ready for the delay between agreeing on a consequence and following through with it, and it brings us back to
the original question of whether the punishment truly facilitates learning that makes the meltdown worth inducing. I'm
also enthusiastic about engaging children in discussions about
how they can "make amends" for an act committed in the
midst of frustration. Such discussions should not take place
during or right after meltdowns but rather when coherence
has been fully restored. Here's what such a discussion might
sound like:

*Parent: Carlos, we need to talk a little about the table
you broke yesterday.*

Child: I said I was sorry.

Parent: I know, and it was very nice of you to say that. But I still feel very bad about the broken table, and we still need to figure out what you can do to help me feel better.

Child: Like what?

Parent: I don't know. Can you think of anything you could do that would make me feel better?

Child: You could punish me.

Parent: I don't know if punishing you would make me feel better. I was thinking there might be some things you could help me with around the house.

Child: I could sweep the floors.

Parent: That's an idea. That would be very helpful. Is that something you'd do to help me feel better?

Child: Yes. Or I could help you take out the trash.

Parent: I think it would be most helpful for you to sweep the floors. That would make me feel a lot better. Maybe next time you get frustrated you could let me help you instead of breaking the table.

Child: I'll try.

Whether it's punishment or making amends, children are often capable of coming up with outstanding ideas, which helps their parents become "solution facilitators," rather than "solution imposers."

Question: "What about time-out?"

Some children find time-out to be a good place to calm down when they're frustrated; most of the ones I work with don't. Indeed, the meltdowns of many of the kids I work with are actually exacerbated—sometimes dramatically so—if someone makes any kind of physical contact with them when they're frustrated. So if your child tends to calm down in time-out and will go to and stay in time-out without having to be restrained and without destroying property, go for it. If time-out simply fuels your child's meltdowns, forget it. Even under optimal circumstances, time-out is typically not recommended for older children and adolescents.

On the other hand, I've often found it productive to help parents and children agree to go their separate ways—with each going to different designated rooms of the house—when it becomes obvious that a disagreement or discussion is going poorly. Not all inflexible-explosive children will follow through on this plan, but a surprising number will. The discussion resumes after everyone has regained sufficient coherence.

Question: "But I still have the feeling that some of my child's behavior is planned and willful. What now?"

The last thing I'd want you to try to do at times when your child is in vapor lock is to quickly try to figure out whether his behavior is planned or unplanned. You don't have a whole lot of time to spare. So there are essentially two possible mistakes you can make at such moments. The first is to think your child's behavior is unplanned and unintentional when it really isn't. The second is thinking your child's behavior is planned and intentional when it really isn't. If you have to make an error, I'd rather see you make the first error. In other words, when in doubt, respond as if your child's behavior is unplanned and unintentional. I don't think you have all that much to lose. The ramifications of the second error are much more serious.

Question: *"What about lying? Basket A?"*

A while ago I heard an interesting idea about why kids with ADHD tell lies. Imagine being a child who has a whole bunch of knowledge stored in your brain about appropriate ways of behaving. Also imagine being so impulsive that this store of knowledge seldom prevents you from behaving inappropriately. In other words, you're continuously behaving in ways you "know" are inappropriate, but you aren't gaining access to the knowledge that your behavior is inappropriate rapidly enough to keep you out of trouble. It's like there's two of you—the you who engages in inappropriate behavior and the you who clearly knows better. The stage is now set for lying.

Here's how. You behave inappropriately. Then, after a brief delay, your knowledge about appropriate behavior finally kicks in, and you find yourself in the position of having to explain why you just behaved in a way you already "knew" was inappropriate. Most children with ADHD don't have the presence of mind to say, "I know I shouldn't have done that; I just didn't access the information in time." What many do instead is fall back on one of the most primitive of defense mechanisms: denial. So what comes out of their mouths is "I didn't do it." This pattern can lead to some fascinating conversations:

Parent: Peter, why did you just push your sister?

Peter: I didn't.

Parent [incredulous]: Peter, I just watched you push your sister.

Peter: No, you didn't.

Parent: Peter, what are you talking about? You're lying!

Peter: No, I'm not.

Is this a manipulative, lying child or a child who is struggling to comprehend why he does things he knows he should not?

Other children with ADHD are not good at reflecting long enough to come up with accurate information, but they are good at quickly figuring out what adults want to hear. The resulting "lie" sounds something like this:

Mother [entering her daughter's bedroom]: Roberta, is your homework done?

Roberta [whose mind was not on homework]: Yes.

Mother [scanning Roberta's homework assignment sheet]: All of it?

Roberta [still barely accessing the "Did I do my homework?" file in her brain]: Yes.

Mother: Roberta, there's a good hour's worth of homework here. You haven't even been home an hour.

Roberta [unable to say, "Gee, mom, I guess I wasn't able to access my 'Did I do my homework?' file as quickly as my 'What does my mother want to hear?' file and my 'What will my mother do if she knows I've now lied?' file"]: Oh, I did it all at school.

Mother: When did you have a chance to do it all at school?

Roberta: Oh, Mr. Stearns always gives us time to do our homework.

Mother: Mr. Stearns gives you an hour to do your homework?

Roberta: Yep.

Mother: You're telling me the truth?

Roberta: Yep.

Since lying generally does not involve safety and is often a highly impulsive, unplanned act, my tendency is to put it in

Basket B. I'd much rather deal with lying in the context of a discussion about parent-child trust than simply toss it into Basket A.

As long as we're on the topic of impulsivity, a brief remark about the word *manipulative*, which I've found to be a remarkably overused, overrated explanation for the behavior of inflexible-explosive children. To me, the act of manipulating requires a fair amount of forethought, planning, affective modulation, and calculation—qualities that are in short supply in the vast majority of the inflexible-explosive children I know. Given that few of us enjoy being manipulated, believing that a child is being manipulative often causes adults to behave in counterproductive ways and hinders their consideration of more accurate explanations.

And as long as we're on the topic of overused terminology, I've always been curious about what adults are really up to when they tell a child he has to "take responsibility" for his actions. I'm certainly not interested in having adults and children fight over it. If a child is taking his difficulties seriously and actively trying to change—even if he has trouble saying "OK, I did it"—I'm happy.

Question: "I don't always have time to work things out—like when my child is getting ready for school, or when it's time to go to bed at night. What then?"

Time pressure is one of the great fuelers of frustration in both parents and children and most commonly comes into play during morning and evening routines. Unfortunately, training a child who's underaroused in the morning or overaroused at night to be more sensitive to issues of time is extremely difficult. Once again, your best hope during these times of the day is to make adaptations—often by judiciously establishing priorities and removing as many frustrations as possible—to make these things more manageable for your child. Another option is to increase your involvement during these times of the day, not by badgering but by performing some tasks for your child that he seems unable to perform in a timely way by himself right now. Don't forget: It takes a lot less time to help your child get moving than it does to deal with a meltdown. A third option is to create some mechanism for the child to improve his awareness of time in general.

> Question: "My child becomes frustrated about things that don't involve interactions with me or other people. He just gets really frustrated with something he's doing, like playing Nintendo, or about something that makes no sense. Or sometimes he has a delayed response to a frustration that happened earlier in the day. What then?"

It's true, there are times when there's nothing to work out because your child's frustration didn't involve you or another person. And there are instances in which a child's frustration at the moment is a delayed response to an earlier frustration, like something that happened in school. Such delayed responses are probably even more difficult for a child to artic-ulate. But your role remains the same: to find out what's frus-trating your child by helping him stay coherent enough to tell you what the problem is, or by suggesting plausible hypothe-ses and helping him figure it out, and then showing him that you can help him think things through well enough to come to a resolution. Eventually—when he's able—the goal is for him to figure it out and resolve it on his own.

Mother [standing on the front walk to the house]: Charlotte, we're waiting for you to get in the car so we can go to the beach.

Charlotte [standing in the front doorway—vapor lock]: I'm not going.

Mother: What? Charlotte, you love the beach.

Charlotte [backing into the house—crossroads]: I said I'm not going!

Mother [moving toward the front door]: Charlotte, your brother and father are already in the car, we're in a hurry, and I don't feel like going through this with you right now! Go get me my keys and let's go!

Charlotte [slamming and locking the front door to the house—meltdown]: Stay away from me! I'm not going!

Mother [outside the locked front door]: Charlotte, you unlock this door right now! [Turning to husband in car]: Honey, do you have your keys?

Husband: No. Why?

Mother [pulse pounding, turning back to the locked front door]: Charlotte, open the door dammit! This isn't funny!

No response from inside the house.

Father [arriving at front door]: What's going on?

Mother [through gritted teeth]: Your daughter has informed me that she's not going to the beach and has locked us out of our house.

Hmmm. That looks like an example of how not to do it. Now, through the magic of book writing, let's do something that you don't have the luxury of doing in real life: rewind the tape and try a user-friendlier tack.

Charlotte [vapor lock]: I'm not going.

Mother: You're not going?

Charlotte [crossroads]: No, I'm not going!

Mother [recognizing vapor lock but at an absolute loss for what might be frustrating her daughter]: What's the matter, honey?

Charlotte [rubbing her eyes]: I just don't want to go.

Mother [squatting down to Charlotte's level]: Is there something about going to the beach today that's frustrating you? You usually can't wait to go to the beach.

Charlotte: It's too early to go to the beach!

*Mother [still at a loss]: I don't know what you mean that
it's too early to go to the beach.*

*Charlotte: We don't usually go to the beach until after
church. We never go to the beach in the morning.*

*Mother [hiding her incredulity]: It's bothering you that we
don't usually go to the beach in the morning?*

*Charlotte: We never go to the beach in the morning. We
can't go right now.*

*Mother [light bulb now on]: I'm glad you told me what
was the matter. Let's think about this a little. Maybe we
can figure out what to do.*

No meltdown. Much nicer.

*Question: "My child has to have each solution spelled
out in perfect detail. Is this reasonable?"*

Many inflexible children don't handle ambiguity in their
lives well, and this extends to their solutions to problems. So
statements like, "OK, we'll do that later" or "We'll go there
soon" or "You can do that for a while" have the potential to
fuel their frustration, even in the context of collaborative
problem solving. For such children, clarity is your friend and
ambiguity your enemy.

*Trent [sitting in the back seat of the family car—vapor
lock]: I need something to eat.*

Mother [perking up in the passenger seat, and immediately recalling the potentially unpleasant ramifications of prolonged hunger in her son but failing to remember the dangers of ambiguous courses of action]: We'll stop for something very soon.

Trent [vapor lock deferred]: OK.

Five minutes of silence elapse.

Trent [with agitation—vapor lock déjà vu]: I thought you said we were stopping to eat!

Mother: I said we'd stop soon.

Trent [with significantly greater agitation—advanced vapor lock]: I can't wait! You said we were stopping!

Father [from the driver's seat]: Your mother said we'd stop soon; now put a lid on it!

Trent [very loudly, kicking the back of his father's seat]: You guys are such freaking liars! You always do this! You say you'll do something and then you don't!

Mother: Look, we'll stop for food as soon as we can.

Kaboom.

On a related topic, some kids don't adapt well when a solution doesn't go exactly as planned. Mike, a remarkably rigid thirteen year old, had agreed with his mother over when (12 noon on Saturday) and how (with her help) he'd clean his room. Mike was actually eager to get his room straightened up, but lacked the organizational skills to do it on his own. Unfortunately, the mother was delayed by another commitment and wasn't around at 12 noon to help Mike clean his room. This change in plan proved to be a major obstacle for Mike. When the mother arrived home at 1:30 p.m. and suggested that they begin cleaning the room, Mike entered vapor lock. At 1:31, the mother insisted that they clean the room. Mike's agitation increased. The mother insisted further. At 1:32, Mike melted down. What Mike needed was a complete renegotiation of the original agreement. He was just that rigid.

Some children can handle greater ambiguity. You have to figure out what your kid can handle.

Question: "Is language therapy helpful for inflexible-explosive children? How about occupational therapy?"

For children with linguistic impairments, language therapists can be very helpful at facilitating many of the skills I've been discussing throughout the book; specifically, helping children label their emotions, articulate their frustrations, and think through solutions. I've also seen a talented occupational or physical therapist be very helpful. Such therapists can help children feel a greater sense of mastery over the barrage of sensory stimuli coming at them from the world, thereby reducing their cumulative levels of frustration.

Other similar types of therapies can be useful as well. I was recently sitting in a meeting at a school discussing one of the children I was working with and his adapted physical education teacher—a wonderful man named John Passarini, who works in the Wayland, Massachusetts, public schools—was describing his work with the boy. He was talking about how far the boy had come in learning how to shoot a basketball, but that he had to be taught in very slow, very gradual steps. John was commenting that this gradual training of skills had greatly reduced the boy's frustration during basketball games, and that the boy had become a more active participant in other sports as well. I remember thinking, "My goodness, this man is doing exactly what I try to do with these kids!" Clearly, there's more than one way to skin a cat.

Question: "Many of the examples you've given relate to younger children. My inflexible-explosive child is fifteen. Any special suggestions?"

My emphasis on younger children reflects my bias that the best time to help an inflexible-explosive child is well before his level of alienation reaches its peak, he's begun affiliating with similarly alienated peers, and he's become much harder to reach. Ultimately, the language we'd use to help an inflexible-explosive child would probably be more sophisticated for a fifteen-year-old than for a four-year-old, but the emphasis on training the skills necessary for improved flexibility and tolerance for frustration would be the same. The precise skills we'd try to train would, of course, depend on each individual child no matter what the age.

Older kids may engage in a variety of behaviors that may make basket thinking more of a challenge. For example, parents of many teenagers tend to be very invested in placing drug use and sexual promiscuity in Basket A. While it's absolutely true that these behaviors are unsafe, other components of the Basket A litmus test may not be satisfied, especially as related to enforcing abstinence. So while there are some circumstances in which such behaviors end up in Basket A, it's more typical for them to be placed in Basket B, where parents and teenagers can start talking to each other about them. In other words, I have more faith that rebuilding your relationship with your teenager will reduce self-destructive behavior and keep your child from being arrested than pretending you can enforce the unenforceable.

> Question: "OK, I get the idea that safety is in Basket A. But I'm still not clear about what I'm supposed to do if my child does something unsafe or ends up having a meltdown."

If your child is doing something unsafe, do whatever it takes to defuse the situation and restore safety, even if he melts down in the process. If he's hitting his brother, separate them. If he won't separate, get his brother to leave the situation. If his brother won't leave on his own, perhaps the brother will leave with you. Do whatever it takes to restore coherence. For some children that means a hug. For others it means being left alone.

What you do next is the most important part, though. *Unsafe behavior and meltdowns usually signify that there's more work to be done with your child.* Take a close look at the factors that caused your child to become unsafe or to melt down. Think about how you're going to prepare in advance to keep the same situation from occurring again. Does your implementation of the baskets framework need a tune-up?

Does your child need more skills training? Does his medication need adjusting? Is there some aspect of the environment that is distinctly user-*un*friendly? Does he need to be kept out of certain situations or away from certain people? How can this best be accomplished?

Question: "Things were going really well and then the bottom fell out. What happened?"

Sometimes a minor change can throw a monkey wrench into the works. Sometimes something that happened outside the context of your interactions with your child, for instance, at school, has the same derailing effect. Sometimes medications need to be adjusted. Your goal is to try to get a handle on what's going on so you can help your child get back on track.

Recently I received a phone call from the mother of a very inflexible six-year-old girl I'd worked with about six months before. It was just after New Year's and the mother was beside herself.

"Monica has completely deteriorated," she reported with great distress. "This was an absolutely horrendous Christmas."

"What do you think is going on?" I asked.

"I have no idea," said the mother. "All she could tell us was, 'The Christmas tree is in the wrong place.'"

"What does that mean?" I asked.

"I don't know," said the mother. "Although this was our first Christmas in our new home."

"Is that so?" I said. "And things were going fine before Christmas?"

"Never better," said the mother.

"And how are things now that she's back at school?"

"She's been great the past few days."

"Was she sick during Christmas?"

"Perfectly healthy," said the mother.

Monica wasn't on medication, so I didn't entertain the notion that her medication might need adjusting. And since she'd been fine before and after Christmas, I assumed there wasn't a seasonal component to her sudden difficulties.

"Well, then, my best bet is that spending Christmas in a new place threw her for a loop," I said. "I guess we haven't yet experienced the full repertoire of things she's capable of being inflexible about. And being home from school took her out of her usual routine."

"You know, now that you say that, I think you may be right," said the mother. "Who would've thought spending Christmas in a new house would throw her like that?"

Question: I'm too tired to do this. I'm sick of my child and I don't have the energy to do all the processing and prioritizing you've described. Any advice?

You're underscoring something that is very true about this approach: it requires a lot of parental energy. Which means we've got to find ways to get you your energy back. I've seen the approach described in this book accomplish just that. The parent begins to understand the child's difficulties and respond in a more productive fashion, then the child begins to respond to the parent's new approach, then the parent starts to feel a greater sense of empowerment, then the parent and child begin repairing other damaged parts of their relationship, then the parent begins to feel more energized and optimistic. Basket A feels like less work on the front end but it is actually more work on the back end (meltdowns take a lot of energy to deal with). Basket B feels like more on the front end (because of the energy required to work things out) but is actually less work on the back end (because there's no meltdown). But it's also the case that some parents need to focus on themselves (sometimes with a therapist), find ways to spend time away from the child and recharge, and find ways to focus on other aspects of life besides the child. Support groups, social service agencies, spouses, and relatives can sometimes be of help.

Question: "This whole thing isn't working too well. What's going on?"

There are a few basic explanations for why this approach may not be working well. In some families, screaming and threatening was the main reason a child intermittently complied with adult requests prior to the implementation of the approach you've been reading about in this book. When screaming and threatening is taken out of the equation, it sometimes takes a little while for the new ingredients to kick in.

The first thing you want to do is to make sure you've achieved a comprehensive understanding of the precise factors fueling your child's difficulties. Moving ahead before you've achieved such an understanding makes the baskets framework less effective, provides no guidance on whether your child's difficulties might be better addressed via medication, and makes it very difficult to pinpoint the roadmaps your child may require.

Other components of the user-friendlier environment may be missing. For example, it's possible you've yet to fully revise your vision of who your child is. In other words, you're still determined to create a child who's able to respond to requests and changes in plan with calm compliance and adaptability. Back to Chapter 3: You may need help from a good mental health professional with this one.

You may be falling into any or many of the counterproductive patterns described in Chapter 7.

You may need help from a mental health professional to decide what behaviors should be in the different baskets.

You may be trying to address some issues non-medically that medicine addresses more effectively—or vice versa.

It's possible that the stage has been set for more adaptive interactions within the family, but things are going really poorly at school and this situation carries over to the family. I'll discuss this issue in the next chapter.

12

User-friendlier Schools

As hard as it is to help an inflexible-explosive child within the confines of your home, I think it may be even harder in a classroom. Can you imagine a teacher trying to implement the strategies described in the preceding chapters while simultaneously being responsible for teaching twenty-five to thirty other students, many of whom have other types of special needs? Like parents, most regular education teachers have never been responsible for changing the behavior of an inflexible-explosive child and have never received any specialized training to prepare them for this task (I assure you, my approach to dealing with my first inflexible-explosive child was a lot different than my current approach). How does the teacher keep his or her other students safe and under control while the inflexible-explosive student is falling apart over, say, a spelling test? What can other school staff—the principal, guidance counselor, school psychologist, and so forth—do to help? Does the child need an aide? Should he be in a special education classroom? A special school?

Fortunately, for a lot of inflexible-explosive children, these questions never need to be answered. For reasons that are not entirely clear, many of the children and adolescents with whom I work do *not* evidence serious signs of vapor lock or

meltdowns at school. I've got a few theories about this phenomenon:

- *The embarrassment theory*: They'd be embarrassed if they melted down in front of their friends; they've been melting down in front of their parents practically since the word go, so it's not a big deal. Parents can't hope to replicate the embarrassment factor at home, so embarrassment doesn't prevent the child from melting down at home. It's also possible the child simply feels safer melting down in front of his parents.

- *The tightly wound theory*: The child has put so much energy into holding it together at school that he becomes unraveled the minute he gets home, fueled further by normal late-afternoon fatigue and hunger.

- *The herd-mentality theory*: Because the school day tends to be relatively structured and predictable, it can actually be user-friendlier than unstructured downtime at home. For instance, if the child becomes confused about where he's supposed to be or what he's supposed to be doing while he's at school, he need look no further than his classmates for cues. Parents can't hope to replicate the structure found at school in the home environment.

- *The chemical theory*: Teachers and peers often are the primary beneficiaries of pharmacotherapy, but the medications may have worn off by late afternoon or early evening.

I'm certain there are other possibilities. Of course, just because a child isn't melting down at school doesn't mean that school isn't contributing to meltdowns that occur elsewhere. Lots of things can happen at school—being teased by other children, feeling socially isolated or rejected, feeling frustrated and embarrassed over struggles on certain academic tasks, being misunderstood by the teacher—to fuel meltdowns at home. And homework can extend school frustrations well after the bell rings at the end of the school day. So schools aren't off the hook for helping to achieve a globally user-friendly environment even if they don't see the child at his worst.

Nonetheless, there are kids who actually *do* melt down in one form or another at school. You may recall that Casey, one of the children you read about in Chapter 4, had a pattern of running out of the classroom when he became frustrated by a challenging academic task or difficult interaction with a peer. When he wasn't running out of the room he was melting down in the room, turning red, crying, screaming, crumpling paper, breaking pencils, falling on the floor, and refusing to work. Needless to say, because his low frustration tolerance caused him to shut down quickly on even mildly challenging tasks, there were concerns about whether his learning was suffering.

Danny, another of the children you've read about, was also capable of the occasional meltdown at school. On one particularly memorable day, the teacher designated him to hand out doughnuts to his classmates after recess. Following recess he hurried back to the classroom to hand out the doughnuts. But a parent-aide was already in the room and insisted on being the doughnut distributor. Danny attempted to explain to the parent that he had been assigned the task of giving out the doughnuts, but the parent would not be deterred. The shift in cognitive set demanded by this scenario was more than Danny could handle. Kaboom.

Teachers and schools have little choice but to think about how to handle the Caseys and Dannys. We live in the age of the inclusion movement, which I endorse wholeheartedly.

This movement, which has affected certain parts of the country more than others, has encouraged the practice of providing additional services for children with special behavioral and educational needs inside of the mainstream classroom, thereby reducing—if it's done right—the stigma of having a different style of learning or behaving. Thus, the typical public school classroom now has multiple special needs students, some of whom have disorders their teachers have never even heard of, let alone worked with, before. Teachers must therefore have knowledge not only of the curriculum, but also of the different emotional and behavioral issues presented by some of their students. Unfortunately, in many instances teachers feel—justifiably—that they are not being provided with the kind of support or additional training they need to function effectively with their special-needs students and within the altered composition of their classrooms.

It is against this backdrop that teachers are asked to help inflexible-explosive children overcome their difficulties. And school personnel are as prone to back-end interventions as are any other adults, especially in relation to dealing with children whose frustrations cause them to disrupt the classroom process, behave disrespectfully toward adults, and become physically or verbally aggressive. School-initiated, back-end interventions have the same potential for creating an adversarial process and alienating children as do many parent-initiated interventions. I receive many phone calls from school administrators telling me that their disciplinary practices aren't working very well for the students to whom these practices are most frequently being applied, and asking for help. Thus, the need for a Plan B seems evident to me, for we have little to show for all the consequences—detentions, suspensions, expulsions, and so forth—that have been administered to the inflexible-explosive students who have passed through our schools.

I'm often astounded to hear that the primary reason such interventions are invoked is *for the benefit of the other students.* The rationale goes something like this: "We have to set an example for all our students; even if suspension doesn't help Rickey [whom you'll meet later in this chapter], at least it sets an example for our other students. We need to let them know that we take safety seriously at our school." This rationale begs the following question: "What message do you give the other students at your school if you continue to apply interventions that aren't helping Rickey behave more adaptively?" My answer: "That you're actually not sure how to help Rickey behave more adaptively."

Question: "What's the likelihood that the students who aren't inflexible-explosive will become inflexible-explosive were it not for the example we're making of Rickey?"

Answer: "As a general rule, slim and none."

Question: "What message do we give if we continue to apply strategies that aren't working?"

Answer: "We don't understand you, and we can't help you."

Question: "Under what circumstances do we have better odds of helping Rickey learn and practice better ways of dealing with his inflexibility and low frustration tolerance: in school or suspended from school?"

Answer: "In school."

Question: "Why do many schools continue to apply reactive, back-end interventions that aren't working for their inflexible-explosive students?"

Answer: "They aren't sure what else to do."

Question: "What happens to students to whom these interventions are counterproductively applied for many years?"

Answer: "They become more alienated and fall further outside the social fabric of the school."

Question: "Isn't this the parents' job?"

Answer: "Helping a child deal more adaptively with frustration does not fall exclusively under the parents' purview. In fact, it's the children whose parents are struggling—with poverty, psychopathology, unemployment, and so on—who may need extra help from schools the most. Helping these children is everyone's job."

Question [slightly off-topic]: "In our society, what is the ultimate back-end intervention, and how well does it train flexibility and the tolerance of frustration?"

Answer: "Jail. Very poorly."

Question: "Is there any way in which the other students might actually be able to help Rickey with his inflexibility and explosiveness?"

Answer: "I'm glad you asked!"

Time for Plan B.

Let's take the same principles that we've been applying to inflexibility-explosiveness at home and see how they might look at school. And let's begin with some of our main themes:

- Flexibility and frustration tolerance are *skills*. Some students are predisposed to have difficulty responding to the world in an adaptable, flexible manner. Thus, these students can be exceptionally challenging and frustrating to teach.

- Because inept parenting, poor motivation, attention seeking, and lack of appreciation for who's boss may not be the best explanations for these students' difficulties, standard teaching and motivational practices may be mismatched to their needs. These students may require a different approach.

- How we perceive and understand these students' inflexibility-explosiveness is directly related to how we'll ultimately respond to it (*"Your explanation guides your intervention"*). If we respond to the student in an inflexible, angry manner, then we will increase the likelihood of vapor lock and meltdowns, facilitate adversarial teacher-student interactions, and reduce the likelihood of improving the student's flexibility.

- I am more optimistic about a teacher's ability to respond differently to a student's inflexibility than I am about the student's ability to improve his capacity to be flexible, at least initially.

- If you create a user-friendlier school environment for an inflexible-explosive student and concentrate more on the front end than the back end, interactions between school staff and the student should improve. Once things begin to improve a little, the student should become more receptive to, and have a greater capacity to benefit from, more direct methods for improving his flexibility and tolerance of frustration.

Next, let's apply the components of a user-friendlier environment described in Chapter 6 to the classroom:

A user-friendlier school environment would be one in which all the adults who interact with the child have a clear understanding of his unique difficulties. Before and when an inflexible-explosive child is stuck in the red haze of inflexibility, lots of adults in a school can serve as potential helpers. And lots of adults can take on the role of enemy by failing to take into account the student's limitations in the domains of flexibility and frustration tolerance. Parents are not the only ones who can act as temporary guides to steer an inflexible-explosive child around, or help him think through, frustrations; teachers can step up to the plate as well. Coming to a common view of a child and making sure everyone is on the same wavelength requires a lot of teamwork within the school environment. It's important for all the adults who are likely to interact with the student to be brought into the mix.

Parent-teacher collaboration is absolutely essential. When things are going poorly at school, parents have a tendency to blame the school staff, and school staff have a tendency to blame the parents. This blaming misses the important point: The child is frustrating *all* of us, and *none* of us has done an incredible job of helping him yet, so let's see if we can put our heads together and come up with a plan that incorporates the best we all have to offer.

Some teachers are eager for a quick fix. But there is no quick fix for an inflexible-explosive student. And we can't jump into intervention until we have an answer to the question, "What's this kid's deal?" Restated, we have to put the hard work into looking closely at the pathways that seem to be associated with a student's inflexibility and low frustration tolerance before we'll even have a clue about what interventions might make the most sense. Any attempt to intervene before being able to answer "What's this kid's deal?" is akin to firing a shotgun randomly into the air and hoping to hit something good. And reaching a clear understanding of a child begins with competent assessment.

When assessments are performed by school systems, they are often initiated by the classroom teacher because he or she has some concerns about the child's functioning in the classroom. As you've already read, a diagnosis is not the primary goal of an assessment, although it may be an important by-product. Nor should determining whether a child qualifies for special education services be the main thrust. Once again, the primary goal of an assessment is to achieve the fullest possible understanding of the child and the school environment in which he functions. Even if no learning disabilities are uncovered and no diagnoses are rendered, the assessment process is not complete. We still have a student whose teacher has serious concerns about his functioning! We still need to understand the factors underlying his difficulties in the classroom! Once we truly understand, logical interventions often become evident.

Let's take homework as an example. Many inflexible-explosive children find homework to be remarkably frustrating because they don't have any brain energy left after a long day at school, their medication has worn off, they have learning problems that make homework completion an agonizing task, or because homework—especially long-term assignments—requires a lot of organization and planning. Thus, it's no accident that these children often exhibit some of their most extreme inflexibility and explosiveness while they are trying to do homework.

Do these difficulties render some children incapable of completing the same homework assignments as their classmates? Yes. Is it always possible to effectively address these difficulties? No. Does having a child melt down routinely over homework help him feel more successful about doing homework? No. Are these difficulties a good reason to alter or adjust homework assignments? Yes. I've yet to be convinced that the best way to instill a good work ethic in a child—or to help his parents become actively and productively involved in his education—is by inducing and enduring five hours of meltdowns every school night. The best way to instill a good work ethic is to assign homework that is both sufficiently challenging and doable in terms of both quantity and content.

How can homework be altered or adjusted in a manner that brings it into the doable range for an inflexible-explosive child? Probably in the same ways that are useful for children with other types of disabilities. I've found that once teachers are made aware of the horrific battles that are taking place between parents and children over homework they've assigned, most are willing to make all kinds of adaptations to homework assignments for their inflexible-explosive students. Good teachers know that although it would be nicer and more efficient to have all the students in a classroom have the exact same learning styles and capabilities, it never works out that way. So it's always necessary to adapt lessons and assignments to individual learners. Inflexibility-explosiveness is as good a reason to adapt schoolwork as any other type of learning disability. Thus, when warranted, teachers usually agree to eliminate unnecessary repetition from homework assignments (such as permitting a student to do five multiplication items instead of twenty); to place limits on the amount of time a child spends on homework each night; and to establish homework priorities among assignments, so the more important assignments are completed first, and the child isn't penalized for not finishing the less important assignments.

I've also found that most teachers are willing to allow students to produce work in a manner that keeps them from becoming tripped up by their learning difficulties. For example, if a teacher wanted to have students practice writing skills and an inflexible-explosive student became extremely frustrated by the physical demands of writing, the teacher might permit the student to complete his work on a word processor or by dictating his thoughts to a parent, sibling, or fellow classmate. Although it would be important to make sure that the student continued to work on writing skills, it would be even more important to make sure that our expectations took into account both the student's writing capabilities *and* level of frustration.

> *Inflexibility-explosiveness is as good a reason to adapt schoolwork as any other type of learning disability.*

Finally, it's crucial for parents and teachers to communicate clearly and continuously about homework, so the teacher is well aware of the assignments that routinely frustrate the child. If a teacher isn't aware of a child's frustration on specific tasks, she or he can't be expected to make appropriate adjustments.

These steps often make homework more doable for many inflexible-explosive children. But, in some cases, the battles over homework persist even though homework has been made user-friendlier for the child. Sometimes these continued battles are a signal that the parents are not, and may never be, the ideal homework monitors. In such instances, I often recommend that the child complete homework either at school, under the supervision of an adult whose feedback and assistance is less objectionable to the child (many schools have "homework clubs" that can serve this purpose), or at home, with the assistance of a high-school aged "homework helper" or hired tutor. Such assistance often improves communication between the parents and child and permits the parents to focus on the more important aspects of parenting.

In a user-friendlier school environment, the adults try to reduce the overall demands for flexibility and frustration tolerance being placed on the inflexible-explosive student. In other words, there has to be a Basket B and C in the classroom. I'm told by my educator colleagues that good teachers are able to maintain a balance between the common needs of all their students and the specific needs of individual students. In other words, good teachers do a good job of teaching individual students within the context of a group. I've seen that it is possible to reduce demands for some students without stigmatizing them and without alienating others. One way to do so is to create a "responsive" classroom, which you'll read about later in this chapter.

A user-friendlier school environment would also be one in which adults try to identify—in advance—specific situations that may routinely lead to inflexible-explosive episodes. This theme is critical to your attempts to intervene proactively, on the front end. As you've read, it's important for the adults who interact with the student at school to take a close look at the specific situations—content areas, methods of producing work, contexts (large- and small-group discussion and instruction, independent seat work, working with a partner, story and circle time, recess, and lunch)—that may cause significant frustration.

Then the options are the same: In Basket A, go important issues (such as safety) that are worth inducing and enduring meltdowns over. In Basket B, go important issues that require collaborative problem solving or roadmapping. In Basket C, go unimportant issues that aren't even worth bringing up.

In a user-friendlier school environment, adults read the warning signals and take quick action when these signals are present. As you've read, some inflexible-explosive students refuse to work when they're challenged by certain tasks. Danny would slump down in his seat, cross his arms, and announce that he could do no more (at those moments, he was probably right). Those were the warning signals. Danny was lucky: His teacher didn't push him when it was clear he was in vapor lock; instead, she tried to help him articulate what he was frustrated about. Sometimes Danny was able to explain the problem immediately; sometimes he couldn't. Sometimes his attempts to explain were spiced with inappropriate language (luckily, none of his classmates had virgin ears). Once in awhile, Danny's agitation seemed to worsen when his teacher tried to help him. At these times, the teacher would back off, give Danny some time to chill, and come back to the issue when the odds of successful thinking improved. Over time, Danny began to trust that his teacher understood his tendency to get stuck and that she had a good sense about when he was apt to do so. He became better at verbalizing his difficulties and came to appreciate that the teacher seemed able to help him get unstuck. Often, before the teacher introduced an assignment to the entire class, she would quietly let Danny know she thought he'd have some trouble with it and reassured him that she would help him get started (this, of course, is an example of the *sine qua non* of proactive, front-end thinking: intervening *before* there's trouble). Sometimes she had another student help Danny.

Just remember, the burden for recognizing the early warning signs falls on the adults who are interacting with the student. It's critical to read these early warning signs and take action while there's still some coherence to work with to prevent these hints from turning into something much bigger, uglier, time-consuming, and disruptive to the teaching process.

In a user-friendlier school environment, adults can interpret incoherent behaviors for what they really are: incoherent behaviors. The same theme as before: A lot of the words that come out of a student's mouth when he's frustrated are just mental debris. Your job is to get past the style of delivery and get to the actual message: I'M STUCK! HELP!

RING OUT THE OLD

Rickey [age thirteen]: I'm not working on this assignment right now.

Teacher: Well, then your grade will reflect both your attitude and your lack of effort.

Rickey: I don't give a damn about my grades, man. I can't do this crap.

Teacher: Your mouth just got you a detention, young man. And I don't want students in my classroom who don't do their work. Anything else you'd like to say?

Rickey: Yeah ... This class sucks.

Teacher: Nor do I need to listen to this. You need to go to the assistant principal's office ... now.

BRING IN THE NEW

Rickey: I'm not working on this assignment right now.

Teacher: Well, there must be something about the assignment that's hard for you. Let's see if we can figure it out.

Rickey: Forget it ... I can't do this! Just leave me alone! Damn!

Teacher: Rickey, listen a second ... I know you have trouble with writing and spelling and you get very frustrated when you have to do assignments where you have to write and spell. Let's see if we can find a way for you to do the important part of the assignment—letting me know what you thought of the story you just heard, *which is something you're very good at—without you getting all frustrated about the writing and spelling part.*

Rickey: How?

Teacher: Well, maybe Darren would help you write down your thoughts. You could sort of dictate your thoughts to him.

Rickey: It's not worth it. No way.

Teacher: Oh yeah . . . I sometimes forget you're embarrassed about how you spell. Why don't we have you and Darren do the assignment as a team and just make sure he does the writing part?

Rickey: You won't tell him I can't spell?

Teacher: Not if you don't want me to.

Rickey: Darren, let's do this thing together!

BETTER STILL

Rickey: I'm not working on this assignment right now.

Teacher: Why, because it has spelling and writing? Are you forgetting how we've decided to help you when you have to do assignments like that?

Rickey: Oh, yeah. Darren, get your butt over here and let's do this thing together!

In a user-friendlier school environment, adults can also understand how they themselves may be fueling a student's inflexibility-explosiveness. Are there any teachers out there who have, in one way or another, fueled a student's inflexibility and explosiveness? By misjudging his true capabilities? By assuming that compliance and flexibility and a tolerance of frustration are skills all children automatically possess? By believing that the student's difficulties all trace back to the home environment? By not being an especially wonderful role model for the other children in the class on how to interact with a child whose needs differ from the norm? By believing that a student's difficulties were totally accounted for by poor motivation, a bad attitude, or attention seeking? By creating a classroom environment that was distinctly *un*friendly? By communicating with the student in a manner that promoted an adversarial pattern of interactions? By expecting administrative staff to pull out the sledgehammer every time a student was sent down to the office? OK, so maybe you hadn't read this book yet. Do it differently the next time.

In a user-friendlier school environment, adults try to use a more accurate common language to describe various elements of the student's inflexibility-explosiveness. Once again, the terminology we use for describing these students to themselves is crucial; since they don't necessarily have a well-developed vocabulary for describing themselves, they may start to use—and believe—our vocabulary. That can be good or bad, depending on the accuracy and usefulness of our vocabulary. I strongly encourage the use of certain terms to describe these children: *easily frustrated, difficulty thinking things through, difficulty shifting gears,* and so forth.

The vision thing. In my research, my colleagues and I have interviewed many teachers, so we know that different teachers have different visions for what they hope to achieve during a school year, both with individual students and with the class as a whole. Because teachers often spend more time with a child than his own parents do, they can have a very potent impact. In this important respect, I envy teachers because they get a lot more time each day with the child, while I get him, on average, only for an hour a week. Can an inflexible-explosive student be a productive, respected member of the class? Is it possible for one teacher in a class of twenty to thirty students—many of whom also have special needs—to devote the time to meet the needs of such a student?

The concept of the responsive classroom is an intuitively appealing vision that can help teachers answer these questions in the affirmative. This vision is described more fully in *Teaching Children to Care: Management in the Responsive Classroom*, by a teacher, Ruth Sidney Charney. Responsive classrooms are those in which teachers place as heavy an emphasis on a "social curriculum" as they do on the academic curriculum (mathematics, reading, writing, and so on). In such classrooms, individual differences, such as great reading skills, poor writing skills, great athletic skills, poor spelling skills, and—why not?—inflexibility and low frustration tolerance—are celebrated and accentuated.

Some of the same themes I discussed with regard to families apply to responsive classrooms as well. Everyone in the classroom has strengths that can be used to help other students, and everyone has areas of weakness on which they need help. In the responsive classroom, everyone gets what he or she needs. Thus, no one is singled out and stigmatized. Indeed, because of the emphasis on individual differences, students learn to help one another and learn that each classroom is an integral thread in the fabric of a community of learners. Planned and unplanned discussions (sometimes called "social conferences") focusing on social interactions are common. Teachers interrupt other ongoing lessons to process important social issues that have suddenly erupted in the classroom. Conflict resolution—negotiating, dealing with frustration, and generating alternative solutions to problems—can be an integral focus of such discussions. All students benefit from such discussions, but especially those who need it most. In such classrooms, teachers act as role models and provide frequent opportunities for practicing social interactions and helping one another, including peer tutoring, judicious seating arrangements, and cooperative learning. A responsive classroom sets the stage for the teacher to have a different Basket A, B, and C for each student. Rather than being overwhelmed (exhausted is probably still in the mix!), the teacher has a sense about the unique needs of each student and a framework for trying to meet those needs within the context of the a larger group.

I was in a responsive classroom observing one of the inflexible-explosive children with whom I was working and was pleased to see him helping another student with her math (the child with whom I was working was strong in math). Several minutes later, it was time to switch activities, and, predictably, this child became stuck. The girl he'd been assisting calmed him down, talked to him, and helped him move on to the new activity, all under the watchful gaze of the teacher. Then the girl, apparently recognizing that the stranger (me) observing the class might not have comprehended what was going on, came over to me and said softly, "He just gets a little frustrated sometimes." I nearly fell over.

Because of the severity of their behavior, inflexible-explosive students tend to be "defined" by this behavior, rather than by their many positive characteristics. A classroom is, without question, one of the ideal places to accentuate the positives and build alliances between these students and adults. Alienation is the by-product of the failure to do so.

So when teachers tell me that they'd like to be helpful to the inflexible-explosive student in their classroom but simply can't devote sufficient time to him, given the demands of the other students, I tell them about the responsive classroom and how it's possible to get help from the least likely but most available and willing candidates: the other kids.

Teacher: "I can't have different sets of rules for different kids. If I let one child get out of or get away with something my other students will want to as well."

First off, you probably have different expectations for different children already, so in classrooms, as in families, fair does not mean equal anyway. For example, while it would be nice if all your students could read at grade level, not every student can. So you probably make accommodations and provide assistance for those who can't. If one of the other students inquires about why a student is receiving such accommodations and assistance, you have the perfect opportunity to do some educating: "Everyone in our classroom gets what he or she needs. If someone needs help with something, we all try to help him or her. And everyone in our class needs help with something."

Talking the talk and walking the walk are no different when the developmental deficit is inflexibility and a low tolerance for frustration. So our response to the student who asks why an inflexible-explosive classmate is receiving some sort of special accommodations and assistance would sound very similar: "Everyone in our classroom gets what he or she needs. If someone needs help with something, we all try to help him or her. Because you're very good at handling frustration, I bet you could be very helpful to Johnny the next time he gets frustrated."

I've yet to come across a situation in which a child who typically behaved adaptively decided to behave inappropriately because accommodations were being made for an inflexible-explosive child in the classroom. As I already mentioned, it follows that punishing a child to set an example for or to be fair to the others—especially when there's no expectation that the punishment will be an effective intervention for the child being punished—makes little sense. In a community of learners, the academic or behavioral idiosyncrasies of one student are an opportunity for his or her classmates to help and learn, not to follow suit.

Children are actually pretty good at understanding the "fair does not mean equal" concept and at making exceptions for children who need help; in my experience, it's much more common that adults are the ones struggling with the principle.

Except for some extreme circumstances—discussed in Chapter 13—inflexible-explosive children *can* function in regular education classrooms, often without a great deal of support. As you know, this usually requires a highly collaborative effort involving the child's parents, special education coordinator, school and outside psychologists, guidance counselor, principal, occupational therapist, speech therapist, and psychopharmacologist. All these adults have important and unique pieces of information to add to the understanding of the child and treatment picture.

The teachers know what they see at school and what they're doing to help the child be more successful and manage frustration more adaptively. The parents know best how things are going at home, can provide insight as to the child's perceptions of how things are going at school, and often have a clear sense as to which homework assignments are causing the greatest frustration. The special education coordinator knows what services the school system may be able to provide over and above those already being offered. The psychologists, speech and language therapist, occupational therapist, and guidance counselor can offer additional insights into specific areas of concern and the factors that seem to be fueling the child's frustration, whether through psychoeducational testing, neuropsychological testing, psychological testing, additional evaluations, or conversations with the child. The principal can open a lot of doors in a school; if special arrangements need to be made for a child, the principal is the person who can oversee the logistics. And you already know what a psychopharmacologist can do. It's important that the psychopharmacologist be an integral part of the process; I've never been enthusiastic about secondhand information, especially with regard to the adjustments required for optimal medical care. Why so few school systems have an established relationship with a consulting psychopharmacologist has always been a mystery to me.

With all that talent in the room, an understanding of a child and a consensus regarding a cohesive treatment plan—what the child is capable of right now, what issues are essential to address right now, what situations to avoid, what situations to adjust, what skills to build, when to increase supervision, and what treatments to bring to bear—should emerge, guided, I hope, by many of the principles in this book. Even if the initial treatment plan goes well, the whole crew should reconvene every two to four weeks or so to revisit the issues, adjust the intervention strategies, and revise the goals. Over time, if things go really well, fewer meetings will be necessary. Before the beginning of each school year, the new teachers should be brought into the loop to ensure the smoothest possible transition.

The tragic shootings that have occurred recently in our public schools underscore several important points: 1) there are many students who are capable of committing acts of unimaginable violence; 2) identifying children at risk for such acts must become a high priority and must involve the entire student body (most of the students who were involved in these shootings gave advance warning of their intentions to their fellow students); 3) we must redouble our efforts to find ways of ensuring that all students feel they are an important part of the social fabric of their schools; 4) if they are to remain in public school, such students will require the type of collaborative teamwork described above; and 5) suspending or expelling such students, or handing them over to the police, does not satisfactorily address their difficulties. Are any of the students who have committed these horrific acts inflexible-explosive? Not knowing any of them personally, I can't say for sure. Is it fairly clear that they weren't able to think of better ways to handle whatever problems they were having at school? The evidence is before us.

It is indeed the case that some inflexible-explosive children aren't able—despite everyone's best efforts—to stay safe within the school environment. More on this in Chapter 13.

DRAMA IN REAL LIFE
EDGAR'S BASKETS

Edgar was an inflexible-explosive fourth grader with ADHD, expressive language delays, and sensory integration issues. Though he was apparently well medicated, he still struggled with tasks requiring sustained attention, particularly those involving written expression. His school system had provided him with a part-time classroom aide, with whom Edgar had worked reasonably well since second grade. But in the fourth grade, he was assigned to a different aide. Early on, he began refusing the help she offered, insisting that he didn't want to be different from the other children. As the school year progressed, Edgar's resistance to being helped worsened, and his academic performance and behavior suffered as a result. When his teacher and aide permitted him to try working independently on lessons with which Edgar had difficulty, he completed very little work and tended to wander around the room, interrupting the work of other students. When his teachers insisted that he accept help, he often exploded and ended up in the principal's office.

Needless to say, Edgar's teachers, principal, and school psychologist were eager to see Edgar receive the help he needed. They were curious about the "basket thinking" that was helping Edgar explode a lot less at home.

"Basket thinking is a way of prioritizing our goals for children who aren't able to meet all our priorities," I explained. "It also helps us train some very important skills, such as perspective-taking and problem solving."

"How would we use this system with Edgar?" asked his teacher.

"Well, we need to think about what Edgar is capable of and what our priorities are for him," I said. "Because he's so easily frustrated, and has difficulties in so many areas—social, academic, and behavioral—we need to be really judicious about what we're asking of him. In Basket A are very high priorities that Edgar must do. In Basket B are important things on which there's some give and take. And Basket C includes things we're not going to pay much heed to right now. There are a lot of things that Edgar needs help with, but what are our top priorities?"

"He's so sensitive about looking different," said the school psychologist. "But I don't know if there's any way around it."

"He really needs the help," said the teacher. "Without it, he gets practically nothing done. I'm really becoming concerned about whether he's learning anything."

"He won't even try to write in cursive," said the aide. "Even when he's willing to write, it's in print. And he refuses to show his work in math. He gets correct answers, but he can't tell you how he got them."

"I can't let him keep disrupting the classroom," said the principal. "I have other students in there whose learning is suffering because of Edgar's outbursts."

"I'm very worried about how his peers react to him," said Edgar's father. "He hasn't had a kid over to the house to play in a very long time."

"Well," I said, taking a deep breath. "That's quite an agenda. Edgar's not going to be able to work diligently on all those things at once. My personal opinion is that his accepting help is probably our top priority. He's not learning anything or getting any work done without help, and he's being disruptive to the learning of others when he's not working. I think accepting help goes in Basket A."

"I agree," said the teacher. "That would be like killing several birds with the same stone."

"Now, the last time I talked to Edgar," I said, "he told me that looking different isn't the only reason he doesn't like getting help. He said the help is provided at unpredictable times. So I think Edgar would experience the help as user-friendlier if it was provided on a predictable schedule."

"That's easy enough," said the principal. "We just have to decide what work he needs the most help on and what work he can do on his own. Then we can schedule the help during the times he needs it the most."

"Great," I said. "What work won't he even attempt without help?"

"Anything involving writing," said the teacher.

"Do we want the help provided in the class or outside the class?" I asked.

"He hates leaving the classroom," said the aide. "But he hates having me work with him in front of the other kids even worse. And he gets less done when he gets help in the class."

"It sounds like leaving the room for help is in Basket A," I said. We then discussed a daily schedule for receiving help. We also agreed that writing in cursive was, for the time being, in Basket C. In other words, we concurred that it was more important to have Edgar complete more work than to have him write in cursive.

"How are we going to get him to accept the help without getting upset?" asked the father.

"Ah, that's where you come in," I said.

"Me? What can I do?" asked the father.

"If Edgar doesn't cooperate with leaving the room to get help as scheduled, these good folks here at school are going to call you so you can talk to him," I said.

"Better you than me," the mother said under her breath.

"What would I say to him?" asked the father.

"You'll remind him of the necessity of accepting help and tell him you expect him to go work with the aide the minute he gets off the phone with you," I said. "If he balks, you'll let him know that he has no choice and that he won't be a happy camper if you get home from work and hear that he didn't accept the help."

"That's powerful," said the principal. "That's a lot more potent than my having him sit in the office."

"I can do that," said the father.

"I'd be surprised if he balks at accepting help from now on," I said. "But that's probably the only thing that's in Basket A for now," I said.

"I don't know," said the teacher. "I think his saying mean things to other kids belongs in Basket A, too."

"I'm not sure about that," said the principal. "He's a very impulsive kid, and I'm not sure he's aware that he's saying something hurtful before he does it."

"What's he say?" I asked.

"Often he'll say, right out loud, in front of the entire class, that someone's answer was stupid," said the teacher. "Stuff like that."

"To tell you the truth, knowing Edgar, I'd probably put that in Basket B," I said. "My bet is that Edgar is simply being too 'honest.' He's certainly not very good at being politically correct."

The parents laughed. "There isn't a politically correct bone in his body," said the mother.

"My bet is that Edgar would be better off if we gave him different words for saying the same thing," I said.

"Like what?" asked the aide.

"Well, a lot of us would love to tell people that something they just said was pretty stupid," I said. "But what we say instead is something like, 'I'd like to add something to that answer.' " I just don't think Edgar has the language wherewithal to say what he's thinking in a way that isn't so honest. But I also think that's a lesson the entire class could benefit from—you know, not saying exactly what you're thinking but getting the point across in a kinder manner."

"So you mean we could have class discussions about the issue?" said the teacher. "I like that idea. But what should I do if Edgar says something mean in the middle of a lesson?"

"Stop the lesson briefly, suggest what you think Edgar—or anyone else—might have been trying to say," I said.

"This I can do," said the teacher. "I like it much better than sending him out into the hall."

"Sending him out in the hall would be fine if you thought he had good political skills that you were trying to motivate him to use," I said. "But, you're exactly right, sending him out into the hall doesn't help much if the real problem is that he doesn't have the words."

"OK, one last issue," said the aide. "What do we do about his wandering around the room?"

"Well, we're already doing something about that by having him do his most difficult work with you," I said. "But my sense is that Edgar needs more frequent breaks than other kids. I think we ought to give him a certain number of discretionary breaks every day, so he'll know we're aware of the fact that he needs breaks. And I think we need to identify certain things that are OK for him to do during these breaks. But he needs to know that the instant he disturbs other students, the break is over. Are there things in the room he can do during these breaks?"

"He loves the science center," said the teacher. "If he'd go to the science area and not disrupt other kids, I'd be very happy."

"Would the other kids mind that he gets breaks and they don't?" I asked.

"They're accustomed to his being out of his seat," said the teacher. "I think they'd be relieved just to have him not bothering them."

"I think we've got a plan," I said. "There are some things we're not attending to right now. But I think we've identified the most important issues. By being very judicious about what's most important, and by thinking about how we're going to deal with each issue on the front end, I think the stage is set for things to go well."

"When should we meet again?" asked the school psychologist.

"Let's give this two weeks," said the principal. "We still need to present all of this to Edgar. But I like the idea of having a plan to deal with these issues before he falls apart, rather than responding after he falls apart. Let's give it a shot."

DRAMA IN REAL LIFE

"RUNNING ON EMPTY"

"Dr. Greene, we can't let Casey keep running out of the room," the school principal said gravely. "It's dangerous, and we're responsible for his safety."

It was March of Casey's first-grade year, and the principal was presiding over a meeting that included Casey's teacher, occupational therapist, guidance counselor, special education coordinator, parents, and me. Casey was blowing up a lot less often at home, but there were still some kinks to work out at school.

"Well," I said, "as you know, in some ways Casey's leaving the classroom is more adaptive than some of the other things he could be doing in response to frustration—like tearing the room apart. But, I agree, it's very important that he stay safe."

"What's making Casey act this way?" asked the classroom teacher. "What's his diagnosis?"

"Let's just say that Casey is very poorly self-regulated—like a lot of students with ADHD—and that he is easily frustrated and easily overwhelmed," I said.

"So why does he run out of the room?" asked the teacher.

"His running out of the room is probably a signal that his frustration with a particular task has become overwhelming," I said. "Does that correspond to your experiences with him?"

"Oh, absolutely," said the teacher. "He does fine on the things he's good at. But when he's confronted with something that challenges him or requires extra effort, he seems to become frustrated very quickly."

"I think we need to think about how to help Casey 'hang in there' when he's frustrated so he doesn't run out of the room," I said. "I also think we need to hone in on the specific situations that are causing him significant frustration, so we can decide which ones to avoid, which ones to adapt, and which ones to work harder on. But he may not stop running out of the room completely yet, so we may need a place where he can go to settle down when he does run out, so he doesn't end up in the parking lot."

The special education coordinator chimed in. "I think we should have consequences for leaving the classroom," she said. "I don't think it's good for the other kids to see him leave when he gets frustrated."

"Why, have any of the other kids expressed a desire or shown an inclination to leave the classroom when they're frustrated?" I asked.

"No," said the teacher.

"Do we think Casey is leaving the classroom because he'd rather be out in the hallway all by himself?" I asked.

"I don't think so," said the teacher. "He's always very eager to come back in as soon as he's settled down."

"Do we think that punishing him after he leaves the classroom will have any effect on his behavior the next time he's frustrated and feels the need to leave the classroom?" I asked.

"I don't know," said the teacher. "It's almost like he's in a completely different zone when he's frustrated."

"Then I'm not certain why we'd punish Casey for leaving the classroom," I said. "Especially if the main reason we're doing it is to set an example for the other kids."

"So what do you suggest we do when he gets frustrated?" asked the special education coordinator.

"I think most of our energy should be focused on what to do before Casey gets frustrated, not after," I said. "When Casey's frustration with a particular task or situation is predictable, we can anticipate his frustration and steer him around it. We can do things to make those tasks more doable for him, making them more stimulating, limiting the amount of time he has to spend on them, seeing if he'll accept help from one of his classmates . . . I think there are a lot of ways to make these tasks more manageable for him. When the frustration is unpredictable, I think we need a place for Casey to go to calm down if your initial efforts to calm him down don't do the trick. I don't think he's at the point yet where he's able to talk things through when he's frustrated, although we're working on it. Luckily, he's pretty good at calming down on his own if we leave him alone for a while. We have to find ways to let him do that while still making sure he's safe. So for now, our top priority is to keep meltdowns to a minimum, even at the expense of his learning. It's the meltdowns that are getting in the way of Casey's learning anyway."

Things went quite well for Casey for the last few months of that school year. At the beginning of the next school year, the group reassembled, including his old and new teachers, reviewed what worked and what didn't the previous school year, and agreed to try to do more of the same, while focusing on helping Casey complete more schoolwork. Although we expected some rough moments as Casey adjusted to his new teachers and classmates, it wasn't until two months into the school year that he had his first series of meltdowns. The special education coordinator hastily called a meeting.

"We think Casey has regressed," the principal said. "He looks as bad as he did last school year."

"Actually, we think he looks a lot better than he did last school year," said Casey's father. "In fact, we were happy he started off as well as he did. He was really looking forward to going back to school."

"I think we need to revisit the idea of consequences," said the special education coordinator. "Do you folks say anything to him about this behavior at home?" she asked the parents.

"Of course we do!" said the mother, a little offended. "We let him know very clearly that it is unacceptable, and he gets very upset because he knows that already. Believe me, this is being addressed at home."

"Is he melting down a lot at home?" asked the principal.

"We haven't had a major meltdown in months," said the father. "We'd almost forgotten how bad things used to be."

"I still think Casey needs to know that at school, life doesn't just go on like nothing happened after he has a meltdown," said the principal.

"I agree," said the special education coordinator.

"What did you have in mind?" I asked.

"I think after he blows up, he needs to sit in my office and talk it over," said the principal. "And until he does, he shouldn't be permitted to rejoin his classmates."

"I don't think he's ready for that yet," I said.

"Well," said the special education director, "whether he's ready or not, it's important that the other students see that we disapprove of Casey's behavior."

"His classmates don't already know you disapprove of his behavior?" I asked.

"We think we need to send a stronger message," the special education coordinator said. "We think he can control this behavior."

"I think he needs something more than a stronger message," I said. "Just remember, we shouldn't use consequences just for the sake of using consequences or just because it's the first intervention that comes to mind but, rather, because we believe consequences will put something in the forefront of Casey's brain that will help him refrain from doing things we wish he wouldn't when he becomes frustrated. If we don't believe that will happen, consequences are only likely to make him more frustrated."

"We have to do what we think is right in our school," said the principal, ending the discussion.

Casey had a minor meltdown two weeks later. He was escorted to the principal's office. The principal tried hard to get Casey to talk about his frustration. Casey couldn't. The principal insisted, setting the stage for a massive, one-hour meltdown that included spitting, swearing, and destroying property in the principal's office. Another meeting was hastily called.

"I've never been treated that way by a student!" said the principal.

"Casey's going to have to understand that we can't accept that kind of behavior."

"Casey already knows that behavior is unacceptable!" said the mother. "Sometimes he can talk about what's frustrating him right away—and that's a recent development—but most of the time he can't talk about it until much later, and then we have to give him some time to collect himself before we try to help him."

"I tried that," said the principal. "When he was in my office I told him that I wasn't going to talk to him until he was good and ready."

"How did he respond to that?" I asked.

"That's when he spit on me," said the principal.

"I guess that tells you that something about what you said made him more frustrated, not less," I said.

"You don't think having him sit in my office will eventually help?" asked the principal. "I'm very uncomfortable having him blow up and then watch him go happily out to recess and rejoin the other kids without there being some kind of consequence. I'm struggling with this."

"I think sitting in your office would work great if Casey experienced it as a place where he could calm down, rather than as a place where he's asked to do something he can't do yet—namely, talk about things immediately—or where he feels he's being punished for something he already knows he shouldn't have done."

"So why doesn't he just tell me he knows his behavior is unacceptable?" asked the principal.

"I don't think Casey can figure out why he behaves in a way he knows is unacceptable," interjected the father. "After this recent episode, he was very upset. That night, he practically begged me to give him more medicine so he wouldn't act that way anymore."

The assembled adults were silent for a brief moment.

"But I can't give the other children in his class the idea that they can do what he does and get away with it," said the principal.

"I honestly don't think," I said, "that the students who are flexible and handle frustration well are going to starting exploding just because they see Casey getting away with it. They do need some help knowing the best ways to respond to him. And they're not going to see Casey getting away with anything—they're going to see that you take safety seriously and that you're doing everything you can to help Casey handle frustration more adaptively. I think Casey would be very willing to discuss how he can make amends for what he's done, so long as the discussion takes place later—when coherence has been restored—and so long as he perceives that you understand how hard this is for him."

Did Casey run out of the classroom again during the school year? Yes—to a designated desk in the hallway he knew was his "chill-out" area. Did he begin returning to the classroom much more rapidly after he left? Absolutely. Did he hit his principal again? No. Did he hit his classmates a few times? Yes—which placed him somewhere in the average for boys in his class. Did he continue to have trouble shifting gears? Of course. But his teacher demonstrated to Casey that she could help him when he became frustrated, and Casey thrived in her class. One day, I asked the teacher, "Do you think Casey's difficulties affect his relations with his peers?" She replied, "Oh, I think he's well-liked despite his difficulties. I think the other kids can tell when Casey's having a rough day, and they try to help him make it through."

13

Change of Venue

Just in case you didn't notice, I'm optimistic about the capacities of inflexible-explosive children to begin responding to frustration more adaptively. Yes, it's often difficult to create user-friendlier environments at home and school. Yes, sometimes old habits and knee-jerk, back-end interventions die slow deaths. And yes, sometimes it takes a while to get the psychopharmacology piece squared away. But these are resilient kids—they do respond to being understood and to good treatment.

Most of the time. There are, unfortunately, children who do not have access to, refuse to participate in, or do not respond as favorably to treatment and who continue to behave in an unsafe manner at home, at school, and/or in the community. Many started a downward spiral early, became increasingly alienated, began exhibiting more serious forms of societally inappropriate behavior, and began to hang out with other children who have come down a similar path.

First, a warning. Society—schools, the justice system, social service agencies, the mental health profession—isn't well prepared to help these children. As you've read, although school systems establish the priorities of safety and respect for authority, they often don't have high-quality programs for students who may have difficulty adhering to expectations in these domains. And many alternative day-school placements still have motivational programs as their primary therapeutic ingredient. The police and courts aren't equipped to provide the type of monitoring and intervention needed by many families. Often, the best the judicial system can do is hold the threat of a significant back-end consequence over a child's head. Many social service agen-

Once alienation and deviance become a child's identity and a means of being a part of something, things are a lot harder to turn around. Many such children ultimately need treatment that is more intensive than the kind that can be provided on an outpatient basis or in a regular education setting.

cies are overwhelmed; the problems of an inflexible-explosive child and his family may pale in comparison to the problems of other children and families that are referred to and followed by these agencies. Mental health professionals aren't especially effective in working with individuals who won't come in for treatment or whose needs require attention outside the boundaries of a fifty-minute session in a therapist's office. And managed care issues are sometimes a significant obstacle. Finally, most states don't devote tons of money to the development of quality services for children whose inflexible-explosive behavior prevents them from fitting into the mainstream. That's why there's a building boom in new jails.

After all else has been tried—therapy, medication, perhaps even alternative day-school placements—what many of these children ultimately need is a change of environment. A new start. A way to start working on a new identity. One way to give them this new start is by placing them in a residential facility. As horrible as that may sound, there are some outstanding residential facilities in the United States that do an exceptional job of working with such children. The half dozen kids I've ended up placing in residential settings came out a lot better than they went in, and most maintained their gains once they went back home.

The big problem: These facilities tend to cost a lot of money—as much as $120,000 a year per child. For the vast majority of families, that's an obscene amount of money. No school system, department of mental health, or social service agency is eager to part with that kind of money, either. And the political winds in many states are making it even more difficult to place children in these facilities when necessary.

Let's put money aside for the moment to dispel a few misconceptions. The better residential facilities have excellent academic programs, so a child's chance of being accepted to college isn't sacrificed. Although many of these facilities have a behavior management component for maintaining order, the better ones also have a strong therapeutic component through which many of the thinking and communicating skills described in the preceding chapters can be developed. Many also have a family therapy component (remember, the goal is for the child to return to his own home and community). As you may imagine, I'm generally not enthusiastic about residential programs whose primary agents of change are large human beings who make sure your child knows who's boss.

The prospect of placing one's child in a residential facility can feel like a nightmare to many parents, although parents who have been living a constant nightmare at home are often more open to the idea. Our instincts are to keep our families together, even when they're being torn apart. Our instincts are to keep our children under our supervision, even when our supervision is no longer sufficient. We don't like to feel like we're throwing in the towel, even when all the evidence suggests we cannot provide everything a child needs. We don't like asking someone else to take care of our child, even when we think it may be for the best. So our every instinct is to hang on, tough it out, and try something else. A new drug. A new therapist. A new program. A new school. A new book.

Back to money. If a child is acting out in school, it is sometimes possible to convince or compel a school system to pay for a placement outside the school system. Under the Individuals with Disabilities Act, a federal law (and it's a good one) that applies to public schools, school systems are obliged to place their students in the "least restrictive" setting appropriate to their needs; residential placements are considered the *most* restrictive setting, so such placements are generally held out as a last resort. School systems vary widely in their resources for children who need more than the mainstream can provide. If it becomes apparent, after adjustments and accommodations are made, that a regular education program is not sufficient for your child's needs, the first consideration in many school systems is a classroom aide. The next stop is often a special classroom for children with behavioral problems. A day-school placement outside the school system is frequently the next stop. If these alternatives fail to achieve the desired effect, a residential program may become a more serious consideration. In some cases, if it's sufficiently clear that these intermediate placements are insufficient for a child's needs, a residential program may be considered earlier in the process.

In general, public school systems require a student to pass the following litmus test before a residential facility is considered: (1) the child's current program is thought to be inappropriate to meeting his educational needs (or the child's emotional issues are preventing his educational needs from being met); (2) there is no program within the system appropriate to the child's needs; and (3) the child's needs require the intensity or safekeeping of a twenty-four-hour program. As you may imagine, this is a pretty subjective litmus test, and it's fairly common for parents and school systems to come to radically different opinions on these issues. Some parents end up hiring lawyers or educational consultants who are familiar with the special education laws to help with the persuading. I've not seen many parents successfully navigate this process alone.

Your other option is to ask to have your child placed in the custody of the state. The state then decides what the best facility for your child may be. Often, the state's decision is based more on funding and the availability of space and less on what a child actually needs. Unfortunately, the parents who end up pursuing this route are often those who lack the financial resources or wherewithal to advocate for themselves. Raising an inflexible-explosive child is difficult enough without the added burdens of financial hardship, dangerous neighborhoods, poor role models, and so forth. There are some organizations that can be helpful to such parents, and these organizations are listed in the Additional Resources and Support section in the back of this book.

If you end up seriously considering placing your child in a residential facility, try to visit any of the places to which you're thinking of sending him. Make sure you feel comfortable with the staff, the philosophy of the program, and the other children at the facility. Make sure the facility has lots of experience working with children whose profiles are similar to your child's. Make sure the staff of the facility are open to your ideas about your child.

Placement won't be forever. With luck, only a year or two. That gives you some time to get your house in order. To have your child in a controlled, safe environment where he can learn how to think more flexibly and handle frustration more adaptively. To get his medication straight. To help him come home. It's not the end of the world. It can be a new beginning.

DRAMA IN REAL LIFE
HARD TIMES

You met Jennifer—star of the "waffle episode"—in Chapter 1. By the end of fifth grade, her teachers were just beginning to see signs that all was not right with Jennifer. Jennifer began to miss more school, usually because of some mild physical ailment. Some days she simply refused to go. Sometimes her mother would try to force Jennifer to go to school, subjecting herself to a barrage of verbal and sometimes physical attack. A truancy officer had come to the home on several occasions; during one visit, Jennifer locked herself in the bathroom and refused to come out. Her teachers began to comment on the forced, "wooden" quality to her social presentation and noted that she came off as very bossy. Several new combinations of medication had been tried, with little change.

Our therapy sessions often went something like this:

"Jennifer," I'd begin, "from what I hear, you got very frustrated about something at home yesterday. Maybe I can help out."

"WHAT DID YOU TELL HIM?!" she'd scream at her mother.

"Well, he knows I called him from a pay phone while you were tearing the house apart," the mother replied.

"WHY DID YOU TELL HIM THAT?!" Jennifer would thunder, kicking her mother's chair.

"Because he can't help us unless he knows what goes on in our house," the mother would reply with some irritation.

"I DON'T WANT HIS HELP!"

"I do," the mother would say, "because I think we can get along better than we do."

"THEN YOU COME HERE BY YOURSELF! IF YOU KEEP TALKING ABOUT ME, I'M LEAVING THE ROOM!"

"Jennifer," I'd interject, "I was just interested in what you were so frustrated about . . ."

"I WAS JUST INTERESTED IN HAVING YOU SHUT UP!"

". . . before you started tearing the house apart."

"I WASN'T FRUSTRATED! THE ONLY THING THAT'S FRUSTRATING IS THAT YOU AND MY MOTHER AND MY FATHER ARE ALL FREAKING A--HOLES!"

"Let's talk about school, then," the mother said, trying what she thought would be a less inflammatory topic.

"SCHOOL IS NONE OF HIS FREAKING BUSINESS EITHER!"

Sometimes we'd get some glimmer of hope that Jennifer might be able to participate in a meaningful conversation about her difficulties or be capable of some kernel of insight, but not for long and not often.

"Do you think she's ever going to 'open up?' " her mother would ask me privately.

"I don't know," I'd say. "The only emotion we ever get from Jennifer is anger. It's hard to tell what other feelings she has or whether Jennifer has any meaningful insight about her feelings because she becomes so anxious and frustrated the instant she's uncomfortable talking about something."

"She's been like that since she was born," said the mother. "It's always been hard to tell what she feels. Do you think she even knows what she feels?"

"Hard to tell," I said.

"Can you imagine?" asked the mother. "All I've ever wanted from this kid is some sense of what's going on inside her head . . . some sense that she actually cares about the people around her . . ."

"If she was the least bit receptive to seeing a different therapist, we could see whether she might be more open with someone else," I pondered.

"She's been to almost a dozen therapists already!" the mother would remind me. "Believe it or not, this is the most 'open' she's ever been, if you can call it that."

"That may be true, but we're not getting very far," I said. "Given her propensity for physical aggression, we don't have tons of time to figure it out. If she can't at least be a lot safer than she's being right now, I'm afraid we're going to have some very difficult decisions to make. I have this sinking feeling that starting middle school next year is only going to magnify her level of discomfort and make things even tougher all the way around."

This turned out to be prophetic. When Jennifer entered sixth grade, things headed downhill fast. She had difficulty adapting to the heightened social pressures of middle school, and rapidly alienated many of her peers (when she perceived that a classmate disliked her, she'd spread vicious lies about the child). By winter, the police had to be called to the home several times because of her violent behavior. Jennifer continued to have massive difficulties engaging in any discussion that emphasized the necessity of safety or that was aimed at helping her develop some basic skills for dealing with frustration. Her mother called me from a pay phone on more than one occasion: Jennifer was destroying the house; Jennifer's siblings were in the car, scared to death. Despite everyone's best efforts, she was deteriorating.

In one session, Jennifer's mother tried to talk about a problem Jennifer had with a classmate at school during the week.

"Jennifer, Mrs. Johnson called me from school," the mother began. "I think it would be a good idea to talk with Dr. Greene about what happened between you and Eileen this week."

"I CAN'T BELIEVE SHE CALLED YOU!" Jennifer screamed, turning red. "IT'S NONE OF YOUR FREAKING BUSINESS!"

"We can't help you if you won't let us," said Jennifer's father.

"I DON'T NEED YOUR FREAKING HELP!" Jennifer screamed, becoming more agitated. "IF YOU KEEP TALKING ABOUT THIS, I'M LEAVING."

"Jennifer," said the father, "in the last month your mother has called me from a pay phone while you tore up the house, the police had to come to our house because the neighbors could hear you screaming at your mother, and—"

"I TOLD YOU I'M NOT LISTENING TO THIS!" Jennifer screamed. With that, Jennifer picked up a paper weight from the end table and hurled it, barely missing her mother's head. The father leaped out of his seat and wrestled his daughter to the ground. I called for hospital security.

"You cannot hurt your mother!" the father yelled. Jennifer struggled to escape his grasp.

Security arrived and Jennifer and her parents were escorted to the emergency room. Jennifer calmed down quickly; ultimately, the emergency room staff did not think it was necessary for her to be hospitalized. The parents and I met the next day.

"I don't think you guys are going to be surprised by what I'm about to say," I began. "We've been at this for quite a while now. Jennifer's been on just about every psychiatric medication known to mankind. I'm afraid it's becoming obvious that we are not going to achieve our goals through outpatient treatment. I think we should consider looking for a placement outside your home."

The mother began to cry. She seemed relieved. The father wasn't quite ready.

"Maybe if we tried a new therapist," he said. "Maybe you're not the one."

"That could be," I said. "Don't forget, you've been to many different therapists already. Jennifer is unsafe, and you guys and your other children continue to be traumatized."

"Maybe she needs a female therapist," said the father.

"She's had a ton of female therapists," said the mother, tearfully.

"What kind of place are we talking about?" asked the father.

"A place with kids just like Jennifer," I said. "Kids who can't seem to deal with frustration, who become violent, who need a safe place to work on things."

"You mean a place with a lot of crazy kids running around?" the father asked.

"No," I replied. "Far from it. Anyway, it would be a good idea for you to visit some of these places. I think you'd be pleasantly surprised."

"She'll leave if she's put in a place she can escape from," the mother said.

"There are places that are prepared for kids who are likely to try to split," I said.

"She won't go on her own," the father said.

"Some kids have to be brought to these facilities involuntarily, sometimes in an ambulance," I said.

"How long will she have to be there?" the father asked.

"If we're lucky, only a year or two," I said. "It depends on how she progresses."

"How much do these places cost?" the father asked.

"A lot," I said.

"Who pays for it?" the father asked.

"That's something we'll need to explore," I replied. "Her teachers are well aware that her emotional issues are preventing her from learning, and her guidance counselor has been hinting that she doesn't think Jennifer is able to function in a regular education setting right now. So it's possible her school system will see the need for, and be willing to fund, a twenty-four-hour placement."

The father ran out of questions. He sat quietly while his wife cried. Tears began welling up in his eyes.

"This is my daughter you're talking about here," he said.

"I know."

"We love her."

"Yes, you do."

"We . . . uhm . . . we can't . . . live like this anymore."

"I agree."

The parents tearfully hugged each other and said nothing for several minutes. Finally, the father wiped his eyes and said, "Tell us what we need to do."

14

Children Do Well If They Can

Back when our daughter was born, my wife and I felt strongly that she should be breast-fed. When things didn't go quite as well as planned, I was struck by the tremendous disparity of opinions and advice that began flying our way.

"You guys need to let the baby know there's a feeding schedule very early on. You don't want to spoil her."

"You should feed her whenever she wants. Maybe she's just a baby who likes to breast-feed every half-hour."

"Feed her whenever she wants and you'll never know a moment's peace."

"Babies know what they're doing. Just relax."

"Babies don't eat when their mothers are too nervous."

"What that baby needs is some fennel tea—her stomach is too upset for her to eat."

"The problem is that there's simply not enough milk."

"The problem is that the milk is too light."

"You need to make sure she stays awake while she's eating from the breast. Otherwise, she won't consume enough at each feeding and she won't have the energy to breast-feed the next time."

"You should let the baby cry for awhile when she's hungry. It's good for lung development."

What did we know? We'd never done this before. Fortunately, we had some decent feeding alternatives, such as formula, available to us. So if we had to forego our breast-feeding vision, at least we'd know our child would be relatively well-nourished.

Parents of inflexible-explosive children are usually similarly unprepared. Most parents have never had an inflexible-explosive child before. As you've read, such children are not what most parents hope for and dream of when they envision having a child. What a disparity between vision and reality! When faced with such a circumstance, some parents diligently pursue their original vision and apply the same parenting strategies that were effective for themselves or their other children. And who can blame them? There has been no revised vision for them to work toward and no alternative technology to apply in the pursuit of this different vision.

My hope is that this book helps fill the void on both counts.

The vision and technology described in the preceding pages are guided by a simple philosophy that has evolved over the years in my work with all different kinds of children:

Children do well if they can.

If they can't, we need to figure out why, so we can help.

This philosophy—"children do well if they can"—is in the forefront of my brain when I'm listening to parents' first description of the problems that have prompted them to seek help for their child. It energizes me to move beyond the standard motivational explanations and to identify the skills deficits or neuro-bio-chemical issues that underlie the child's difficulties. It reminds me that if a child *could* interact with other people in a more adaptive manner, he *would*. The very vast majority of children do not get their jollies by making themselves and those around them miserable.

Problem is, a very different philosophy—*"children do well if they want to"*—often guides adults' thinking in their interactions with inflexible-explosive children. Adherents to this philosophy believe children are already capable of behaving more appropriately but simply don't want to. This belief leads to interventions aimed at making such children "want to" do well, typically through implementation of reward and punishment programs.

As you now know, my sense is that "poor motivation" is perhaps the most over-rated, over-invoked explanation for why children do not meet our expectations. Unfortunately, for many adults, it tends to be the knee-jerk explanation. My advice: *Hold on to your knees.* For the most part, children are already motivated to do well. Poor motivation is only one possibility within a whole universe of explanations for why a child might be inflexible and explosive.

The explanation I've been advocating in this book is that, due to a variety of factors, some children are compromised in their capacities to be flexible and tolerate frustration adaptively. Compliance is a skill that does not come naturally to all children.

Given the disparate pathways that may give rise to inflexibility and explosiveness, there is no "one-size-fits-all" approach to helping. In other words, being a better motivator is only one possibility within a whole universe of things adults can do to help. There's a wide range of additional skills that are even more important: understanding who your child is, what his capabilities are, and under what circumstances his relative inefficiencies are likely to cause him difficulty; being sensitive to the ways your child communicates that he's stuck; and being responsive to these difficulties in a way that your child experiences as helpful and that fosters a parent-child relationship that is rewarding to you both. One of the most important roles we play in the lives of children is to set our expectations just within reach continuously throughout their development. When they become more capable of clearing higher hurdles, we can start raising the bar, slowly but surely.

Your new vision for your child? That's up to you, but I'm hoping that he'll come to view you as an ally rather than as the enemy. That he'll eventually be interested in understanding himself a little better. That he'll start handling frustration more adaptively, communicate more effectively, and participate more actively and independently in the process of problem-solving. That he'll feel better about himself and his relationship with you. That he'll feel more optimistic and competent and start to show the world his wonderful qualities without being tripped up by his inflexibility and explosiveness.

Your new vision for yourself? That, too, is up to you, but I'm hoping you'll get back in touch with why you became a parent in the first place. That you'll feel like you finally understand your child and feel a greater sense of mastery in responding to his difficulties in ways that reflect this understanding. That you can communicate with your child. That you'll be able to accept his difficulties and feel confident that you can move toward a more productive, loving relationship. That you'll relinquish goals you weren't ever going to achieve, and feel like you can finally be who you really are when you're with your child. That realistic optimism will feel good. That you'll have a new definition of "good parenting" that goes something like this: *Good parenting means being responsive to and making the most of the hand you've been dealt.*

You must be curious about what happened to many of

the children and parents you met in the preceding pages. Casey's parents continue to implement many of the strategies described in this book, and he continues to do well at home. Unfortunately, medicines that have been prescribed to help Casey think more clearly and explode less rapidly have had variable success, and his behavior at school deteriorated dramatically over one 2–3 month span. Ultimately, Casey had to leave public school for a while so he could be stabilized. But he has successfully transitioned back into mainstream classes.

Danny never hits anymore. His mother is much better at helping him find different words to express his frustration, and Danny has become much better at using these words. He does still swear occasionally, but things are so much better that his mother barely notices. Danny is off medication completely.

Joseph didn't come for many more sessions. His parents had a lot of trouble getting to the sessions and were really hoping someone could help him in individual therapy. I'm more of a family therapy guy, and I didn't believe I could give Joseph tools in individual therapy that would be potent enough to overcome the frustrations he faced in his different environments.

Anthony's anxiety over the weather has waned, and, through medication and road-mapping, he's a lot less anxious these days in general. The focus has now shifted from explosiveness to concerns about his social functioning and academic progress.

Mitchell and his parents caught on to their rules of communicating—no sarcasm, no one-upsmanship, and no mind-reading—faster than I thought they would, and began communicating much more effectively. They're now actually able to discuss things with each other and resolve difficult issues.

Mitchell began trusting me enough to agree to a trial of an antidepressant medication, and then a mood stabilizer, to which he responded very nicely. We weren't able to get him up and running academically at school, so we've been looking at less traditional options.

Ryan is doing fabulously in school. In fact, recent testing indicates he's eligible for a gifted program. Ryan's very hesitant about participating, though. He's very nervous about how new classmates would handle his tics.

I haven't seen much of Jack and his parents lately. Over time, they got pretty good at Basket B: the number of meltdowns declined significantly, and the number of productive discussions increased dramatically. At one point, Jack's mother looked at me and said, "I don't see what the big deal is about this approach . . . all you're really saying is that some things just aren't worth fighting over." No, I didn't fall out of my chair, though I came close. It's nice to know they're doing so well.

Finally, Jennifer—star of the waffle episode and subsequent participant in two residential programs—is living at home again. As it turns out, she possessed a wide range of emotions (in addition to anger), many of which she is now able to express in an adaptive manner. She just needed a very intensive therapeutic program to learn how. So did her parents. I'm delighted they were able to get the help they needed. One of the crucial tasks facing our society is to make sure all the other Jennifers out there are able to access the same kind of help.

Children do well if they can. If they can't . . . well, now you know the rest.

Additional Resources and Support

Additional Resources

A variety of resources are available to provide additional information on various topics covered in this book. Here are some of my favorites:

About Parenting Difficult Children

Gordon, Thomas. *P.E.T.: Parent Effectiveness Training*. New York: Plume/Penguin, 1975.

Turecki, Stanley. *The Difficult Child*. New York: Bantam, 1989.

About Problem-Solving Training

Shure, Myrna B. *Raising a Thinking Child*. New York: Pocket Books, 1994.

About Sibling Issues

Faber, Adele, and Elaine Mazlish. *Siblings without Rivalry: How to Help Your Children Live Together So You Can Live Too*. New York: Avon Books, 1998.

About Right-Hemisphere Dysfunction/Nonverbal Learning Disabilities

Rourke, Byron P. *Nonverbal Learning Disabilities: The Syndrome and the Model*. New York: Guilford, 1989.

About Deficits in Executive Functions

Lyon, G. Reid, and Norman A. Krasnegor. *Attention, Memory, and Executive Function*. Baltimore: Paul H. Brookes, 1996.

About Children with Tourette Syndrome

Haerle, Tracy, ed. *Children with Tourette Syndrome: A Parents' Guide.* Rockville, MD: Woodbine House, 1992.

About Sensory Integration Dysfunction

Kranowitz, Carol Stock. *The Out-of-Sync Child: Recognizing and Coping with Sensory Integration Dysfunction.* New York: Perigree Publishing, 1998.

About Psychopharmacology

Koplewicz, Howard W. *It's Nobody's Fault: New Hope and Help for Difficult Children and Their Parents.* New York: Times Books, 1996.

Wilens, Timothy E. *Straight Talk about Psychiatric Medications for Kids.* New York: Guilford Press, 1998.

About Homeopathic Treatment of Difficult Children

Reichenberg-Ullman, Judyth, and Robert Ullman. *Ritalin-Free Kids: Safe and Effective Homeopathic Medicine for ADD and Other Behavioral and Learning Problems.* Rocklin, CA: Prima Publishing, 1996.

About Legal Issues in Children with Disabilities

Latham, Peter S., and Patricia H. Latham. *Attention Deficit Disorder and the Law* (2nd ed.). Washington, DC: JKL Communications, 1997.

Latham, Peter S., and Patricia H. Latham. *Learning Disabilities and the Law.* Washington, DC: JKL Communications, 1993.

About Prosocial Classrooms

Charney, Ruth Sidney. *Teaching Children to Care: Management in the Responsive Classroom.* Greenfield, MA: Northeast Foundation for Children, 1992.

Dornbusch, Marilyn P., and Sheryl K. Pruitt. *Teaching the Tiger: A Handbook for Individuals Involved in the Education of Students with Attention Deficit Disorders, Tourette Syndrome, or Obsessive Compulsive Disorder.* Duarte, CA: Hope Press, 1995.

Levin, Diane E. *Teaching Young Children in Violent Times: Building a Peaceable Classroom.* Cambridge, MA: Educators for Social Responsibility, 1994.

Richardson, Rita C. *Connecting with Others: Lessons for Teaching Social and Emotional Competence.* Champaign, IL: Research Press, 1996.

About Helping Difficult Children Get the Most out of School

Anderson, Winifred, Stephen Chitwood and Deidre Hayden. *Negotiating the Special Education Maze: A Guide for Parents and Teachers* (3rd ed.). Bethesda, MD: Woodbine House, 1997.

Cutler, Barbara Coyne. *You, Your Child, and "Special" Education: A Guide for Making the System Work.* Baltimore, MD: Paul H. Brookes, 1993.

Siegel, Lawrence M. *The Complete IEP Guide: How to Advocate for Your Special Ed Child.* Berkeley, CA: Nolo, 1999.

Additional Support

Parents and Teachers of Explosive Kids (PTEK)
www.explosivekids.org

Children with Attention Deficit Disorders (CHADD)
8181 Professional Place, Suite 201
Landover, MD 20785
800-233-4050
www.chadd.org

Tourette Syndrome Association (TSA)
42-40 Bell Boulevard
Bayside, NY 11361
718-224-2999
800-237-0717
http://tsa.mgh.harvard.edu/

The Child and Adolescent Bipolar Foundation (CABF)
1187 Wilmette Avenue PMB#331
Wilmette, IL 60091
847-256-8525
http://www.cabf.org

Learning Disabilities Association of America (LDAA)
4156 Library Road
Pittsburgh, PA 15234
412-341-1515
888-300-6710
http://www.ldanatl.org

National Information Center for Children and Youth with Disabilities (NICHCY)
Box 1492
Washington, DC 20013
800-695-0285
http://www.nichy.org

Obsessive Compulsive Foundation
P.O. Box 70
Milford, CT 06460
203-878-5669
http://pages.prodigy.com/a/willen/ofc.htm/

Anxiety Disorders Association of America
11900 Parklawn Drive, Suite 100
Rockville, MD 20852
301-231-9350
http://www.adaa.org

National Depressive and Manic-Depressive Association
730 North Franklin Street, Suite 501
Chicago, IL 60610
800-826-3632
http://www.ndmda.org

National Foundation for Depressive Illness
P.O. Box 2257
New York, NY 10116
800-248-4344
http://www.depression.org

Depressive and Related Affective Disorders Association
Meyer 3-181
600 North Wolfe Street
Baltimore, MD 21287-7381
410-955-4647
http://www.med.jhu.edu/drada/

American Occupational Therapy Association, Inc.
P.O. Box 31220
Bethesda, MD 20824-1220
800-668-8255
http://www.aota.org

American Speech-Language-Hearing Association
10801 Rockville Pike
Rockville, MD 20852
800-638-TALK
http://www.asha.org

Federation of Families for Children's Mental Health
1021 Prince Street
Alexandria, VA 22314-2971
703-684-7710
http://www.fcmh.org

Asperger Syndrome Coalition of the United States (ASC-US)
P.O. Box 49267
Jacksonville Beach, FL 32240-9267
http://www.asperger.org

Online Asperger Syndrome Information and Support (OASIS)
http://www.udel.edu/bkirby/asperger

Nonverbal Learning Disorders Association (NLDA)
999 Asylum Avenue
Hartford, CT 06105
860-293-1800
http://www.nlda.org

Index

discipline
    punishment, 99, 242–47
    in school, 267–68
disconfirming, 210
disintegrative rage, 22–23
distraction, 114
divorce, 54, 70–75
Dodge, Ken, 38
dopamine, 28, 183
downshifting, 115–17
drugs. *See* medication
drug use, 258
Duke, Marshall, 39–40
Durant, Steve, 21

Edgar (child), 287–91
Eduardo (child), 150–51
electrocardiograms, 185
embarrassment theory of
    meltdowns, 265
Emily (child), 142–43
Emotional Intelligence
    (Goleman), 22
empathy, 112–14
    ADHD and, 37
    in problem solving, 141,
        152–53
Eric (child), 75–78, 229–30
executive functions, 14, 28–37
    assessment of, 107
    brain development and, 13,
        28
    organization and planning,
        29, 31–33
    sensory integration
        dysfunction and, 53
    separation of affect, 29,
        36–37

shifting cognitive set, 29–31
    working memory, 29, 33–36
explosive children. *See*
    inflexible-explosive
    children
explosive episodes. *See*
    inflexible-explosive
    episodes
expulsions, 267–68
extrapyramidal symptoms, 188

Faber, Adele, 222
family dynamics and
    interactions, 107, 217–37,
    240. *See also* parents
    communication patterns,
        217, 224–32, 234–37
    grandparents, 233–34
    siblings, 125, 141–42,
        217–24, 240
    stepparents, 232–33
family therapy, 300
feedback
    about homework, 275
    in restructuring automatic
        thoughts, 210–15
fish oil, 188
flaxseed oil, 188
flexibility
    Basket B and, 132, 133
    as developmental skill,
        10–11, 17, 24–25, 96–97,
        270
    limited capacity for, 17,
        20–21
flight anxiety, 47–50
fluoxetine (Prozac), 186
fluvoxamine (Luvox), 186

About the Author

Ross W. Greene, Ph.D., is Director of Cognitive-Behavioral Psychology at the Clinical and Research Program in Pediatric Psychopharmacology at Massachusetts General Hospital in Boston, where he specializes in the treatment of inflexible-explosive children and adolescents and their families. He is also Associate Clinical Professor of Psychology in the Department of Psychiatry at Harvard Medical School.

Dr. Greene's research focuses on the classification and treatment of inflexible-explosive children and adolescents and their families; the classification, longitudinal study, and treatment of severe social impairment in children with ADHD; and the influence of teacher characteristics on school outcome for elementary school students with ADHD. He has authored and co-authored numerous articles, chapters, and scientific papers on behavioral assessment and social functioning in children, school- and home-based interventions for children with disruptive behavior disorders, and student-teacher compatibility. Dr. Greene's research has been funded by the Theodore and Vada Stanley Foundation; the National Institute on Drug Abuse; and the U.S. Department of Education. He is on the editorial boards of the *Journal of Clinical Child Psychology* and the *Journal of Psychoeducational Assessment*.

Dr. Greene received his doctorate in clinical psychology from Virginia Tech in 1989 after completing his predoctoral internship at Children's National Medical Center/George Washington University Medical School in Washington, DC. Prior to his current position at Mass General, he served as Visiting Assistant Professor on the clinical psychology faculty at Virginia Tech and as Assistant Professor in Psychiatry and in Pediatrics at University of Massachusetts Medical Center.

He lives outside Boston with his wife, daughter, and son.

As seen on DATELINE NBC

Listen to

THE EXPLOSIVE CHILD

as read by the author
ROSS W. GREENE, PH.D.

**"An insightful, sensitive protrayal of children
who need help – and how to help them."**
—Myrna B. Shure, Ph.D., author of *Raising a Thinking Child*

Dr. Ross W. Greene now gives a new approach to
understanding and helping children who suffer intense
outbursts of temper, extreme noncompliance, and verbal
and physical aggression. This informative audio edition of
The Explosive Child provides the entire family with the
valuable tools necessary for coping – complete with ways to
regain sanity and optimism while rebuilding the confidence to
handle a child's difficulties competently and lovingly.

ISBN 0-694-52190-6 • $18.00 ($26.00 Can.)
3 hours • 2 cassettes
ABRIDGED

Available wherever books are sold, or call 1-800-331-3761 to order.

HarperAudio
A Division of HarperCollins*Publishers*
www.harperaudio.com